Preventing the Next Financial Crisis

The collapse of Lehman Brothers, the oldest and fourth-largest US investment bank, in September 2008 precipitated the global financial crisis. This deepened the contraction in economic activity that had already started in December 2007 and has become known as the Great Recession. Following a sluggish and uneven period of recovery, levels of public and private debt have recently been on the rise again making another financial crisis almost inevitable. This book answers the key question: can anything be done to prevent a new financial crisis or minimize its impact?

The book opens with an analysis of the main elements responsible for the 2007/2009 financial crisis and assesses the extent to which they are still present in today's financial system. The responses to the financial crises – particularly the Dodd-Frank Act, the establishment of the Financial Stability Board and attempts to regulate shadow banking – are evaluated for their effectiveness. It is found that there is a high risk of a new bubble developing, there remains a lack of transparency in the financial industry and risk-taking continues to be incentivized among bankers and investors. Proposals are put forward to ameliorate the risks, arguing for the need for an international lender of last resort, recalling Keynes' idea for an International Clearing Union.

This book will be of significant interest to scholars and students of financial crises, financial stability and alternative approaches to finance and economics.

Victor A. Beker is Professor of Economics at the University of Belgrano and the University of Buenos Aires, both in Argentina. He has been Director of the Economics Department at the University of Belgrano and of the Economics Program at the University of Buenos Aires. He was awarded several prizes for his works in economics. He is a former Associate Editor of the *Journal of Economic Behavior and Organization*. He is author of several economics books and papers, co-author of *Modern Financial Crisis* (Springer, 2016), co-editor of the *European Crisis* (WEA Books, 2016) and editor of *Alternative Approaches to Economic Theory* (Routledge, 2020).

Routledge Frontiers of Political Economy

The Political Economy of State Intervention
Conserving Capital over the West's Long Depression
Gavin Poynter

Intangible Flow Theory in Economics
Human Participation in Economic and Societal Production
Tiago Cardao-Pito

Foundations of Post-Schumpeterian Economics
Innovation, Institutions and Finance
Beniamino Callegari

Distributive Justice and Taxation
Jørgen Pedersen

The China–US Trade War and South Asian Economies
Edited by Rahul Nath Choudhury

Politics and the Theory of Spontaneous Order
Piotr Szafruga

Preventing the Next Financial Crisis
Victor A. Beker

Capital Theory and Political Economy
Prices, Income Distribution and Stability
Lefteris Tsoulfidis

Value and Unequal Exchange in International Trade
The Geography of Global Capitalist Exploitation
Andrea Ricci

Inflation, Unemployment and Capital Malformations
Bernard Schmitt
Edited and Translated in English by Alvaro Cencini and Xavier Bradley

Democratic Economic Planning
Robin Hahnel

For more information about this series, please visit: https://www.routledge.com/Routledge-Frontiers-of-Political-Economy/book-series/SE0345.

Preventing the Next Financial Crisis

Victor A. Beker

Routledge
Taylor & Francis Group
LONDON AND NEW YORK

First published 2021
by Routledge
2 Park Square, Milton Park, Abingdon, Oxon OX14 4RN

and by Routledge
52 Vanderbilt Avenue, New York, NY 10017

Routledge is an imprint of the Taylor & Francis Group, an informa business

British Library Cataloguing in Publication Data
A catalogue record for this book is available from the British Library

Library of Congress Cataloging-in-Publication Data
Names: Beker, Víctor A., author.
Title: Preventing the next financial crisis / Victor A. Beker.
Description: Milton Park, Abingdon, Oxon ; New York, NY : Routledge, 2021. | Includes bibliographical references and index.
Identifiers: LCCN 2020048694 (print) | LCCN 2020048695 (ebook) | ISBN 9780367483982 (hardback) | ISBN 9781003039686 (ebook)
Subjects: LCSH: Financial crises–Prevention. | Global Financial Crisis, 2008–2009. | Economic policy.
Classification: LCC HB3722 .B438 2021 (print) | LCC HB3722 (ebook) | DDC 338.5/42–dc23
LC record available at https://lccn.loc.gov/2020048694
LC ebook record available at https://lccn.loc.gov/2020048695

ISBN: 978-0-367-48398-2 (hbk)
ISBN: 978-0-367-75842-4 (pbk)
ISBN: 978-1-003-03968-6 (ebk)

Typeset in Galliard
by Taylor & Francis Books

Contents

Boxes

Acknowledgements

I am very grateful to Routledge, the publisher of this volume, and particularly to Andy Humphries, Emma Morley and Cherry Allen, who assisted me at different stages involved in the creation of this book. Comments by two anonimous referees were particularly useful. I also appreciate the efforts of the copyeditor, Sarah Fish, as well as everyone who took part in the production of this book and I hope the readers will too.

Some parts of the volume were inspired by comments by Jane D'Arista to a previous paper on the subject. I am indebted to her for this although, of course, the usual caveats apply.

I want to especially thank my wife Dora, my son Pablo, his wife Luciana and my grandson Tomas for their patience and support during the process of writing this book.

Foreword

Malcolm Sawyer

The global financial crisis (GFC) was one, albeit a large and global, of many financial crises. As Victor Beker remarks in the preface, 'crises are a recurrent event in economic history' and economic and financial crises have become frequent features of capitalist economies – with over 400 recorded around the world since 1970. It is well known that financial crises, and particularly those which can be labelled banking crises, have substantial economic costs in terms of unemployment, lost output and slower post-crisis growth alongside the social costs. Can financial crises be avoided? – the central question of this book. The past histories of financial crises and their frequent occurrence and the analyses of authors such as Hyman Minsky suggest such prevention will prove very difficult. Or should the approach be more of allowing a financial boom to proceed and then cope with the financial bust?

The two decades or so prior to the GFC attracted the phrase 'great moderation' of low inflation and avoidance of recession and it generated the false hope of the end of economic and financial crises. Yet there were continuing financial crises around the world; and there was the booming financial sector with financialisation running rampant. The author explains in the appendix how the processes of financialisation have developed new financial products including derivatives which facilitate speculation and instabilities. The subprime mortgages and the mortgage backed securities derived from them were a central feature of the financial crisis, particularly in the USA.

The 2007/2009 financial crisis involved interconnections of financial crises in a number of countries and the contagion effects spreading those crises and recessionary effects around the world. Whilst most attention is paid to the USA, there were major crises in countries such as the UK, Ireland and Iceland which had national origins (in so far as there can be national origins in a globalised world) and occurred close in time with the American financial collapse (though, for example, there were earlier signs such as the collapse of Northern Rock in the UK). Many other countries were pulled into crisis through a range of contagion effects including purchase of 'toxic assets' and spill-over demand effects. Chapter 5 of this book examines the channels of transmission of shocks through interconnectedness, contagion and panic, and these were very much in evidence in the GFC as spreading the crisis across the globe. Many elements came together for the financial crisis – as this book reminds us major elements of financialisation such as securitisation, the so-called shadow banking, i.e. largely unregulated, system and the role of credit rating agencies.

The nature of neo-classical economic analysis and what can be termed mainstream economic analysis more generally does not readily enable any understanding of economic and financial crises (Chapter 9). The use of equilibrium analysis reduces crises to some sudden shift in the key parameters leading to a major shift in the equilibrium position. Stock market crashes come from a sudden adjustment in profit expectations leading to a revaluation of stock prices. There have though been many strands of analysis which have stressed that capitalism is a crisis prone system. The chapter 'concludes that economic crisis is one of the pathologies economics has yet to study in order to provide society with an answer about its deep causes and how to prevent their occurrence'.

The growth of the so-called shadow banking system was (and continues to be) an important dimension of financialisation and illustrates how the financial system grows outside the regulatory system and an important source of instability. It played a central role in the generation of the financial crisis and was itself subject to crisis. The failures of the Dodd-Frank Act in the USA in 2010 are well explored in Chapter 4 particularly in respect of not bringing the shadow banking system under systematic regulation.

The re-emergence of regulation (and attitudes towards regulation) are a notable feature post-crisis, even if there may be doubts on their effectiveness in addressing financial instability. The financial industry is a powerful lobby in limiting the degree and effectiveness of regulation. The pursuit of financial stability has often been added, formally or informally, to the objectives of the central bank. Micro-prudential supervision seeks to protect consumers of the financial institutions and to try to limit the risks which the institutions engage in. Macro-prudential supervision has to address the overall level of risks and instabilities of the financial system. One proposal made here is for central banks to establish acceptable limits of concentration risk and the ways to monitor and control such risks. The concentration of loans can refer to a sector of the economy, a region or kind of assets, exposing the financial system to transmission of crisis in the event of difficulties in the areas where loans have been concentrated.

The global financial crisis was played out on the international stage, and with the globalisation especially in the financial sphere future financial crises will have international dimensions and require co-ordinated international responses. Finance has become increasingly global, with regulation and supervision remaining essentially set and implemented at the national level, albeit with attempts at co-ordination of the regulations as under the Basle agreements. The author notes the attempts in the direction of co-ordination in regulation and supervision. He argues for a new global monetary system to provide at least for an international lender of last resort and to remove the 'exorbitant privilege' which allows the United States to run large external deficits of imports in excess of exports when the corresponding borrowing is in dollars. All the policy proposals for reforms of the financial system at the national level and at the international level face major difficulties of designing the necessary reforms: but the major, perhaps insurmountable, obstacles are the political powers of financial powers. As the author puts it:

> a more balanced global system will have to wait to be implemented until a more balanced relation of forces in the world economy becomes reality and it turns out evident that the present regime is incapable of dealing with a global crisis.

Malcolm Sawyer
Emeritus Professor of Economics, University of Leeds, UK

Preface

Crises are a recurrent event in economic history. They are white swans, not black swans.

In 2016, together with my distinguished colleague Beniamino Moro, I authored a book on *Modern Financial Crises* (Moro and Beker, 2016), which provides a comprehensive overview of the causes and consequences of the financial crises in Argentina, the US and Europe that took place in the 21st century.

Economic theory has paid little attention to the subject of crisis. Most mainstream economists not only did not foresee the depth of the last financial crisis, they did not even consider it possible. In fact, most of the orthodox economists' efforts are devoted to showing the nonexistence of economic problems. The bulk of their papers are aimed at showing how the market solves any potential conflict or difficulty on its own. If so, there is no economic problem to work on. Most scholars' efforts are devoted to study "health" and very little to analysing "illness" in economics. Considerable effort is invested in showing why the economy works smoothly most of the time and very little effort to the analysis of why, from time to time, the economic mechanism breaks down or – more importantly – what is needed to fix it. However, these failures in the economic mechanism have huge economic and social costs. Economic illness rather than economic health should be the focus of economists' efforts (Beker, 2016: 194).

Up to 1930, crises were mainly considered in mainstream economic literature as an adjustment process to correct existing distortions in the economy. With Keynes's General Theory crises started to be considered as an economic illness requiring treatment.

During the optimistic years of the Great Moderation the study of economic and financial disruptions have been practically expelled from the economic theory arena and confined to the economic history field. They were just considered an antiquity to be housed at the museum of economic archaeology. Kindleberger's seminal book on the subject was blatantly ignored or looked at with a mixture of contempt and *condescension*. Minsky's model simply did not exist for most of the economics profession.

In the following pages there is an analysis of the regulatory reforms that took place after the global financial crisis of 2007/2009 and an evaluation of to what an extent they can avoid a new financial crisis. Most of them go in the right direction but they are insufficient. What can be done to try to prevent a new financial crisis or minimise its consequences is the main subject of this book.

Along these pages I always adopt the real-world point of view in sharp contrast with theoretical approaches which are hopelessly at odds with reality and how economies do function in the real world.

It is true that every model implies a certain degree of unrealism in the assumptions – a model is a simplification of the real world. But it is one thing to simplify reality and quite another to overtly distort it.

This was the great methodological contribution made by Keynes to economic analysis. He was a practical-minded economist. In contrast to many past and present economic theorists, he had great practical experience in economic policy. He did use simplifications of economic reality but they allowed him to reach significant practical results. He was well aware that the real world is quite different from what some academics sitting in their comfortable ivory towers imagine.

If this book contributes to shedding light on what should be done to avoid a new economic catastrophe like the one witnessed in 2007/2009, its main purpose will have been achieved.

References

Beker, V. A. (2016). From the Economic Crisis to the Crisis of Economics. In B. Moro and V. A. Beker, *Modern Financial Crises: Argentina, United States and Europe*. Financial and Monetary Policy Studies 42. Switzerland: Springer International Publishing.

Moro, B. and Beker, V. A. (2016). *Modern Financial Crises: Argentina, United States and Europe*. Financial and Monetary Policy Studies 42. Switzerland: Springer International Publishing.

1 Introduction

On September 15, 2008 Lehman Brothers filed for Chapter 11 bankruptcy protection in what has been the largest bankruptcy filing in US history, far surpassing previous giant bankrupts as WorldCom or Enron. As a matter of fact, it was the largest bank failure ever as well as the largest bankruptcy ever.

The collapse of Lehman, which was the fourth-largest US investment bank, was followed by a global financial crisis. This deepened the contraction in economic activity that had already started in December 2007 and has been known as the Great Recession. The world economy was brought to the brink of collapse.

Between December 2007 and June 2009 US GDP fell 4.3% while unemployment increased from 5.0% to 9.5%, peaking at 10.0% in October 2009. Most advanced economies followed suit. In the United States, the stock market plummeted, wiping out nearly $8 trillion in value between late 2007 and 2009.

The main issue addressed in this book is whether a new financial crisis can be avoided. In this respect, the former US Federal Reserve Chair J. Yellen, in a lecture at The British Academy on June 2017, gave an optimistic point of view: "I do think we're much safer and I hope that it (another financial crisis) will not be in our lifetimes and I don't believe it will be."

However, contrary to Janet Yellen's hopeful assertion, Blanchard and Summers (2019: 12) claim that "financial crises will probably happen again." Steve Keen (2017), one of the very few economists who anticipated the last financial crisis, warns that ever-rising levels of private debt make another financial crisis almost inevitable. The key issue is what can be done to try to prevent a new financial crisis or minimize its consequences. As the Vice-President of the Deutsche Bundesbank Claudia Buch (2017) stated, "reducing excessive risk-taking, making crises less likely and reducing their costs should be the ambition of policymakers."

However, it seems that these goals are far from being attained. Adrian et al. (2018) warn that the $1.3 trillion global market for so-called leveraged loans may be approaching a threatening level.[1] These authors remark that "yield-hungry investors are tolerating ever-higher levels of risk and betting on financial instruments that, in less speculative times, they might sensibly shun." Even worse, underwriting standards and credit quality have worsened.

> This year (for 2018), so-called covenant-lite loans account for up 80% of new loans arranged for nonbank lenders (so-called "institutional investors"), up from about 30% in 2007. Not only the number, but also the quality of covenants has deteriorated.
>
> (Adrian et al., 2018)

Moreover, according to a report by the Financial Stability Board, assets of collective investment vehicles with features that make them susceptible to runs have grown by around 13% a year since end-2011 (FSB, 2018: 3). It goes on to warn that greater attention is needed on collecting liabilities data to better assess funding vulnerabilities although it admits that some progress has already been made (FSB, 2018: 5).

The October 2019 IMF's Global Financial Stability Report warns that "vulnerabilities among nonbank financial institutions are now elevated in 80% of economies with systemically important financial sectors (by GDP). This share is similar to that at the height of the global financial crisis" (IMF, 2019).

Already, in July 2013, Governor Daniel Tarullo, Member of the Board of Governors of the Federal Reserve System, warned that "a major source of unaddressed risk emanates from the large volume of short-term securities financing transactions in our financial system, including repos, reverse repos, securities borrowing, and lending transactions" (Tarullo, 2013).

Then, the key question is to what an extent the financial system is prepared to avoid systemic risk i.e. the spreading of losses, illiquidity and/or other forms of financial distress across financial institutions with serious consequences for the economy as a whole as we witnessed in 2007/2009.

The subject of financial crisis has deserved very little attention in the economic literature during the last 50 years. Minsky (1992) together with Kindleberger (1978) were lonely voices during the years of the so-called Great Moderation when the possibility of a financial crisis had been discarded and its study considered just a waste of time, at least in developed countries.

After the latest financial crisis, the issue became of public interest and several accounts of the crisis and its lessons were published, among them Paulson (2010), Bernanke (2015), Geithner (2014), Gorton and Metrick (2012), Mian and Sufi (2014), Pilkington (2013), Keen (2017) and Blanchard and Summers (2017). Most of them either focus on the events which led to the financial meltdown or deal with some particular issue such as the monetary or macroeconomic policies or the level of private debt. On the contrary, this book – after reviewing the main factors behind the 2007/2009 financial crisis – is focused on what has been done up to now to avoid a new one, to what an extent those measures have or have not removed the main factors which led to the last financial crisis and what should be done to avoid a new one.

The remainder of the book is structured as follows. In Chapter 2, the main elements which contributed to the 2007/2009 financial crisis are analyzed. Four main elements which led to the 2007/2009 financial crisis are identified: irrational expectations, securitization, the "shadow" banking system and the credit rating agencies. A brief explanation is given on how each of these four factors contributed to the financial crisis.

Chapter 3 summarizes the main reforms which took place after the crisis. The chapter starts with an analysis of the concept of moral hazard and its implications for the financial industry. It is argued that the negative externalities of bank failure and the economic and social costs associated with the chain reaction it may trigger weigh a lot more in policy decisions than the moral hazard argument. Then some of the key reforms in regulation and supervision since the crisis are examined.

The role played by the shadow banking system in the financial crisis and the regulatory reforms dealing with it are the subjects of Chapter 4. It is noticed that the Dodd-Frank Act fails to recognize that a significant part of the funding of the financial system is no longer in the form of insured deposits and fails to bring the shadow banking component of the financial system under the regulatory umbrella in a systematic way.

Systemic risk and run vulnerability are the contents of Chapter 5. The three different channels of transmission of a certain shock to the rest of the financial system – interconnectedness, contagion and panic – are analyzed.

In Chapter 6 it is argued that to prevent a new financial crisis the real issue is to avoid excessive concentration of loans in any one sector, region or kind of assets of the economy. Besides that, legislation should eliminate incentives for financial institutions to take risks that may be excessive from a social perspective. With respect to credit rating agencies (CRAs), it is argued that, with today's technology, there is no obstacle to implement the investor-pay model in place of the present issuer-pay model and thus avoid a possible conflict of interest.

Micro- and macro-prudential regulation are examined in Chapter 7. The areas on which the regulation reform has focused are detailed. It is proposed that, as part of their macro-prudential policy, central banks should establish the acceptable limits of concentration risk and the mechanisms to monitor and control that the system behaves within them.

Chapter 8 is devoted to the need of reforming the international monetary system. It is argued that a new global monetary system is required to provide at least for an international lender of last resort and to remove the "exorbitant privilege" that allows the United States to run large external deficits while financing them with its own currency.

The treatment given by economic theory to economic and financial crises is the subject of Chapter 9. The analyses done by different authors, from Wicksell to Keynes to Minsky, are presented. The chapter concludes that economic crisis is one of the pathologies economics has yet to study in order to provide society with an answer about its deep causes and how to prevent their occurrence.

An Epilogue is devoted to the central banks' and governments' responses to the COVID-19 crisis. Some lessons the pandemic crisis taught are remarked upon.

A summary of the main conclusions arrived at in the book is detailed under the title of Conclusions.

An Appendix is devoted to the subject of financialization and the impact this process has had on the functioning of the economy; in particular, the fact that the production of goods has become for corporations just a by-product of their main activity focused on valorizing capital through mergers, acquisitions, takeovers and other financial instruments of the kind is remarked.

Box 1.1 Crises in economic history

Crises are a recurrent event in economic history. In their extensive review of economic crises, Reinhart and Rogoff refer to at least 250 episodes of sovereign external default episodes and at least 68 cases of default on domestic public debt between 1800 and 2009 (Reinhart and Rogoff, 2009: 34). The United Kingdom, the United States and France suffered 12, 13 and 15 banking crisis episodes, respectively. Virtually no country has escaped unscathed from economic crises of one form or another. Crises are white swans, not black swans.

The first financial crisis recorded in economic history took place in 33 AD. Not only Jesus was crucified that year but there was also a financial panic that struck the Roman Empire. The panic started in Rome and spread throughout the Empire.

In modern times, the tulip mania which peaked in 1637 is considered the first speculative bubble. The panic of 1792 is the first financial panic recorded in US economic history. It started with a run on the Bank of the United States, just created in 1791. The then Treasury Secretary Alexander Hamilton was in charge of maneuvering to contain the credit crisis. For this purpose, liquidity was injected to banks until normalcy was restored.

The Wall Street crash of 1929 signaled the beginning of the Great Depression which lasted until the late 1930s and is considered until now the *most devastating* economic downturn in economic history.

Source: Reinhart and Rogoff (2009)

Note

1 A leveraged loan is a type of loan that is extended to companies or individuals that already have considerable amounts of debt or poor credit history.

References

Adrian, T., Natalucci, F. and Piontek, T. (2018). Sounding the Alarm on Leveraged Lending. *IMF Blog*, November 15.

Bernanke, B. S. (2015). *The Courage to Act: A Memoir of a Crisis and its Aftermath*. New York: W. W. Norton & Company.

Blanchard, O. J. and Summers, L. H. (2017). Rethinking Stabilization Policy: Evolution or Revolution? National Bureau of Economic Research. Working Paper 24179 http://www.nber.org/papers/w24179.

Blanchard, O. J. and Summers, L. (2019). *Evolution or Revolution? Rethinking Macroeconomic Policy after the Great Recession*. Cambridge, MA: MIT and Peterson Institute for International Economics.

Buch, C. (2017). How Can We Protect Economies From Financial Crises? Deutsche Bundesbank. https://www.bundesbank.de/Redaktion/EN/Reden/2017/2017_07_08_buch.htm.

Keen, S. (2017). *Can We Avoid Another Financial Crisis?* Cambridge, UK: Polity Press.

Financial Stability Board (FSB) (2018). Global Shadow Banking Monitoring Report 2017. http://www.fsb.org/wp-content/uploads/P050318-1.pdf.

Geithner, T. F. (2014). *Stress Test: Reflections on Financial Crises*. New York: Crown Publishers.

Gorton, G. and Metrick, A. (2012). Getting Up to Speed on the Financial Crisis: A One-Weekend-Reader's Guide. *Journal of Economic Literature* 50(1), 128–150.

IMF (2019). *Global Financial Stability Report*. https://www.imf.org/en/Publications/GFSR/Issues/2019/10/01/global-financial-stability-report-october-2019.

Kindleberger, C. P. (1978). *Manias, Crashes and Panics: A History of Financial Crises*. 1st edition. New York: Basic Books.

Mian, A. and Sufi, A. (2014). *House of Debt: How They (and You) Caused the Great Recession, and How We Can Prevent It from Happening Again*. Chicago, IL: University of Chicago Press.

Minsky, H. P. (1992). *The Financial Instability Hypothesis*. Working paper No. 74. New York: The Jerome Levy Economics Institute of Bard College. http://www.levyinstitute.org/pubs/wp74.pdf.

Paulson, H. M. Jr. (2010). *On the Brink: Inside the Race to Stop the Collapse of the Global Financial System*. New York: Business Plus.

Pilkington, M. (2013). *The Global Financial Crisis and the New Monetary Consensus*. Abingdon, Oxon: Routledge.

Reinhart, C. M. and Rogoff, K. S. (2009). *This Time Is Different: Eight Centuries of Financial Folly*. Princeton, NJ: Princeton University Press.

Tarullo D. K. (2013). Dodd-Frank Implementation. Testimony before the United States Senate Committee on Banking, Housing, and Urban Affairs, Hearing on "Mitigating Systematic Risk Through Wall Street Reforms," Washington DC, 11 July.

2 Key elements in the 2007/2009 financial meltdown

The subprime mortgage meltdown

Financial crises have been defined by Mishkin and Eakins (2015: 164) as "major disruptions in financial markets characterized by sharp declines in asset prices and firm failures." In Beker (2016: 45) I have asserted that "the core of the 2007/09 financial market crisis has been the discovery that many securities were actually far riskier than people originally thought they were."

In fact, the epicenter of the crisis was the meltdown in the subprime mortgage market that started in the United States in mid-2007, affected most of the financial industry and eventually spread around the world triggering a global deep contraction in economic activity known as the Great Recession.

In the years previous to the crisis, the financial world had been manufacturing vast quantities of triple-rated securities with attractive yields. The star protagonist of this process was the subprime mortgage market.

The subprime mortgage market developed in the early 1990s; the government-sponsored Fannie Mae and Freddie Mac played an active role in it.

Fannie Mae stands for the Federal National Mortgage Association while Freddie Mac is the Federal Home Loan Mortgage Corporation. Their aim is to help banks make more mortgage loans and keep interest rates low.

Fannie Mae was established by Congress in 1938. Its purpose was to buy Federal Housing Administration mortgages from banks, giving them more money to lend. Fannie then packaged the mortgages into mortgage-backed securities and sold these derivatives to hedge funds, pension funds and individual investors. In 1968, it was transformed into a company. The purpose was to stop using tax dollars to fund it; the government allowed Fannie to sell stocks to shareholders in an initial public offering but it retained what has become known as an implied government guarantee of its debt.

By acquiring mortgages and securitizing them into residential mortgage-backed securities, Fannie could transfer default risk from the originator's books onto its own and in the process encourage further mortgage lending.

Freddie Mac was established in 1970. Unlike Fannie Mae, Freddie Mac could buy any type of mortgage and not just FHA ones. As a government-sponsored enterprise, its loans also benefit from the implied government guarantee.

Since the late 1990s both agencies gradually lowered the underwriting standards in their securitization business actively purchasing high-risk loans. The "affordable housing goals" established by Congress in 1992 have been pointed out as responsible for this shift because they determined targets for the share of Fannie- and Freddie-backed lending that went to low-income and minority borrowers.

By 2007 both government-sponsored enterprises represented 40% of the entire mortgage market.

In the early and mid-2000s high-risk mortgages became widely available from private lenders who funded mortgages by pooling and repackaging them into securities that were sold to private investors. Rising house prices protected lenders from losses; in case subprime mortgage borrowers could not make loan payments they could either sell their homes at a gain and pay off their mortgages or borrow more against higher market prices.

Securitization is the process through which loans are removed from the balance sheet of lenders and transformed into debt securities purchased by investors. In other words, it is a process through which an illiquid asset or group of assets are transformed into a financial security. The investment bank Lehman Brothers was one of the active issuers of securitized subprimes.

The process of securitization allowed trillions of dollars of risky assets – subprime mortgages in the first place – to be transformed into securities that were widely considered to be safe.

The problem is that subprime mortgage securitization models relied on assumptions and historical data that turned out to be incorrect and therefore made incorrect valuations. Substantial lending to subprime borrowers was a recent phenomenon; historical data on the defaults and delinquencies of this sector of the mortgage market were scarce (Coval et al., 2009: 15). Some models were not even based on historical data because they referred to transactions for which there was no active trading market.

When the housing bubble exploded in 2007, real estate markets went down together and mortgage defaults soared in Florida as well as in California. Subprime mortgage-backed securities carried the dual risk of high rates of default due to the low credit quality of borrowers, on the one hand, and the high level of default correlation as a result of pooling mortgages from similar geographical areas and vintages, on the other. When prices fell in the home market, subprime-related assets deteriorated and the financial crisis blew up.

What is the essence of a financial crisis? According to Furceri and Mourougane (2009: 5),

> financial crises are generally characterized by a collapse of trust between financial institutions and their creditors. Increased uncertainty materializes into soaring premia on short-term liabilities and a squeeze on liquidity. When premia reach a very high level, the liquidity problem becomes a solvency and capital shortage problem, unless public authorities intervene.

The 2007/2009 financial crisis was triggered by the discovery that many AAA-rated securities were absolutely unsafe. People rushed first to liquidate these assets and next to withdraw their money from those institutions known or suspected of holding those toxic assets.

As a matter of fact, there were four main elements which led to the 2007/2009 financial crisis:

1 Irrational expectations.
2 Securitization.
3 "Shadow" banking system.
4 Credit rating agencies.

The presence of these four elements was absolutely necessary to produce the cocktail which led to the crisis. Let us have a look at each of them.

Irrational expectations

A usual assumption in mainstream economics is that agents act rationally. It is a useful assumption; it would be very difficult to build an economic theory under the assumption that individuals always behave in a non-rational way. However, one should always keep in mind that rationality is just an assumption, not a description of the real world.

There are many examples of non-rational behavior in the real world. Some cases of herd behavior are an example: individuals act collectively as part of a group, blindly following the behavior of some of its members. Individuals find it hard to believe that a large group could be wrong. If I don't understand why all my friends are buying a certain asset I guess that it must be because they know something I don't know. Just in case, I follow their behavior although it may happen that they are as uninformed as I am.

In a 1995 paper, the German economist Thomas Lux formalized herd behavior in speculative markets as a self-organizing process of infection among traders. Mutual mimetic contagion among traders leads to the existence of positive or negative bubbles. One example of herd behavior is speculative manias, which appear from time to time in economic history.[1]

Speculative manias happen when an increasing number of economic agents start dreaming of ever-increasing prices of a certain kind of assets.

As it happened with the different speculative manias that emerged since the 1630s Dutch tulip one, all the actors involved in the last financial crisis drama were convinced that prices – in this case house prices – could only rise.[2] In fact, throughout the early 2000s, housing prices kept rising. For many homeowners, rising values made it attractive to refinance their mortgages and use their home equity to pay for other things – investment properties, remodels, cars. Bankers acted as if they believed that housing prices would rise forever. Irrationality pervaded key parts of the economic system.

Subprime mortgages were granted under the premise that background checks were practically unnecessary: a borrower in difficulties could always refinance a loan using the increased value of the house. Many subprime mortgages debtors were "ninja" people – standing for no income, no job and no assets. This behavior was stimulated by the "originate-to-distribute" model implemented through a system of off-balance-sheet investment vehicles and conduits.

Historically, banks originated loans and kept them on their balance sheets until maturity. Over time, however, banks began increasingly to distribute the loans they originated.

With this change, banks limited the growth of their balance sheets but maintained a key role in the origination of loans, and contributed to the growth of nonbank financial intermediaries.

The originate-to-distribute model of lending gives banks the flexibility to change quickly the volume of mortgages they make without having to make large adjustments to their equity capital or asset portfolio.

Banks repackaged loans and passed them on to other financial investors, thereby off-loading risk. In some cases, banks created conduits or structured investment vehicles with this purpose. However, "to ensure funding liquidity for the vehicle, the sponsoring bank grants a credit line to the vehicle, called a 'liquidity backstop'" (Brunnermeier, 2009: 80). Therefore, the bank was still bearing the liquidity risk even though it did not appear on the banks' balance sheets. But while commercial banks fully guaranteed their conduits' borrowings, they did not at the same time make any equivalent capital provision for these guarantees.

Off-loading loans allowed banks to lend while holding less capital than if they had kept loans on their balance sheets. In this way banks enhanced their return on equity while regulations regarding minimum capital ratios were bypassed. This process enhanced the return on equity of banks, or, more precisely, of their holding companies.

As He and Krishnamurthy (2019: 32) point out, "there was a great deal of leverage 'hidden' in the system" thanks to the off-loading of loans. According to these authors, this hidden leverage explains why financial market indicators did not signal a crisis as agents were unaware of the real size of leverage in the financial system.

Cheap credit and weak lending standards resulted in a housing frenzy that led to the financial crisis. Once a bank off-loaded the risk of a certain mortgage it could offer a new loan to another homeowner. The cycle restarted, fueling a housing boom. Home prices skyrocketed. That house prices would rise forever became a self-fulfilling prophecy.

Securitization

Securitization is the mechanism by which loans are turned into bonds. "The process of securitization allowed trillions of dollars of risky assets – subprime mortgages in the first place – to be transformed into securities that were widely considered to be safe" (Beker, 2016: 45). Buiter (2009: 5/6) clearly explains how it worked:

> Uncertain future cash flows from mortgages or from business loans were pooled, securities were issued against the pool, the securities were tranched,

> sliced and diced, enhanced in various ways with guarantees and other insurance features. The resulting asset-backed securities were sometimes used themselves as assets for backing further rounds of securitization. Banks sold their previously illiquid loans and used the proceeds to make new loans. A "money machine" had been invented.

In fact, assembling bonds from different bond pools allowed a second round of securitization (Coval et al., 2009: 7). A gigantic interlinked structure of securities was thus created, which has been characterized by Brunnermeier (2009: 98) as "an opaque web of interconnected obligations."

As Ordoñez (2018: 34) rightly asserts, "banks increasingly devised securitization methods to bypass capital requirements."

The most direct path from origination to securitization is when a bank pools the loans it originates and then makes them the collateral for a securitization it issues. But it is also possible that a mortgage is sold several times before ending up in a mortgage-backed security pool.

The complexity of the structured mortgage products which bundled together traditional asset-backed securities and new products based on subprime mortgages favored the opacity of the whole process and the development of a hidden risk which was difficult to detect.

It is really surprising to learn how misinformed even Fed authorities and regulators were about what was going on within the financial system under their supervision before the crisis burst.

Timothy Geithner, who at the time of the crisis was President of the Federal Reserve Bank of New York, declares that:

> We couldn't foresee how the ongoing "run" might evolve, and how rapidly and broadly it might spread. We had only limited knowledge about the potential severity of losses and which parts of the financial system were most exposed to losses, because of the limited reach of our supervisory authorities and the fundamental uncertainty that complicated any assessment of the likely depth of the recession and the incidence of losses.
>
> (Geithner, 2019: 11)

The former Fed's Chairman, Alan Greenspan, candidly admits that:

> We at the Federal Reserve were aware earlier in the decade of incidents of some highly irregular subprime mortgage underwriting practices. But, regrettably, we viewed it as a localized problem subject to standard prudential oversight, not the precursor of the securitized subprime mortgage bubble that was to arise several years later. On first being told in the early months of 2005 by Fed staff of the quarterly data for 2004, I expressed surprise given that our most recently official Fed data – those of the Home Mortgage Disclosure Act (HMDA) compilations for 2003 – exhibited few signs of problems. I had never heard of the private source

> *Inside Mortgage Finance* before. But, in retrospect, those data turned out to be right.
>
> (Greenspan, 2014: 63/64)

Therefore, the then Chairman of the Fed and President of the Federal Reserve Bank of New York apparently ignored that trillions of dollars of mortgage-backed assets were a time-bomb ready for detonation under their feet. Had they known it perhaps they would have put a bit more attention on the statistics on subprime mortgage delinquency even if they were not familiar with the source of that information as Greenspan declares.

In his defense, Greenspan – who served as Chairman of the Federal Reserve between 1987 and 2006 – argues that "in early 2007, the composition of the world's nonfinancial corporate balance sheets and cash flows appeared in as good a shape as I can ever recall" (Greenspan, 2014: 37). The only thing this proves is that he was looking at the wrong indicators.

Greenspan (2014: 46) goes on to admit that in spite the fact that "ten to fifteen largest banking institutions have had permanently assigned on-site examiners to oversee daily operations, many of these banks still were able to take on toxic assets that brought them to their knees."

As far as investors in asset-backed and mortgage-backed securities are concerned, they mainly relied on the assessments of credit rating agencies. The key role played by these agencies can be clearly understood if we take into consideration that more than 90% of securitized subprime loans were turned into securities with the top rating of AAA (International Monetary Fund, 2008). I come back below to this.

Although securitization was intended to disperse risks associated with bank lending,

> in reality, securitization worked to concentrate risks in the banking sector. There was a simple reason for this. Banks and other intermediaries wanted to increase their leverage – to become more indebted – so as to spice up their short-term profit. So, rather than dispersing risks evenly throughout the economy, banks and other intermediaries bought each other's securities with borrowed money. As a result, far from dispersing risks, securitization had the perverse effect of concentrating all the risks in the banking system itself.
>
> (Adrian and Shin, 2009: 11)

"Shadow" banking system

In the process of securitization and off-loading of risk a key role was played by what has been baptized as a "shadow" banking system. The term was coined by the economist Paul McCulley.

In August 2007, most of the US's central bankers met in Jackson Hole, Wyoming, for the Federal Reserve Bank of Kansas City's annual Economic Policy Symposium. The meeting took place just after two hedge funds sponsored by Bear Stearns that had invested heavily in subprime mortgages collapsed and BNP Paribas suspended withdrawals from three money market mutual funds. It was at that meeting where McCulley, who was the chief economist of PIMCO (Pacific Investment Management Company), spoke of shadow banking to refer to a highly complex web of financial entities and activities that had developed outside of the regulatory realm. This was its official baptism although, as a matter of fact, already in the late 1980s and early 1990s, the economist Jane D'Arista had begun warning of the emergence of a "parallel banking system" which practically remained unnoticed until the financial crisis made it quite visible.

The main activities in this system include secured funding, hedging (primarily with over-the-counter (OTC) derivatives) and repurchase agreements (repos).

Box 2.1 Repos

Although repos have been in existence since at least the early part of the 20th century, it was not until the late 1970s and early 1980s that the market expanded rapidly thanks to major changes in repo contracting conventions.

Repo, which stands for repurchase agreement, implies direct lending between borrower and creditor.

In a repo contract, a firm borrows funds by selling a collateral asset today and promising to repurchase it at a later date. The 2003 decision by the SEC to allow mortgage asset-backed securities to be used for repos and the 2005 legal amendment excluding repos from bankruptcy processes led to a huge increase of the repo market in the US. Similar changes took place at the same time in Europe. However, there are at least two important differences between the US and the EU in relation to the repo markets. First, in the US, tri-party repos dominate the market. In a tri-party repo market a third party (a clearing bank) holds the collateral and is responsible for returning the cash to the creditor whereas a bilateral repo is directly settled between the two parties to the transactions (collateral and cash provider) without the interposition of a third party. In the EU, bilateral repos absolutely dominate the market. The second difference is that around 80% of the collateral used in the European repo markets is government securities while in the US they are mostly structured securities (Nabilou and Prüm, 2017: 13).

The repo rate is the rate at which cash is lent against collateral and it is agreed upon by the parties.

By the mid-1980s, a number of different dealers and clearing banks in the US had adopted the tri-party structure that had been introduced in the late 1970s, with tri-party repo gradually rising to prominence. The tri-party agent is in charge of services like collateral selection, payment and settlement, custody and management during the life of the transaction.

The majority of repos are for short terms, typically overnight. The performance risk on a repo is typically mitigated by a "haircut" that reflects the risk or liquidity of the securities. For instance, a haircut of 10% allows a cash loan of $900 million to be obtained by posting securities with a market value of $1.000 million.

Although shadow banks perform similar functions to those of depository banks there is a main difference: they do not rely on deposits but on securities markets to fund loans. In fact, they fund themselves in capital markets by issuing commercial paper, asset-backed commercial paper, asset-backed securities, collateralized debt obligations (CDOs)[3] and repurchase agreements (repos). Money market funds, investment funds and some other securities lenders are the main purchasers of these instruments. "The joining together of the supply of asset-backed securities with the demand for private alternatives to insured deposits led to the shadow banking system" (Gorton and Metrick, 2012: 137).

As shadow banks do not accept insured deposits, they were not subject to regulatory rules. As Ordoñez (2018: 34) points out, it was only after BNP Paribas suspended withdrawals from three funds invested in mortgage-backed securities that most of the public realized that shadow banking involved higher risks than more traditional banking.

Shadow banking is something difficult to define. It consists of a complex web of both institutions and activities but there is not a one-to-one correspondence between them. Most activities conducted by shadow banks are also developed by regulated banks and vice versa. Synthetically, shadow banking has been defined as "money market funding of capital market lending" (Mehrling, 2017).

> Shadow banking activities consist of credit, maturity, and liquidity transformation that take place without direct and explicit access to public sources of liquidity or credit backstops. These activities are conducted by specialized financial intermediaries called shadow banks, which are bound together along an intermediation chain known as the shadow banking system.
>
> (Pozsar et al., 2013: 1)

Ferrante (2015: 1) describes this system as "as a network of financial subjects that replicated the credit intermediation process by decomposing it in different activities, while heavily relying on securitization and sophisticated financial products."

Pozsar et al. (2013) identify seven steps in the process: 1) loan origination, 2) loan warehousing, 3) asset-backed securities (ABS) issuance, 4) ABS warehousing, 5) ABS CDO issuance, 6) ABS "intermediation," and 7) wholesale funding. Each step is handled by a specific type of shadow bank and through a specific funding technique.

Shadow banks competed with commercial banks by offering maturity transformation services too but they were not subject to regulatory rules as they do not accept insured deposits. The rationale behind regulation was that if the government was to insure bank deposits, it should also have some say in the risks that insured banks were allowed to take. As shadow banks do not accept insured deposits, regulation was considered unnecessary for them.

These lightly regulated institutions began to displace commercial banks as the primary funders of mortgage-related securities.

The shadow banking system is the child of the marriage celebrated at the end of the twentieth century between deregulation and financial innovation. As a result of this marriage, at the beginning of the 2000s the "originate-to-distribute" model became an extended practice in banking activity.

Deregulation allowed the appearance of universal banks which had been prohibited in the US following the 1930s legislation. Banks became large financial institutions dealing with a variety of clients and originating a variety of loans; among them, subprime mortgages became more and more significant in banks' portfolios. However, the risk associated with these loans could be shifted to other institutions (shadow banks) thanks to one of the financial innovations: securitization.

As stated before, shadow banks raised funds by selling short-term papers primarily to money market funds or through short-term repos. On the other hand, most of its assets – mortgage-backed securities in particular – had maturities measured in decades. Therefore, these credit intermediaries relied on short-term liabilities to fund illiquid long-term assets.

> In summary, leading up to the crisis, commercial and investment banks were heavily exposed to maturity mismatch both through granting liquidity backstops to their off-balance sheet vehicles and through their increased reliance on repo financing. Any reduction in funding liquidity could thus lead to significant stress for the financial system, as we witnessed starting in the summer of 2007.
> (Brunnermeier, 2009: 80)

Maturity mismatch has been a regular feature in banking industry because maturity transformation is precisely one of the main functions the financial system fulfills by borrowing money on short time frames and lending on longer ones.

This mismatch causes problems for banks if too many depositors attempt to withdraw at once – a situation known as a bank run. Government deposit insurance can avoid runs because it guarantees the bailout of depositors no matter how many depositors simultaneously withdraw. But investors′ dollars collected through the shadow banking industry were not protected by any kind of insurance. Shadow banking institutions did not have access to short-term, government-backed funding; the only way they had to return money to investors was by selling their assets.

The presence of maturity mismatch combined with the absence of an explicit safety net implied that small shocks could lead to large repercussions due to contagion effects.

Maturity mismatch has been increasing over time. In old times, banks:

> lent overwhelmingly over the short term, primarily for self-liquidating, trade-related working capital, as "real bills" financing trade. Even in the early German banking model where banks were supporting long-term capital investment, the key funding came from bond issuance placed by the banks themselves.
> (Goodhard and Perotti, 2015: 1)

A major contributor to maturity mismatch has precisely been the unprecedented expansion in long-maturity mortgage lending. "The share of mortgage loans in banks' total lending portfolios has roughly doubled over the course of the past century – from about 30% in 1900 to about 60% today" (Jordà et al., 2014: 2).

However, even more important than the maturity mismatch is the liquidity mismatch. If financial intermediaries hold long-term assets but they can sell them in case of necessity without incurring in significant losses or can borrow from money markets by pledging those assets as collateral, the maturity mismatch would not be a problem. But:

> when the financial sector runs into liquidity problems, triggered by runs by lenders, the sector sells assets whose prices then reflect an illiquidity discount. The lower asset prices lead to losses that deplete capital, further compromising liquidity. The critical point that emerges from this literature is that the liquidity of assets is endogenous.
>
> (Brunnermeier et al., 2014: 100)

At the same time, if the value of the assets used as collateral becomes too volatile, these can no longer be pledged. Moreover, as Brunnermeier and Sannikov (2016: 45) point out, the micro-prudent behavior by individual institutions may turn out into macro-imprudent results – the Paradox of Prudence. The sale of assets to improve individual institutions' liquidity depresses their prices leading to higher endogenous risk in the economy as a whole.

When the funds of shadow banks plunged because of the collapse of repos and asset-backed commercial paper, it became extremely difficult for them to reissue their securities as they matured. As a result, their funds dried up and they were forced to liquidate their assets at fire-sale prices, eroding their capital and tightening funding even further.

Credit rating agencies

John Moody founded the first rating agency in 1909. In 1916 the Poor Company followed suit. In 1941 it merged with Standard Statistics to form Standard and Poor's. Fitch Publishing Company started publishing financial information in 1913 and in 1924 introduced the now familiar AAA to D rating scale.

In 1931 the US Treasury Department adopted credit ratings as a measure of the quality of the bond accounts for the national banks. In the mid-1970s the Securities and Exchange Commission created the category of "nationally recognized statistical rating organization" and immediately recognized Moody's, Standard & Poor's and Fitch as the only firms within this category. These regulatory rules made the three rating agencies a central actor in the bond market. Banks and other financial institutions could satisfy the safety requirements of their regulators by just following the bond raters' pronouncements whatsoever their own evaluations of the risks of the bonds might be.

> Although there appear to be roughly 150 local and international credit rating agencies worldwide (…) Moody's, Standard & Poor's, and Fitch are clearly the

> dominant entities. All three operate on a worldwide basis, with offices on six continents; each has ratings outstanding on tens of trillions of dollars of securities.
> (White, 2010: 216)

Credit rating agencies played a key role in the incubation of the financial crisis. They "were an essential input into the process of manufacturing vast quantities of triple-rated securities with attractive yields. In a period of low interest rates, they were eagerly bought up by investors unaware of the real risks they entailed" (Beker, 2016: 48).

Without the generous ratings assigned by credit rating agencies to subprime mortgage-backed securities these assets would not have been so highly demanded by investors.

Credit rating agencies were ill-prepared for assessing this sort of assets. Traditionally, credit rating agencies had focused the majority of their business on single-name corporate finance – where there is only one company to be assessed. However, by having these new securities rated, the issuers created an illusion of comparability with existing single-name securities.

When the process of securitization started, credit rating agencies included the nascent field of structured finance in their business portfolio. Issuers of structured finance products combined mortgages and other financial assets and then sliced the securitized asset into tiers (tranches) grouping assets with similar underlying risks. The various tranches would be paid principal and interest from the funds received from the collateral pool in order of seniority. Thus, any shortfall would be allocated first to the lowest tranche and then to the next lowest tranche and so on up the capital structure. The same is true for any losses. Credit rating agencies were contracted to assess the risk of each of the tranches thus manufactured.

Rating of a structured financial product is, however, qualitatively different from a corporate bond rating where securities are assessed independently of each other. In the case of structured financial products, the rating process involves estimating the extent to which defaults in the underlying collateral pool might be correlated.

The problem is that "with multiple rounds of structuring, even minute errors at the level of the underlying securities that would be insufficient to alter the security's rating can dramatically alter the ratings of the structured finance securities" (Coval et al., 2009: 9). The estimates of risk depend crucially on whether default correlations have been estimated correctly.

The agencies' overly optimistic forecasts were based on historically low mortgage default and delinquency rates. However, substantial lending to subprime borrowers was a recent phenomenon and some models used by credit rating agencies were not even based on historical data because they referred to transactions for which there was no active trading market as there is in mature markets. On the other hand, past downturns in housing prices were mainly local phenomena but when the housing bubble exploded in 2007, real estate markets went down together and mortgage defaults soared across the US.

The high ratings assigned by credit rating agencies explain why a huge amount of dollars were invested in what proved to be highly risky assets. "The three credit rating agencies were key enablers of the financial meltdown. The mortgage-related securities at the heart of the crisis could not have been marketed and sold without their seal of approval" (FCIC, 2011: XXV). In fact, important financial institutions are not permitted to hold assets with less than an AAA rating from one of the major rating companies. There was thus a strong demand for high ratings which were generously provided by the credit rating agencies to illiquid, opaque, highly risky mortgage-related securities.

A theoretical argument advanced by Kartik et al. (2007) may help explain rating agencies' behavior. In the context of an analytical model of communication games, the authors assume a setting in which the sender of a message is interested in the average response of a population of receivers characterized by heterogeneous strategic sophistication. They demonstrate that in such cases there is a unique equilibrium that has the important property that in every state of the world, the sender induces a belief in naive receivers such that the average population response is in fact his/her bliss point.

A sophisticated receiver correctly infers the true state by inverting the observed message according to the equilibrium language. A credulous receiver instead interprets the equilibrium messages with some non-equilibrium-based rule and is accordingly deceived, taking biased actions. If naive receivers are on one side of the playing field and sophisticated ones are on the other one, the result may be something like what was observed in the subprime meltdown.

Concluding remarks

The interaction of these four factors – irrational expectations, securitization, shadow banking, and credit rating agencies – led to the subprime mortgage crisis. When house prices started falling most borrowers who could not afford their monthly payments had no alternative but to default their subprime mortgages; many of them found themselves holding mortgages in excess of the market values of their homes. Subprime-related securities experienced large losses; investors learned the hard way how risky those assets were in spite their almost risk-free ratings.

In the summer of 2007, panic started in the repo market, triggered by the increase in subprime mortgage defaults. Borrowers were forced to raise repo rates and haircuts to calm the lenders' concerns about the value and liquidity of the collateral should the counterparty bank fail.[4] However, even higher rates were insufficient to keep repo lenders in the market.

Lenders in the repo market massively abstained from rolling over the financing, just like depositors did in traditional runs on banks.

The effect of deleveraging in this sector on the market value of mortgage-backed securities further impaired the capital of financial intermediaries more broadly, requiring further deleveraging, in a vicious spiral. Brunnermeier (2009) provides a detailed description of this process. A liquidity crunch took place: asset-backed securities lost 40% of their value overnight (Gorton and Metrick, 2012). All of a sudden, assets which were considered highly liquid became absolutely illiquid.

A liquidity crunch is something which neither general equilibrium nor monetary theory has taken into consideration (Calvo, 2013: 1). A liquidity crunch is difficult to explain for mainstream economics. Economic fundamentals cannot explain why an asset has today a price 40% below the value it had yesterday. Economic fundamentals do not change overnight but fundamentals are useless when panic is on. Conventional economic theory cannot explain how billions of dollars of wealth can evaporate in 24 hours. This merely cannot happen in a world governed by the holy trinity of rational expectations, competition and efficiency. However, it did happen in the real world despite being a phenomenon that mainstream economic theory cannot explain.

Notes

1 Kindleberger and Aliber (2005) devote chapter 3 of their penetrating book on financial crisis to recall the different speculative manias which took place in economic history.
2 Likewise, the savings and loan industry had assumed that interest rates would remain low forever. When funding costs rose dramatically in the early 1980s, nearly 750 firms failed (Greenspan, 2014: 386).
3 CDOs are securities that hold different types of debt, such as mortgage-backed securities and corporate bonds, which are then sliced into varying levels of risk and sold to investors. While asset-backed securities have as their collateral a single class of loans the securities backing CDOs consist of many different types of asset classes.
4 Moro (2016) thoroughly describes the run on the repo market.

References

Adrian, T. and Shin, H. S. (2009). *The Shadow Banking System: Implications for Financial Regulation*. Federal Reserve of New York. Staff Report no. 382. July.
Beker, V.A. (2016). The American Financial Crisis. In B. Moro and V. A. Beker, *Modern Financial Crises: Argentina, United States and Europe*. Financial and Monetary Policy Studies 42. Switzerland: Springer International Publishing. doi:10.1007/978-3-319-20991-3_3.
Brunnermeier, M. K. (2009). Deciphering the Liquidity and Credit Crunch 2007–2008. *Journal of Economic Perspectives* 23(1): 77–100.
Brunnermeier, M. K., Gorton, G. and Krishnamurthy, A. (2014). Liquidity Mismatch Measurement. In M. Brunnermeier and A. Krishnamurthy (eds.), *Risk Topography: Systemic Risk and Macro Modeling*. Chicago, IL: University of Chicago Press.
Brunnermeier, M. K. and Sannikov, Y. (2016). The I Theory of Money. NBER Working Paper 22533. http://www.nber.org/papers/w22533.
Buiter, W. H. (2009). *Lessons from the Global Financial Crisis for Regulators and Supervisors*. Discussion Paper No 635. LSE Discussion Paper Series.
Calvo, G. (2013). *Puzzling Over the Anatomy of Crises: Liquidity and the Veil of Finance*. IMES discussion paper series.
Coval, J., Jurek, J. and Stafford, E. (2009). The Economics of Structured Finance. *Journal of Economic Perspectives* 23(1): 3–25.
FCIC (2011). *Final Report of the National Commission on the Causes of the Financial and Economic Crisis in the United States*. https://www.govinfo.gov/content/pkg/GPO-FCIC/pdf/GPO-FCIC.pdf.

Ferrante, F. (2015). *A Model of Endogenous Loan Quality and the Collapse of the Shadow Banking System*. Finance and Economics Discussion Series 2015–2021. Washington: Board of Governors of the Federal Reserve System. doi:10.17016/FEDS.2015.021.

Furceri, D. and Mourougane, A. (2009). *Financial Crises: Past Lessons and Policy Implications*. OECD Economics Department Working Papers, No. 668. Paris: OECD Publishing. doi:10.1787/226777318564.

Geithner, T. (2017). Are We Safe Yet? How to Manage Financial Crises. *Foreign Affairs*, January/February.

Geithner, T. (2019). The Early Phases of the Financial Crisis: Reflections on the Lender of Last Resort. *Journal of Financial Crises* 1(1).

Goodhard, C. and Perotti, E. (2015). Maturity Mismatch Stretching: Banking Has Taken a Wrong Turn. *CEPR Policy Insight* 81, May.

Gorton, G. and Metrick, A. (2012). Getting Up to Speed on the Financial Crisis: A One-Weekend-Reader's Guide. *Journal of Economic Literature* 50(1): 128–150.

Greenspan, A. (2014). *The Map and the Territory 2.0. Risk, Human Nature and the Future of Forecasting*. London: Penguin Books.

He, Z. and Krishnamurthy, A. (2019). Systemic Risk and the Macroeconomy. *American Economic Journal: Macroeconomics* 11(4): 1–37. doi:10.1257/mac.20180011.

International Monetary Fund (2008). *Global Financial Stability Report. Containing Systemic Risks and Restoring Financial Soundness*. World Economic and Financial Surveys. April.

Jordà, Ò., Schularick, M. and Taylor, A. M. (2014). *The Great Mortgaging: Housing Finance, Crises, and Business Cycles*. NBER Working Papers 20501.

Kartik N., Ottaviani, M. and Squintani, F. (2007). Credulity, Lies, and Costly Talk. *Journal of Economic Theory* 134(1): 93–116.

Kindleberger, Ch. P. and Aliber, R. Z. (2005). *Manias, Panics, and Crashes A History of Financial Crises*. Fifth Edition. Hoboken, NJ: John Wiley & Sons.

Lux, T. (1995). Herd Behaviour, Bubbles and Crashes. *The Economic Journal* 105(431): 881–896.

Mehrling, P. (2017). *Financialization and its discontents*. Conference CFP: Intersections of finance and society. http://financeandsociety.ed.ac.uk/ojs-images/financeandsociety/FS_EarlyView_Mehrling.html.

Mishkin, F. and Eakins, S. (2015). *Financial Markets and Institutions*. 8th Edition. Harlow: Pearson.

Moro, B. (2016). The Run on Repo and the Policy Interventions to Struggle the Great Crisis. In B. Moro and V. A. Beker, *Modern Financial Crises: Argentina, United States and Europe*. Financial and Monetary Policy Studies 42. Switzerland: Springer International Publishing. doi:10.1007/978-3-319-20991-3_3.

Nabilou, H. and Prüm, A. (2017). Shadow Banking in Europe: Idiosyncrasies and Their Implications for Financial Regulation. https://ssrn.com/abstract=3035831 or doi:10.2139/ssrn.3035831.

Ordoñez, G. (2018). Sustainable Shadow Banking. *American Economic Journal: Macroeconomics* 10(1): 33–56.

Pozsar, Z., Adrian, T., Ashcraft, A. B. and Boesky, H. (2013). Shadow Banking. *Economic Policy Review* 19(2). Available at SSRN: https://ssrn.com/abstract=2378449.

White, L. (2010). Markets: the Credit Rating Agencies. *Journal of Economic Perspectives 24*(2): 211–226.

3 What has been done during and after the crisis

Changes in bank regulation and supervision

During and after the 2007/2009 financial crisis a major process of reform of regulation and supervision of the banking industry took place. These reforms had two main aims: increasing the resilience of the financial system and overcoming what is known as moral hazard.

As pointed out in Chapter 2, the crisis was caused by excessive risk-taking by financial institutions.

From the onset of the crisis, emphasis was placed on the need for better regulation of banking systems and on enhancing the tools available to supervisory agencies with the declared purpose of realigning incentives so as to discourage excessive risk-taking.

This chapter starts with an analysis of the concept of moral hazard and its implications for the financial industry; then examines some of the key reforms in regulation and supervision since the crisis. However, some other reforms – in particular, micro- and macro-prudential regulatory reforms – will be analyzed in Chapter 7.

The moral hazard issues

Why did the federal government rescue Bear Stearns, a large Wall Street investment bank that was sinking under the weight of its subprime mortgage holdings, but refused to follow suit in the Lehman Brothers case?

The loan to Bear Stearns to facilitate its acquisition by JPMorgan Chase was the first time the Federal Reserve used its authority to lend to non-banks since the 1930s. The Bear rescue was criticized because – it was argued – it created a moral hazard problem: other financial institutions in trouble would interpret that the Fed was ready to rescue them as it did with Bear. Their managers could not be forced to do their best to keep their institutions safe if they expected the Fed to rescue them in case of failure.

"Moral hazard" is a concept borrowed by economics from insurance which refers to the fact that someone increases their exposure to risk because someone else bears the cost of risks. The typical example is someone who, after the fire insurance contract is signed, ignores safety measures knowing that they are safeguarded against the risk and there is the other party who will incur all the losses.

The Fed action was justified with the argument that if an investment giant like Bear Stearns failed, it could spark a run on other financial institutions with sizable exposure to troubled credit markets, creating a domino effect of defaults.

On the opposite side of the spectrum, the Fed action was criticized arguing that it could incentivize other investment banks and financial institutions to take excessive risks as they would interpret that the Fed was ready to step in to rescue them in case of difficulties.

When the time came to take a decision in the Lehman Brothers case, the moral hazard argument led the federal government not to bail it out in an attempt to teach financial markets a lesson.

The consequences of the decision were devastating. Lehman's failure sent financial markets and mortgage markets into a panic of unprecedented proportions.

One day after Lehman's bankruptcy, in an unprecedented move, the Fed had to inject an $85 billion two-year loan to AIG to prevent its bankruptcy. Additional funds would flow in the coming months. Why did a central bank have to rescue an insurance company? AIG had become a major seller of credit default swaps (CDS); these swaps insured the assets that supported corporate debt and mortgages. Lehman had over $400 billion in credit default swap contracts with AIG; Lehman's failure triggered a run on AIG, who had to pay out big money as a seller of protection on Lehman CDS. If AIG went bankrupt, it would have triggered the bankruptcy of many of the financial institutions that had bought these swaps. AIG's swaps on subprime mortgages pushed the company to the brink of bankruptcy. As the mortgages tied to the swaps defaulted, AIG lacked enough cash to pay the swap insurance. In the end, AIG's bailout had a cost of $182 billion.

After rescuing AIG, later that same week, the US Congress was asked for a $700 billion bailout to buy mortgage-backed securities that were in danger of defaulting; this finally became the Troubled Asset Relief Program (TARP) which, by the time it was completed, had been used in five areas: automotive, banking, credit, housing and insurance industries. Any talk against moral hazard had gone out the window in just one week.

Box 3.1 TARP

On September 20, 2008, the Secretary of the Treasury Henry Paulson submitted to Congress a request for $700 billion for the purchase of troubled mortgage-related assets. Congress rejected the proposal and replaced it with a bill which was passed on October 3 that included an expanded definition of the troubled assets the Treasury could purchase. It authorized the immediate spending of $350 billion and an additional $350 billion at a later date.

A couple of days later, the Treasury announced that it would make $250 billion available to financial institutions through purchases of preferred stock instead of buying trouble assets as was the original purpose of the law. At the same time the Treasury announced the purchase of $40 billion of newly issued AIG preferred shares under the Troubled Asset Relief Program (TARP). This came in addition to a previous $85 billion Fed loan to keep the insurance company from collapsing. In March 2009 the Treasury committed another $29.84 billion in AIG. These and other changes made the total AIG financial bailout package $182 billion.

In December 2008, President Bush used his executive authority to declare that TARP funds could be spent on any program deemed necessary to alleviate the financial crisis.

The Homeowner Affordability and Stability Plan set aside $75 billion in TARP funds to help homeowners refinance or restructure their mortgages.

A total of $80.7 billion from TARP funds was devoted to bail out General Motors and Chrysler who had asked Congress for help arguing there were one million jobs at stake. The Treasury Department lent money and bought stock ownership in GM and Chrysler. The federal government took over GM and Chrysler in March 2009.

On December 2014 TARP came to an end when the Treasury sold its last remaining shares of Ally Financial, formerly known as General Motors Acceptance Corporation. According to a TARP report to Congress, $427 billion were disbursed and $442 billion were recovered, which left a $15 billion profit.

The next victim of Lehman going bust was the money market funds industry. A rapid exodus from money market funds began after the shares of one of them "broke the buck"[1] due to losses incurred when Lehman Brothers declared bankruptcy. In order to stop the run on the money market funds the Treasury Department had to step in and guarantee that the value of participating money funds would not fall below the standard $1 a share.

In spite of lip service paid to the argument on avoiding moral hazard, the test done in the Lehman Brothers case had dissuaded policy makers from going on holding the line against it and bailouts followed one after the other. It is one thing to talk about moral hazard in a university classroom and another one to implement measures against it from the chair of the Fed or the Department of the Treasury. The real world proved to be quite different from what academics sitting in their comfortable ivory towers imagine.

Financial firms are no longer stand-alone entities but a diverse set of interconnected components that distribute risk and are exposed to it, oftentimes in ways that are not transparent or expected. The negative externalities of bank failure and the economic and social costs associated with the chain reaction it may trigger weigh a lot more in policy decisions than the moral hazard argument.

Only in a contagion-proof world can the government and regulators credibly commit to a policy of allowing any bank to fail regardless of its size.

Too-big-to-fail

In May 1984, Continental Illinois National Bank and Trust Company became insolvent in what at the time was the largest bank failure in US history, and it remained so until the global financial crisis of 2007–2009. The Chicago-based bank was the seventh largest bank in the United States. The fear of spillovers led regulators to extend unusual support to it. Not only did the FDIC guarantee depositors up to the $100,000 insurance limit, but it also guaranteed all accounts exceeding $100,000 and even prevented losses for Continental Illinois bondholders. The unusual treatment of Continental Illinois gave popular rise to the term "too-big-to-fail." The term refers to a financial institution whose failure could spill over to other firms or sectors of the economy, and thus is expected to receive government support in the event of trouble.

When a business fails, it would ordinarily enter corporate insolvency or administration procedures to be sold or liquidated, with any value returned to creditors. Achieving this in a manner that meets financial stability objectives is more difficult in the context of a financial institution. Critical services provided by the institution may need to be continued or wound down in an orderly manner outside normal insolvency processes. In addition, creditors are often other financial institutions – imposing losses on these institutions. If the failure affects a large financial institution not only can this cause immediate failures of its counterparties in both the banking and the rest of the financial system, but it can also lead to a crisis of confidence that may spill over to other banks and financial institutions, leading to a full-scale financial crisis and a large decline in investment and output. Disorderly resolution of one institution of a certain size may create instability in the rest of the financial system as the Lehman's failure illustrated.

However, not everybody is convinced of this. For example, according to the so-called fundamentalist view (Calomiris, 2007), banks are inherently stable. This means that unless they are insolvent, they neither can be victims of deposit withdrawals nor a major source of macroeconomic shocks. Therefore, it may be desirable to limit or even avoid government protection of banks in order to preserve market discipline in banking: banks should be allowed to fail in order to prevent moral hazard. Preserving market discipline encourages good risk management by banks no matter what its costs may be.

In a very ill-timed article published in December 2006, mainstream economist Frederic Mishkin argued that the importance of the too-big-to-fail problem was overstated: the Federal Deposit Insurance Corporation Improvement Act (FDICIA) legislation of 1991 limited the FDIC's discretion to protect bank creditors, and limited the Fed's ability to lend to troubled banks. Thus, the too-big-to-fail problem was no longer a serious one as it has been in the past (Mishkin, 2006). Less than one year later, reality showed how wrong he was.

Mishkin's article was a criticism of the book *Too Big to Fail: The Hazards of Bank Bailouts* by Gary Stern and Ron J. Feldman, at that time president and a vice president, respectively, of the Federal Reserve Bank of Minneapolis. These authors argued that not only had the too-big-to-fail policy been a serious problem in the past but it had even gotten worse because of the increasing size and complexity of banking organizations. They maintained that the presence of too-big-to-fail encourages banks to grow in size to take advantage of the too-big-to-fail subsidy, so that banks are larger than is socially optimal.

Mishkin dismissed this idea with the argument that the passage of FDICIA legislation in 1991 had limited the too-big-to-fail problem. He pointed out that "by 2004, the largest banks have more than doubled their capital ratios and are now well capitalized, more than meeting the Basel requirements" (Mishkin, 2006: 997). The higher capital ratios for large banks were interpreted as a signal that they were no longer willing to take on risk because they were less likely to be bailed out. "Higher capital means that large banks have more to lose if they get in trouble and this also mitigates any incentives to take on risk created by too-big-to-fail" (Mishkin, 2006: 998).

According to Mishkin, the bottom line on the status of the too-big-to-fail problem was that it appeared to be far less severe in the 2000s than it was in the 1980s.

A couple of months after the article was published, the too-big-too-fail argument was used to justify the bailout of investment banks like Bear Stearns, Citigroup, Goldman Sachs and Morgan Stanley, an insurance company like AIG, the federal takeover of the government-sponsored Fannie Mae and Freddie Mac, and even the rescue of non-financial companies like General Motors and Chrysler; in the latter two cases the emphasis was placed on the thousands of jobs that would be lost in case of bankruptcy at both the companies themselves and at suppliers and dealers.

The conclusion is that in the real world the risk of encouraging moral hazard collapses in the presence of the "too-big-to-fail" argument. And the "too-big-to-fail" problem was at least as big in the 2000s as it was in the 1980s when Continental Illinois was bailed out.

This leads us to the systemic risk issue which will be analyzed in Chapter 5.

Meanwhile, let us take a look on the main reforms in the financial architecture which took place after the crisis.

Main reforms in the financial architecture

In response to the crisis, the G20 countries agreed on a large set of financial sector reforms with four core areas:

- building resilient financial institutions
- ending too-big-to-fail
- making derivatives markets safer
- transforming shadow banking into resilient market-based finance

(Buch, 2017)

Improving the resilience of the financial system and enhancing buffers against unexpected shocks have been the declared key goals of post-crisis financial sector reforms. However, the implementation of reforms in the regulation and oversight of shadow banks is still at an early stage (Financial Stability Board, 2016).

As a matter of fact, the main aim of the post-crisis financial sector reforms, particularly in the US, has been to overcome moral hazard in order to avoid taxpayer losses. In the post-crisis anti-bailout environment this became the first objective of the new regulatory framework. This objective only partially overlaps with the one of preventing a new financial crisis. Increasing the capital and liquidity requirements to improve the resilience of the financial system are measures clearly aligned with both targets of avoiding a new crisis and not putting taxpayer money at risk. But in the case that prevention fails and a crisis bursts, both objectives diverge and the legislators have given priority to the one of preventing tax dollars from being used to save failing financial institutions no matter what it may cost to the economy as a whole.

From a theoretical point of view, it has been argued that market discipline ensures that financial institutions do not take on excessive risks. Providing the right incentives to owners and investors – it was argued – is the first step in ensuring a stable banking system. For market discipline to work effectively – the argument goes – everyone needs to feel that they have their money credibly at risk and that they will experience losses if they take excessive risks, instead of being bailed out at the expense of the taxpayers.

Of course, this argument is valid if and only if bankers and investors behave in accordance with the kind of rationality assumed in mainstream economic models. As we have pointed out in the previous chapter, rationality may be a usual assumption in the class room but not always a good description of economic agents' behavior in the real world. Excluding *ex ante* bailouts does not necessarily guarantee that bankers and financial managers will avoid excessive risk-taking especially if this avoidance entails giving up short-run huge profits.

The legislators' message to the bankers is: do not think that the Treasury or the Fed is behind you to save your institutions; so, act responsibly. The message is also addressed to uninsured large depositors: you will suffer losses if the bank fails. But the result may just be that in case of doubt they will probably rush to withdraw their money from the financial institutions with the hope of being the first in doing so. The cure may be worse than the illness.

Financial regulation reform

As mentioned above, the US Dodd-Frank Act passed in 2010 puts the emphasis on prevention while trying to reduce taxpayer exposure to exposure to loss in case of resolution of financial institutions.

Concerning prevention, the Act created two new agencies, the Financial Stability Oversight Council (FSOC) – a committee of regulators in charge of monitoring the entire system for risks and addressing them before they do harm – and the Office of Financial Research (OFR) to support FSOC by collecting and analyzing data.

The new legislation takes into account the expansion of transactions among financial institutions and changes in the kinds of transactions that channel credit flows. In this respect, the National Bank Act was amended to extend the previous limit on loans as a share of capital to include financial as well as non-financial borrowers and created an expanded definition of exposures to include not only loans but also derivatives, repos, reverse repos and securities borrowing and lending.[2]

Limits on the exposure to any client or affiliate in relation to a bank's capital is now based on a broad definition of derivatives that includes contracts, agreements, swaps and options.

In order to reduce the incentives to operate through shadow banking activities, "the Dodd-Frank Act (section 331) requires the assessments of consolidated assets minus tangible equity to compute liabilities instead of just considering deposit liabilities, as used to be the case before the reform" (Ordoñez, 2018: 35).

In 2011, the Securities and Exchange Commission and the Commodity Futures Trading Commission established new confidential information reporting requirements to monitor hedge funds and other private funds, and identify potential systemic risks associated with their activities. As at the end of 2016, approximately 2,800 investment advisers had reported information on 27,000 different kinds of funds. The Private Funds Statistics released quarterly since October 2015 offers to the public aggregated data reported by those private fund advisers.

What is the expected impact of these reforms?

> The most important effect of these provisions will be to rein in the number of transactions between banks and other financial institutions and their credit exposure to any one financial institution. But by enlarging the list of transactions that constitute credit exposure, they also reduce the risk posed to banks by the increased use of transactions with nonfinancial customers outside the previous limits on loans. Limiting exposure to derivatives and contingent liabilities related to any one customer, financial or nonfinancial, will reduce the immense volume of banks' off-balance sheet liabilities and retard their future growth. In addition, limits on banks' credit exposures to other financial institutions will shrink the short-term wholesale funding markets.
>
> (D'Arista, 2011: 6)

The Dodd-Frank Act is meant to reduce the interconnectedness of financial institutions and, as a consequence, systemic risk.

However, the repo market and money market funds, whose functions are not substantially different than demand deposits – and have been shown to be systemically important – remain mostly unregulated.

Volcker rule

The so-called Volcker rule was enacted as part of the Dodd-Frank Act; it limits bank holding companies' investment in proprietary trading activities, such as hedge funds and private equity, and prohibits them from bailing out these investments. It aims to protect bank customers by preventing banks from making certain types of speculative investments that contributed to the 2007/2009 financial crisis. The logic behind the Volcker rule is quite simple: in the years leading up to the financial crisis, Lehman and other banks decided to take positions in mortgage-backed securities, and when those positions went south, so did the firms. By outlawing proprietary trading and restricting banks' abilities to invest in hedge funds and private equity funds, banks would become less risky, and less likely to require a bailout. The rule took effect in 2015 and some changes were already made to it in 2019. One of them is that banks are no longer assumed to be engaging in banned trades when they conduct short-term transactions.

The Volcker rule restriction does not apply to non-bank dealers. So, proprietary trading is not restricted for them.

The "originate to distribute" model

As stated in the previous chapter, in many cases, firms originating subprime mortgages quickly sold them, relieving them of any downside risk if a mortgage borrower ultimately defaulted. Similarly, sponsors pooling mortgage loans quickly passed along the risk of default to the investors of mortgage-backed securities.

Thus, the originators and securitizers seldom retained meaningful "skin in the game" as loans were passed on to other financial investors, thereby off-loading risk. Those market participants received immediate profits with each deal while assuming that they faced little or no risk of loss if the loans defaulted. As a result, securitizers had very little incentive to maintain adequate lending and servicing standards. Moreover, an active market arose in selling and repackaging equity tranches in collateralized debt obligations, thereby removing all risk of loss from the original security issuer.

The problems generated by the "originate and distribute" model were addressed in the Dodd-Frank Act by requiring security issuers to retain no less than 5% of the equity risk, so they have an incentive to more carefully choose the mortgages and other assets they include in the pool. There are some kinds of mortgages which, however, are exempted from risk retention.

An empirical research examines how the implementation of risk retention regulation differentially impacted commercial mortgage loans subject to the new rules relative to those exempted. The findings suggest that risk retention significantly affected the underwriting of mortgages that were securitized. On the one hand, loans subject to risk retention requirements have become safer. On the other hand, borrowers pay significantly higher interest rates. Thus, the implementation of risk retention rules seems to have achieved the policy goal of making securitized loans safer, yet transferring the cost of higher safety to borrowers. The conclusion is that "loans subject to risk retention requirements appear to be less likely to become troubled" (Furfine, 2018: 32).

Bailouts

The Dodd-Frank Act debate took place in an environment of public contempt for too-big-to-fail policies and a strong desire to avoid exposure of taxpayer funds in addressing systemic risk concerns.

Taking into consideration the tide of public opinion, the Dodd-Frank Act prohibits emergency assistance to individual firms as was done in 2008. Any emergency lending program or facility should only be for the purpose of providing liquidity to the financial system as a whole and not to a particular financial company.

The deepening of the financial crisis in 2008 had led the Federal Reserve to revive an obscure provision added to the Federal Reserve Act in 1932: Section 13(3). It was invoked by the Fed in the cases of Bear Stearns and AIG to extend credit to *non-bank* financial firms for the first time since the 1930s.

Concerns in Congress about some of the Fed's actions under Section 13(3) during the financial crisis led to the section's amendment. While preserving some discretion to create broadly based facilities to address unpredictable market-access problems during a crisis, the intention of the provision in the Dodd-Frank Act is to prevent the Fed from bailing out non-bank failing firms. However, it preserves the ability of the Federal Reserve to provide more generally eligible assistance to shadow banking sectors through the Term Asset Backed Liquidity Facility (TALF). Title II of the Dodd-Frank Act allows the FDIC to resolve the failure of any firm, including shadow banking firms, if their failure may pose a threat to financial stability.

The argument to prevent the Fed from bailing out failing firms was that such assistance would not be necessary in the future because the too-big-to-fail issue has been dealt with through the creation of an Orderly Liquidation Authority (OLA). OLA appoints the Federal Deposit Insurance Corporation as a receiver to liquidate any "systemically important financial institution" that fails.[3] To fund these activities, an Orderly Liquidation Fund (OLF) was created to provide a source of emergency liquidity in receivership.

Summarizing, bailouts are explicitly banned and emergency lending is subject to stricter rules than before the crisis. Specifically, the Dodd-Frank Act requires the Fed to ensure

> that any emergency lending program or facility is for the purpose of providing liquidity to the financial system, and not to aid a failing financial company, and that the security for emergency loans is sufficient to protect taxpayers from losses and that any such program is terminated in a timely and orderly fashion.
>
> (Section 1101(a) (6))

Such lending must now be made in connection with a "program or facility with broad-based eligibility," cannot "aid a failing financial company" or "borrowers that are insolvent," and cannot have "a purpose of assisting a single and specific company avoid bankruptcy" or similar resolution. In addition, the Fed needs the prior approval of the Secretary of the Treasury for any emergency lending program.

These provisions aim at mitigating moral hazard problems. However, Geithner (2017) and others argue that it could make an appropriate response to the next crisis more difficult.

The fact is that:

> in the wake of the most recent financial crisis, there has been both a backlash against anything seen as providing assistance to troubled firms and an increased focus by policymakers on extreme losses that leave a financial institution insolvent. The result has been a post-crisis emphasis on providing a mechanism for resolving/restructuring failed firms ... at the expense of other emergency powers.
>
> (Group of Thirty, 2018: 14)

Although the Dodd-Frank Act added restrictions to Section 13(3), attempting to ban future assistance to failing firms, during the COVID crisis the Fed was able to invoke that obscure clause to create some new broadly based facilities and reinstate others.[4]

However, what may happen if a global systemically important bank needs to be resolved is still an untested issue; political costs could be deemed too high and some sort of bailout may be considered necessary in spite of the legal constraints. Broadly speaking, the new resolution and restructuring regimes designed after the crisis "do not reduce to zero the possibility that governments will need to intervene to rescue failing financial firms under some future circumstances" (Group of Thirty, 2018: 12). On the other hand, as Scott (2016: 14) puts it, "the reality is that creditors of financial institutions will run if a large financial institution is put into resolution – better safe than sorry – and we need to be prepared to deal with that."

Derivatives

Derivatives played a key role in the 2007/2009 financial crisis. In fact, they served as a vector for contagion, helping to spread the crisis throughout the financial system.

Credit default swap (CDS) is a derivative tied to debt securities such as bonds that promise certain future payments. A CDS is a sort of insurance against non-payment: the buyer of a CDS is entitled to the par value of the contract by the seller of the swap, should the issuer default on payments.

Many CDSs issued in the 2000s were tied to subprime mortgage-backed securities. Most of them were sold by AIG Financial Products – a subsidiary of AIG with major operations in London. AIG wrote $656 billion in credit insurance on structured finance products with only $54 billion in resources to pay those claims. How was this possible? The performance of AIG Financial Products was guaranteed by its US parent. It was not required to post collateral on its transactions providing AIG's credit rating remained above AA. Only when, all of a sudden, AIG's credit rating fell below AA and it was unable to provide the required collateral, did regulators become aware of the risks that had been taken.

When the mortgage market crashed, payments on CDSs were triggered. As losses on credit default swaps accumulated, AIG's financial position deteriorated; if AIG went bankrupt, it would have defaulted on all of the promised payments on the credit default swaps it had sold on mortgage-backed securities, putting at risk most of the financial industry. As of December 2007, AIG had written credit default swaps with a notional value of $527 billion (McDonald and Paulson, 2015: 18). The US government stepped in and AIG was rescued at a cost of $182 billion.

Derivatives are either traded over-the-counter (OTC), i.e. directly between two parties without intermediation or exchange-traded – traded through specialized derivatives exchanges or other exchanges. Previous to the financial crisis, AIG sold a gigantic amount of OTC credit default swaps.

Derivatives exposures were at the time of the financial crisis an important contributor to systemic risk. In fact, as financial asset prices fell, a complex and under-collateralized web of OTC derivative trades between financial market participants was revealed. The resulting exposures and demands for collateral greatly amplified the stress and uncertainty in the financial system.

After the crisis, the regulation of derivatives in the US was addressed in the Title VII of the Dodd-Frank Act. Its purpose is granting increased access to data by regulators. The law directed the Commodity Futures Trading Commission (CFTC) and the Securities and Exchange Commission (SEC) to draft the appropriate implementing regulations. As a result of the Dodd-Frank Act, the CFTC became the main US federal regulator of derivatives markets. Under CFTC regulations, counterparties to a derivative trade have now the obligation to report in real-time the trade to an approved Swap Data Repository.

The Dodd-Frank Act mandated the central clearing of all standardized derivatives, including the largest category of derivatives, standard interest rate swaps.

In the case of OTC derivatives, its decentralized nature together with the heterogeneity of the instruments traded implies a lack of transparency with the possibility that market participants and regulators may underestimate counterparty risk. For this reason, there has been increased pressure to move derivatives to trade on exchanges. It was understood that improved transparency in the derivatives markets and further regulation of OTC derivatives and market participants would be necessary to limit excessive and opaque risk-taking and to mitigate the systemic risk posed by OTC derivatives transactions, markets and practices.

At the global level, the OTC derivatives reform agenda has been progressing since in 2009 G20 Leaders agreed it would be one of the priorities in the efforts to avoid a future financial crisis. The reform is guided by three main principles: universal supervision, transparency through exchange-trading and price reporting, and central clearing. As a result, there has been a trend away from customized OTC derivatives toward more standard products.

The Financial Stability Board (FSB) was established after the aforementioned G20 meeting in 2009; it replaced the former Financial Stability Forum and brings together national authorities from 23 countries and the European Union. One of its first tasks has been the removal of barriers to trade reporting and the introduction of other reforms to improve transparency in the OTC derivatives market.

At the same G20 meeting, it was decided that a critical mass of dealer banks' derivative-related risks would be moved to derivatives' central counterparties in order to move the risk from OTC derivatives outside the banking system.

An initial result of these initiatives has been that "comprehensive trade reporting requirements have been implemented in 22 jurisdictions; central clearing frameworks in 18 jurisdictions; and platform trading frameworks in 14 jurisdictions" (FSB, 2018a: 13).

This is in huge contrast with the existing situation before 2007 when OTC CDS transactions were barely disclosed. However, challenges to the effectiveness of trade reporting remain, including a lack of harmonization of data formats and other data quality issues, as well as various legal barriers to reporting and to authorities' access to data, according to FSB.

Losses of derivative instruments as a result of the deterioration in the creditworthiness of a counterparty were a major source of losses for banks during the global financial crisis. This is why Basel III introduced a significant increase in the capital requirements for counterparty risk, in particular on OTC derivatives transactions.

A FSB's line of work has been to push FSB jurisdictions to develop frameworks for determining when standardized OTC derivatives should be centrally cleared. A central clearing counterparty (CCP) is a special-purpose financial institution whose only business is to stand in between the original buyers and sellers of OTC derivatives. If credit derivatives are standardized and traded on a central exchange, this institution would be in charge of ensuring that the parties to the transaction have the necessary collateral to make good on their promises. Regulatory authorities are in charge of making sure that the central exchange has the necessary reserves in the event the counterparties fail.

Data shows a significant increase in the notional amount outstanding of centrally cleared OTC derivatives since the crisis. This is especially true for interest rate and credit derivatives whose clearing levels were around 24% and 5%, respectively, in 2009; by the first quarter of 2018 these levels had risen to approximately 60% and 38%. Clearing levels for the most standardized OTC derivatives such as fixed-floating interest rate swaps and default swaps referencing standard credit indices were even higher (FSB, 2018b: 17).

The fact that central clearing is limited to standardized derivatives means that a significant proportion of less standardized OTC contracts will continue to be written on a bilateral basis without the intermediation of a central counterparty. The International Monetary Fund estimates that one-third of interest rate and credit derivatives and two-thirds of equity, commodity and foreign exchange derivatives will not be suited to standardization and will remain non-centrally cleared. One important tool for managing the systemic risks of non-centrally-cleared derivatives is margin requirements. In the event of a counterparty default, margin protects the surviving party by absorbing losses using the collateral provided by the defaulting entity.

In this respect, the then Federal Reserve Vice Chair Janet Yellen argued that "robust and consistent initial margin requirements will help prevent the kind of contagion that was sparked by AIG" (Yellen, 2013).

Besides central clearing, the G20 Leaders have also mandated that standardized OTC derivatives should be traded on exchanges or electronic trading platforms. However, implementation has been rather slow in this respect.

Moreover, it is argued that:

> there is a danger in trying to trade OTC derivatives in the same way as exchange-traded derivatives. This is because there are important differences between the two. OTC derivatives trade intermittently whereas exchange-traded derivatives such as futures trade continuously. The size of a typical OTC derivative is much larger than that of a typical exchange-traded derivative. There are fewer market participants in the OTC market, but they are more sophisticated than the average participant in exchange-traded markets.
>
> (Hull, 2017: 1)

The argument may be true for those OTC traded derivatives that are tailored to the specific needs of the customer but it does not apply to more standardized OTC derivatives.

The fact that there are some countries which are slower in implementing the reform poses the peril that companies may move their derivative trades to those jurisdictions where the reform is yet incomplete.

Anyway, in spite of all efforts to regulate as many derivatives as possible, for sure there will be some which will escape regulation. This should not be a problem for the economy as a whole, provided they are prevented from contaminating with systemic risks the so-called systemically important financial institutions (SIFIs).

On the other hand, it should be taken into consideration the warning by Véron (2016: 4) that the G20 move toward more central clearing may be leading to the concentration of systemic risk in CCPs or clearing houses, creating new forms of systemic risk. In the same direction, Baranova et al. (2017: 37) warn that CCPs are "a potentially new 'too big to fail' entity" which should too be stress-tested and whose resolution plans should be agreed to and implemented.

On this subject, the Financial Stability Board warns in its 2019 Resolution Report that no credible resolution plans are in place for any of the 13 major CCPs identified as systemically relevant in more than one jurisdiction.

In the US, Title VIII of Dodd-Frank Act aims at strengthening the supervision of financial market utilities, including central counterparties designated as systemically important, by requiring annual examinations as well as ex ante reviews of material rule and operational changes. Large US CCPs are designated by the Financial Stability Oversight Council as systemically important.

However, in the case of clearing houses in trouble the restriction on emergency lending from the Fed to them – unless especially authorized by FSOC – forces orderly liquidation as practically the only way out; but this is a process which may take several weeks, if not months. In the meantime, uncertainty may cause some stress in financial markets.

Growing systemic risk concentration in CCPs and the significant potential for contagion risks across CCPs and major banking groups makes Véron's warning absolutely valid. Fabio Panetta (2020), Member of the Executive Board of the ECB, predicts that:

> if prefunded CCP margins and default funds are eroded, CCPs' ability to recover their financial strength depends on the capacity of their clearing members to absorb large and unexpected losses on an ad hoc basis. This may be a challenge in situations of severe market stress, when banks may need to withstand credit and liquidity pressures from multiple sources.

He also draws attention to the diverging interests between banks and CCPs in CCP risk mitigation and comments on the difficulties of developing a credible CCP resolution strategy, in particular the lack of granular data on central clearing interdependencies due to the strict confidentiality of data on the exposures of individual participants.

Money market fund (MMF)

MMFs are mutual funds that invest in short-term debt, such as treasury bills, commercial paper or certificates of deposit, and are used by investors as an alternative to bank deposits.

When the Primary Reserve Fund "broke the buck" after the failure of Lehman Brothers, it precipitated a massive run on prime MMFs, mainly by institutional investors who were concerned about MMF exposures to troubled financial firms. The run would likely have been far more severe had the Treasury not temporarily guaranteed MMF balances. Because large financial firms depend heavily on MMFs for short-term funding, the run on MMFs generated significant additional stresses on the financial system at the peak of the crisis.

Specific reforms were enacted to the money market mutual funds. In the EU, the MMF Regulation effective from January 2019 introduced stricter liquidity requirements for MMFs to meet any sudden withdrawal of investment, established rules on portfolio diversification and valuation of assets, increased the requirements for credit quality, prevented MMFs from receiving any external financial support, and imposed direct obligations on MMF fund managers.

In the US, in 2014, the Securities and Exchange Commission (SEC) issued new rules for MMF management; the new rules place some restrictions on portfolio holdings while enhancing liquidity and quality requirements. The most fundamental change was the requirement for prime MMFs to move from a fixed $1 share price to a floating net asset value (NAV), which introduced the risk of principal where it had never existed. It also introduced redemption gates and fees at the fund's discretion should its weekly liquid assets fall below 30%. However, the SEC rejected the idea of imposing capital requirements to MMFs suggested by FSOC and only accepted a much lighter requirement that only applied to a subset of MMFs. This reform took effect in October 2016.

The fact that the share price is no longer fixed implies that when many investors redeem their shares simultaneously, this can adversely affect the value of the fund shares for the remaining investors. This "first-mover advantage" creates incentives akin to depositors in bank runs: investors have an incentive to move their money out before others do; and the higher the risk of redemptions, the more investors will try to exit ahead of others.

This happened in March 2020 when prime MMFs were hit by large-scale redemptions at the onset of the COVID 19 crisis, as explained in the Epilogue.

Notes

1 When the price of a share in a money market fund dips below the $1-per-share price that it is supposed to hold, the fund is said to break the buck.

2 I am indebted to Jane D'Arista for drawing my attention to this aspect of the financial legislation reform.

3 This portion of Dodd-Frank was repealed by the House in June 2017 although the repeal has not become law. Ex-Chairman Ben Bernanke (2017) firmly opposed to the reform. A report by the Treasury in 2018 recommends retaining OLA although adopting a new Chapter 14 of the US Bankruptcy Code to make resorting to OLA proceedings less likely.

4 See Epilogue for details.

References

Baranova, Y., Coen, J., Lowe, P., Noss, J. and Silvestri, L. (2017). *Simulating Stress Across the Financial System: The Resilience of Corporate Bond Markets and the Role of Investment Funds.* Bank of England Financial Stability Paper No. 42, July, 3–6. https://www.bankofengland.co.uk/-/media/boe/files/working-paper/2018/rethinking-financial-stability.pdf?la=en&hash=6A14C6F12C1DEFFDD57BD5C3255493BFE5F02060.

Bernanke, B. (2017). *Why Dodd-Frank's Orderly Liquidation Authority Should Be Preserved?* Brookings. https://www.brookings.edu/blog/ben-bernanke/2017/02/28/why-dodd-franks-orderly-liquidation-authority-should-be-preserved/.

Buch, C. (2017). *How Can We Protect Economies From Financial Crises?*Deutsche Bundesbank. https://www.bundesbank.de/Redaktion/EN/Reden/2017/2017_07_08_buch.htm.

Calomiris, C. W. (2007). *Bank Failures in Theory and History: The Great Depression and other "Contagious" Events.* NBER Working Paper 13597. https://www.nber.org/papers/w13597.pdf.

D'Arista, J. (2011). *Reregulating and Restructuring the Financial System: Some Critical Provisions of the Dodd-Frank Act.* PERI Working Paper Series N° 272. October. http://citeseerx.ist.psu.edu/viewdoc/download?doi=10.1.1.361.1540&rep=rep1&type=pdf.

Financial Stability Board (2016). *Implementation and Effects of the G20 Financial Regulatory Reforms.* http://www.fsb.org/wp-content/uploads/Report-on-implementation-and-effects-of-reforms.pdf.

Financial Stability Board (2018a). *Implementation and Effects of the G20 Financial Regulatory Reforms: Fourth Annual Report.* https://www.fsb.org/wp-content/uploads/P281118-1.pdf.

Financial Stability Board (2018b). *Incentives to Centrally Clear Over-The-Counter (OTC) Derivatives.* https://www.bis.org/publ/othp29.pdf.

Furfine, C. (2018). *The Impact of Risk Retention Regulation on the Underwriting of Securitized Mortgages.* https://www.fdic.gov/bank/analytical/cfr/bank-research-conference/annual-18th/21-furfine.pdf.

Geithner, T. (2017). Are We Safe Yet? How to Manage Financial Crises. *Foreign Affairs*, January/February.

Group of Thirty (2018). *Managing the Next Financial Crisis.* Washington DC: Group of Thirty.

Hull, J. (2017). *The New Rules for OTC Derivatives.* https://knect365.com/riskminds/article/52a9e957-b2e4-431b-82f5-864b721d1054/the-new-rules-for-otc-derivatives.

McDonald, R. and Paulson, A. (2015). *AIG in Hindsight.* NBER Working Paper No. 21108. http://www.nber.org/papers/w21108.

Mishkin, F. S. (2006). How Big a Problem is too Big to Fail? A Review of Gary Stern and Ron Feldman´s Too Big to Fail: the Hazards of Bank Bailouts. *Journal of Economic Literature*, XLIV (December): 988–1004.

Ordoñez, G. (2018). Sustainable Shadow Banking. *American Economic Journal: Macroeconomics* 10(1): 33–56. https://doi.org/10.1257/mac.20150346.

Panetta, F. (2020). *Joining Forces: Stepping Up Coordination on Risks in Central Clearing.* European Central Bank. https://www.ecb.europa.eu/press/key/date/2020/html/ecb.sp200226~e33a0d0c1c.en.html.

Scott, H. S. (2016). *Connectedness and Contagion: A Global Perspective.* Address to the International Monetary Fund.

Véron, N. (2016). Financial Regulation: The G20's Missing Chinese Dream. *Policy Contribution*, 19. http://bruegel.org/wp-content/uploads/2016/10/PC-19-2016.pdf.

Yellen, J. (2013). *Interconnectedness and Systemic Risk: Lessons from the Financial Crisis and Policy Implications.* Speech at the American Economic Association/American Finance Association Joint Luncheon, San Diego, California, January 4. https://www.federalreserve.gov/newsevents/speech/yellen20130104a.htm.

4 The shadow banking system and the post-2007–2009 regulatory reform

The role of the shadow banking system in the financial crisis

The emergence of a large and diverse shadow banking system, prior to the crisis mainly in the US and subsequent to it elsewhere around the world, deeply changed the shape of financial activity.

"By 2007, over 60 percent of financial sector liabilities were funding shadow banking and less than 40 percent funded 'traditional' regulated liabilities such as bank deposits, checking accounts, interbank loans, and declared reserves of insurance companies" (Stanley, 2015: 2).

Pozsar et al. (2012) document that "the gross measure of shadow bank liabilities grew to a size of nearly $22 trillion in June 2007 (…) total traditional banking liabilities in comparison … were around $14 trillion in 2007."

Although the shadow banking system consists of financial institutions that look like banks, act like banks, and borrow, lend and invest like banks, they were not regulated as banks, as Roubini and Mihm (2010: 77) wisely remark.

During a long period, a largely undetected and opaque web of financial intermediation developed until the 2007/2009 crisis made it emerge to the surface. Because it was out of the scope of regulation there were no reliable data on its size and importance, which were mostly ignored by Fed authorities and regulators until it made a sudden, unexpected and unwanted appearance during the last financial crisis. Depository banks, regulated by the Fed, had become just the tip of the finance industry iceberg.

The shadow banking system grew, in the first place, because large commercial banks found it advantageous to shift increasing amounts of their activities off their balance sheets as it allowed them to conduct lending with less capital than if they had retained loans on their balance sheets thus enhancing the return on equity of banks or, more precisely, of their holding companies.

Commercial banks created special purpose entities (SPE) which:

> used a variety of short-term funding instruments to finance purchases of long-term mortgage and other credit loans that would then be securitized, with the resulting ABS (asset-backed securities) marketed both outside of the

> banking sector to a variety of institutional investors and inside the sector, namely to the SIVs and conduits.
>
> (Lysandrou and Nevestailova, 2014: 11)

Special investment vehicles (SIV) were created by commercial banks as well as investment banks; they specialized in the production of a particular kind of derivatives: collateralized debt obligations (CDOs). For example, a SIV could pool together 5000 different mortgages into a CDO. An investor who purchased the CDO was paid the interest owed by the 5000 borrowers whose mortgages made up the CDO; of course, they also faced the risk that some borrowers might default on their loans. The pooled assets (which might include not only mortgages but also bonds, loans and so on) became debt obligations that made up the collateral for the CDO. The tranches in a CDO varied in their risk profile, with senior tranches having first priority on the collateral in the event of default. The senior tranches of a CDO generally have a higher credit rating with lower coupon rates compared with junior tranches that offer higher coupon rates to compensate for their higher default risk. CDOs were created and sold by most major banks over the counter (OTC), i.e. they were not traded on an exchange but were bought directly from the bank. Usually, each CDO is a unique, customized product that can be sold to a counterparty on privately negotiated terms. The fact that they cannot be widely marketed on standardized terms explains why hedge funds became natural buyers of this complex financial product which requires structural expertise and ability to handle them. The market for CDOs included also conventional institutional asset management firms, and other shadow bank institutions, notably the conduits (Lysandrou and Nevestailova, 2014: 13).

In contrast to SPEs and SIVs, conduits did not typically engage in securitization; they mainly exploited the difference in the interests received on the long-term assets that they held and the interests that they paid on their short-term liabilities (Lysandrou and Nevestailova, 2014: 15).

Both SPEs as well as SIVs were funded by short-term instruments, mainly repos and asset-backed commercial papers.

All these institutions had one feature in common: they were not regulated. However, they kept a close relationship with the regulated banking system. For instance, when the conduits collapsed, the commercial banks took a huge hit because they owned or sponsored 270 out of the 300 or so operating in 2007. While the commercial banks had given a 100% guarantee to their conduits, they had made no corresponding capital provision for the conduits' extensive $1 trillion plus assets (Lysandrou and Nevestailova, 2014: 18).

The two parts of the financial system are closely linked through a network of securities lending, repos and derivatives markets. Regular banks are big players in the shadow banking system, both as collateral providers and as repo participants. Apart from this direct linkage, the risks taken by the shadow banks can also spread to regular banks via indirect channels, such as the massive sale of assets that could cause the decrease of prices of financial and real assets, as happened in 2007/2009. This deep interconnectedness between the shadow banking system and the regular banking system explains why a crisis originated in the shadow banking system had such a formidable impact on many institutions belonging to the regulated one.

As Lord Adair Turner, chairman of the UK's Financial Services Authority during the crisis, observed: "We need to understand shadow banking not as something parallel or separate from the core banking system, but deeply intertwined with it" (Turner, 2012).

In the same sense, Governor Daniel Tarullo referred to the shadow banking activities asserting that "regulated institutions are in fact heavily involved in these activities, both in funding their own operations and in extending credit and liquidity support to shadow banks beyond the regulatory perimeter" (Tarullo, 2013).

The traditional view of the banking system has been that its main funding is provided by household and small- to medium-sized business demand deposits. However, the presence of the shadow banking system allows leverage to rise quickly in both individual banks and the banking system as a whole. Banks intensified their reliance on other financial institutions for funding, increasingly relying on the wholesale capital markets for repos and commercial paper. As a consequence, funding to banks was increasing during the pre-crisis period until it involved much more than just households and their deposits.[1] For example,

> the growth of the market for repurchase agreements zoomed upward from \$1 trillion in 2001 to \$4.3 trillion by the time Bear Stearns went down in March 2008, reflecting a level of borrowing from other financial institutions that fueled leverage and expanded the size of positions taken through proprietary trading.
>
> (D'Arista, 2011)

Although the development of the shadow banking system had its core in the US, off-shore jurisdictions like the Netherlands, Luxembourg and Ireland have been instrumental for providing crucial infrastructural services to large financial agents, in the form of tax avoidance, regulatory arbitrage and the facilitation of what is called "financial innovation," as Engelen (2017: 55) remarks.

The "originate-to-distribute" model developed thanks to deregulation and financial innovation allowed banks to originate a variety of loans and then transfer the risks associated with these loans to non-bank institutions. Securitization allowed bundling up several tranches of illiquid loans together and converting them into liquid financial securities apt to be sold to investors.

The largest investment banks, connecting the different shadow bank entities through their role as dealer, broker and underwriter, were pivotal nodes in the shadow banking system.

Due to the lower quality of the loans they finance, shadow banks make the financial sector highly fragile. Their exposure to bank-like runs reinforces this fragility.

Bank runs

A bank run is a loss of confidence in a particular bank; as deposits are payable on demand on a first-in, first-served rule, depositors rush to withdraw their funds whenever they fear the bank may fail. The run itself may cause the bank's failure because it may be unable to provide cash when too many depositors demand it.

The bank may be solvent – it has more assets than liabilities – but at the same time may be illiquid as normally banks use most of the money they collect from depositors to make loans. They keep minimum reserves in cash to meet any occasional excess demand for withdrawals.

In the case where a bank fails this may create an atmosphere in which depositors lose confidence in other banks; this may cause other banks to fail. If depositors withdraw indiscriminately from both solvent and insolvent banks – due to asymmetric information depositors are usually unable to distinguish which banks fall in each category – the situation can develop into a bank panic in which the loss of confidence hits the country's whole financial system.

To prevent this happening, after the 1930 crisis in most countries the safety of deposits is guaranteed. In the US the FDIC insures deposits in financial institutions up to a limit of $250,000 per covered account.

During the optimistic years of the Great Moderation the study of economic and financial disruptions have been practically expelled from the economic theory arena and confined to the economic history field. They were just considered an antiquity to be housed at the museum of economic archeology. Kindleberger's seminal book on the subject was blatantly ignored or looked at with a mixture of contempt and condescension. Minsky's model simply did not exist for most of the economics profession. In the words of Mankiw's popular textbook, "today, bank runs are not a major problem for the US banking system or the Fed. The federal government now guarantees the safety of deposits at most banks, primarily through the Federal Deposit Insurance Corporation (FDIC)" Mankiw (2016: 621). The problem is that, as mentioned above, during the Great Moderation years the shadow banking system grew exponentially to such an extent that its gross liabilities represented nearly $22 trillion in June 2007, while traditional banking liabilities were only around $14 trillion in 2007 (Pozsar et al., 2012: 9). And the shadow banks lacked something equivalent to deposit insurance, which made them certainly vulnerable if they suffered a run on their liabilities. This means that the risk of runs did not disappear; it mainly moved away from traditional banking to shadow banking. The 2007/2009 crisis was, in essence, a crisis of the shadow banking system.

Bank-like runs

Covitz, Liang and Suarez (2009) argue that the epicenter of the 2007/2009 crisis were runs that began in August 2007 in the asset-backed commercial paper (ABCP) market driven by the weakness in subprime mortgages. Gorton and Metrick (2012: 143) add that the repo markets played a key role in the contagion to the rest of the financial system. Lysandrou and Nevestailova (2014: 16) remark on the role of the CDO market crash when after August 2007 buyers of CDOs almost disappeared.

When house prices fell for several consecutive months in 2007, investors became increasingly worried about the impact this phenomenon could have on mortgage defaults, particularly in the case of subprime mortgages. Their worst fears seemed to be confirmed in the summer of 2007 when two hedge funds sponsored by Bear Stearns that had invested heavily in subprime mortgages filed for bankruptcy and BNP Paribas suspended withdrawals from three money market mutual funds that were exposed to subprime mortgages. Mortgage delinquency rates rose and the level of risk of default on subprime mortgage-backed securities began to rise accordingly. But the main problem was the "unknown corpses below the surface" as one journalist with the Financial Times quoted by Roubini and Mihm (2010: 94) put it. In fact, nobody knew the real magnitude of toxic assets and who held them. As a matter of fact, Gorton (2009) estimates that only 2% of structured investment vehicle holdings were subprime. It may be true but it was irrelevant at the time of the crisis: because of the complexity and opacity of the structured mortgage products, most mortgage-backed assets became under suspicion.

Short-term lending rates between banks rose dramatically, almost overnight, as banks became more uncertain about which of their counterparties held toxic assets and which, if any, did not.

As stated before, the increase in subprime mortgage defaults triggered panic in the repo market. A lender with serious doubts about the underlying value of the collateral can do two things: either ask for more collateral or simply not renew the repo. Borrowers were forced to raise repo rates and haircuts to calm the lenders' concerns about the value and liquidity of the collateral should the counterparty bank fail. However, even higher rates were insufficient to keep repo lenders in the market.

As, in most cases, they could not distinguish between safe and risky mortgage-based securities they massively abstained from rolling over the financing, just like depositors did in traditional runs on banks.

The real issue is that, due to the lack of transparency of the structured mortgage products, the distinction between safe and risky assets became irrelevant. If, in a crowded theater someone shouts "fire" the consequences may be almost the same whether it is true or not.

During the third quarter of 2008, after the failure of Lehman, depositors withdrew significant amounts of money in just days or weeks from different financial institutions. When the crisis blew up nobody knew who was holding toxic assets or how much, not even regulators or Fed authorities, as we have seen in Chapter 2. Bank-like runs were main components of the 2007/2009 crisis which mainly affected shadow banks but it also spread to conventional ones.

Citigroup was declared a systemic risk and rescued by the government; three other large depository institutions (National City, Sovereign and IndyMac) suffered large outflows; IndyMac's failure was responsible for contagion to other depository institutions; the failure of Lehman Brothers caused a general financial turmoil. The deposit runs also forced Wachovia's sale to Wells Fargo and Washington Mutual's sale to JP Morgan Chase after its seizure by the FDIC. Wachovia and Washington Mutual were the fourth and sixth largest depository institutions in the country at the time (Rose, 2015: 5).[2]

Mankiw's assertion on the end of bank runs without even mentioning the 2007/2009 bank-like run and its impact on depository banks paints a too rosy picture of the American financial system.

Shadow banking under the post-2007/2009 crisis regulatory reform.

The clear relationship between the growth of shadow banking and the destructive 2007/2009 financial crisis led to the conclusion that shadow banking plays too critical a role to be kept unregulated.

In this respect, the post-2007/2009 crisis regulatory framework consists of trying to isolate from risk the so-called systemically important financial institutions (SIFIs) which include not only the traditional commercial banks but also some components of the shadow banking system like investment banks or insurance companies considered to be of systemic importance.

Banking companies with over $50 billion in assets were automatically considered SIFIs. This was modified by Section 401 of the Economic Growth Act signed into law in May 2018; it raises the SIFI threshold for bank holding companies from $50 billion to $250 billion in total consolidated assets. However, the Federal Reserve is authorized to apply, by order or rule, enhanced prudential standards to any bank holding company or bank holding companies with total consolidated assets of $100 billion or more if the Federal Reserve makes certain findings regarding the financial stability of the United States or the safety and soundness of the bank holding company. Additionally, the Dodd-Frank Act gives the FSOC the authority to design as SIFI any non-banking financial company that could pose a threat to the financial stability of the United States.

The scope of regulation is always a matter of discussion. I have argued elsewhere that:

> the first issue to be considered is that any regulation means a restriction on the expected rate of return by lowering the level of risk investors or banks are allowed to take. However, this does not necessarily mean a lower *ex post* average rate of return; it only means that the riskier bets are excluded or restricted, precisely those that may result in huge losses.
>
> (Beker, 2016: 253)

In this respect, Ordoñez (2018: 36) discusses the pros and cons of regulation. He argues that, in the absence of regulation, banks take too much risk while in the absence of unregulated shadow banking, efficient investments are lost. That is why he proposes that legislation should "allow banks to decide whether or not they want to be regulated. Banks that choose to avoid regulation would be taxed and the proceedings used to subsidize banks that choose to be regulated and operate under restrictive capital requirements." He admits that "there is a trade-off that regulators face between preventing efficient investments and discouraging excessive risk-taking" (Ordoñez, 2018: 36) and he prefers to leave to the bankers – not to the regulators – to choose which danger to avoid. He expects that:

> banks with access to superior assets would prefer to avoid regulations in order to invest in those superior assets, even after they pay the tax. In contrast, banks with access to inferior assets would rather self-selecting into regulated activities, invest in safe assets and be subsidized.
>
> (Ordoñez, 2018: 36)

Unfortunately, many bankers thought that mortgage-backed securities were superior assets until the 2007/2009 crisis showed how wrong they were.

At an international level, one of the objectives of the FSB is to ensure that shadow banking is subject to appropriate oversight and regulation. With the purpose of assessing global trends and risks in this system, the FSB has been conducting an annual monitoring exercise since 2011. The 2016 peer review on the implementation of the FSB policy framework for shadow banking entities found that implementation of that framework remained still at a relatively early stage (FSB, 2016b).

The FSB underscores the need for a systematic process to bring non-bank financial entities that could pose financial stability risks within the regulatory and supervisory perimeter in a timely manner (FSB, 2016a: 4). It also remarks that data from existing reporting may not be adequate or granular enough to assess shadow banking risks. Gaps in the availability of data are particularly pronounced for non-regulated entities, given that authorities' data collection powers often do not extend to such entities. It proves particularly difficult to assess shadow banking risks arising from non-bank financial entities' interconnectedness with the rest of the domestic financial system and from cross-border activities and exposures.

It is yet unclear whether existing reporting makes a sufficient contribution to enable market participants to fully gauge related shadow banking risks. In this respect, it seems there is still a lot of room for further improvement in the information requirements for non-bank financial entities.

The experience of the financial crisis demonstrated the inadequacy of a safety net limited to commercial banking and its deposits alone and the need to extend the perimeter of the public safety net.

In this respect, the Dodd-Frank Act opens access to public liquidity funding to shadow banking institutions designated as systemically significant.

In return, FSOC has the authority to instruct the Fed to impose regulation on non-bank financial companies that present systemic risk.

As Adrian and Ashcraft (2012: 54) pose,

> the objective of reform should be to reduce the risks associated with shadow maturity transformation through more appropriate, properly priced and

> transparent backstops - credible and robust credit and liquidity "puts." Regulation has done some good, but more work needs to be done to prevent shadow credit intermediation from continuing to be a source of systemic concern.

In particular, "the likelihood of runs on money markets and repo markets remain a real threat in future financial crises" (Acharya et al., 2010: 18). In the absence of a clear plan for resolution of money market funds, investors, in order to exploit the first mover advantage, will probably rush to claim their deposits in case of market distress, as happened during the COVID-19 crisis. Thus, they might contribute to the amplification of systemic risk.

The fact is that, in spite of the key role played by shadow banking in the 2007/2009 crisis, most of the post-crisis reforms have been focused on traditional banks. They just reduced incentives for banks to provide the backstop support for shadow banking activities expecting this will induce more socially efficient levels of these activities. Financial reforms fail to recognize that a large part of the funding of the financial system is no longer in the form of insured deposits but rather in the form of uninsured deposits, money market deposits and repos. In the case of the US financial system, non-bank institutions hold more than double the financial assets of traditional banks; in fact, non-banks hold near 60% of the financial sector total assets (D'Avernas et al., 2020). In the case of the EU, a broad measure of the shadow banking system, comprising total assets of investment funds and other financial institutions, represented €42 trillion at the end of 2015, approximately equivalent to 40% of total EU financial sector assets (ESRB, 2018: 3).

Box 4.1 On terminology: shadow banking and non-bank financial intermediation

2018 was the last year on which statistics on the size of the shadow banking system in Europe were published. Why? Here are the reasons.

> In October 2018 the Financial Stability Board (FSB) announced that it would replace the term "shadow banking" with the term "non-bank financial intermediation".
>
> Consistent with this, the European Systemic Risk Board (ESRB) has relabeled the "EU Shadow Banking Monitor" as the "EU Non-Bank Financial Intermediation Risk Monitor". The new terminology reflects the ESRB's monitoring universe adequately and recognizes the strengthened micro-prudential regulation of non-bank financial intermediation. Parts of the ESRB's monitoring universe, such as equity funds or large parts of the OFI residual, do not engage in shadow banking activities. Moreover, regulatory requirements, data reporting and supervision at the EU and global level have been strengthened in a number of non-bank areas, for example OTC derivatives (EMIR),

alternative funds (AIFMD), securitization (CRA and STS), money market funds (MMFR) and securities financing transactions (SFTR), also with a view to reducing shadow banking risk.

Source: ERSB (2019)

Broadly speaking, the Dodd-Frank Act fails to bring the shadow banking component of the financial system under the regulatory umbrella in a systematic way. In particular, there are no robust mechanisms to deal with runs from short-run creditors in wholesale finance like repos, commercial papers and derivatives that were at the core of the latest financial crisis.

On the other hand, international regulatory coordination is a big challenge. Regulatory agencies in different countries should coordinate their activities to prevent financial institutions from steering their riskiest operations toward the least regulated jurisdiction. This regulatory arbitrage may end up concentrating the highest risks where regulation is weaker.

In this respect, there is an increasing concern about the risks the shadow banking system in China poses. In fact, the shadow banking system expanded dramatically in China since 2009 stimulated by the government measures aimed at alleviating the impact of the global financial crisis in the country. According to Hsu et al. (2013: 6), general shadow financial activity comprises 41.7% of all financial activity in China.

The most popular forms of shadow banking in China are the:

> so-called entrusted loan agreements and trust loans. Under the former, a company lends money to another firm with the bank as the middleman, while for the latter, banks use money raised from wealth-management products to invest in a trust plan, with the proceeds eventually going to a corporate borrower.
>
> (Bloomberg News, 2017)

Such loans benefit from a perception of an implicit guarantee, especially when they were intermediated by the larger state-owned banks. It has been estimated that China's shadow banking industry is worth about $8.5 trillion (Bloomberg News, 2017). The share of shadow banking loans increased from around 11% in 2008 to almost 20% in 2015 according to Chen et al. (2017: 9). Figures differ between experts, depending on what institutions are considered to be included in the shadow banking system in China. Anyway, there is no discussion that it has been growing at an accelerated path after 2009 and that it is a source of increasing concern about the possibility of posing systemic risk on the global financial system.

In Europe, the banking sector has traditionally been the dominant and primary medium of channeling funds from surplus spending units to deficit spending ones. Bank lending constitutes almost 80% of corporate debt in Europe and the rest is raised in corporate bond markets, just the opposite to what happens in the US (Nabilou and Prüm, 2017: 5). In this bank-based financial context, the Euro area shadow banking system has been far smaller than traditional banks. However, the role of shadow banks in granting loans has been increasing while there has been a decline in the growth rate of traditional banks' lending (Nabilou and Prüm, 2017: 4).

Another specificity which has to do with the shadow banking system in Europe is that most of the collateral used in the repo markets is government securities in huge contrast to the US, where structured securities absolutely dominate these markets. Thus, in the absence of sovereign default risk, the risk of a run on the European repo markets can be considered insignificant.

The EU public policy response to the problems in the shadow banking sector has a two-pronged approach. The first prong includes a regulation on transparency of securities financing transactions and of reuse that was adopted in 2015. The second prong consists of new rules adopted in 2018 to make money market funds (MMFs) more resilient against financial market difficulties, reduce the risk of runs and limit cross-border contagion. Among other things, the regulation prohibits all MMFs from receiving external support. The MMF Regulation states that the reason for this prohibition is that the contagion risk between the MMF sector and the rest of the financial sector increases through external support. "External support" is defined as any "direct or indirect support offered to an MMF by a third party, including a sponsor of the MMF, that is intended for or in effect would result in guaranteeing the liquidity of the MMF or stabilizing the NAV [net asset value] per unit or share of the MMF." In fact, the bank sponsorship of MMFs in the EU gives rise to high levels of interconnectedness of the European MMFs to banks. Typically, MMFs are managed by asset management companies and, in the Euro area, more than 50% of large asset management companies are owned by banks (Nabilou and Prüm, 2017: 6). The purpose of the prohibition is to prevent sponsoring banks from bailing out their sponsored MMFs putting in danger their own solvency.

Abad et al. (2017: 35) find "that EU banks have significant exposures to shadow banking entities globally and, in particular, to entities domiciled in the U.S., which represent approximately 27% of the total exposures." In this respect, the EBA's guidelines on limits on exposures to shadow banking entities, effective from January 1, 2017, introduce an approach that allows EU institutions to set internal limits for their exposures to shadow banking entities (EBA, 2015).

Some conclusions on the shadow banking system and its regulation

The 2007/2009 crisis was, in essence, a crisis of the shadow banking system. It proved that shadow banks play a too critical role in today's economic world to be kept unregulated. In this respect, the post-2007/2009 crisis regulatory framework aims at isolating from risk the so-called SIFIs which include not only the traditional commercial banks but also some components of the shadow banking system like investment banks or insurance companies considered to be of systemic importance. Reforms also reduced incentives for banks to provide the backstop support for shadow banking activities expecting this will induce more socially efficient levels of these activities.

However, there is still much to be done to bring non-bank financial entities that could pose financial stability risks within the regulatory and supervisory perimeter. As a matter of fact, most of the post-crisis reforms have been focused on traditional banks.

On the other hand, international regulatory coordination is a big challenge. Regulatory arbitrage may end up concentrating the highest risks in those countries where regulation is weaker.

Notes

1 Singh (2013: 9) provides an illustrative graphic scheme highlighting the non-bank/bank nexus.

2 Large depositors played a key role in the deposit withdrawal because many large accounts were exceedingly far above deposit insurance limits, rendering insurance essentially a non-factor (Rose, 2015: 3).

References

Abad, J., D'Errico, M., Killeen, N., Luz, V., Peltonen, T., Portes, R. and Urbano, T. (2017). *Mapping the Interconnectedness Between EU Banks and Shadow Banking Entities.* ESRB. Working Paper No. 40, April.

Acharya, V. V., Cooley, T. F., Richardson, M. P. and Walter, I. (2010). *Regulating Wall Street.* Hoboken, NJ: Wiley Finance.

Adrian, T. and Ashcraft, A.B. (2012). *Shadow Banking Regulation.* Federal Reserve Bank of New York. Staff Report No. 559, April.

Beker, V. A. (2016). Open Problems and Conclusions. In B. Moro and V. A. Beker, *Modern Financial Crises: Argentina, United States and Europe.* Financial and Monetary Policy Studies 42. Switzerland: Springer International Publishing. doi:10.1007/978-3-319-20991-3_3.

Bloomberg News (2017). China's 8.5 Trillion Shadow Bank Industry Is Back in Full Swing. April 19.

Chen, K., Ren, J. and Zha, T. (2017). The Nexus of Monetary Policy and Shadow Banking in China. *American Economic Review* 108(12): 3891–3936.

Covitz, D. M., Liang, N. and Suarez, G. A. (2009). *The Evolution of a Financial Crisis: Panic in the Asset-Backed Commercial Paper Market.* Finance and Economics Discussion Series. Washington, DC: Federal Reserve Board.

D´Arista, J. (2011). *Presentation.* Central Bank of the Argentine Republic. Money and Banking Conferences. http://www.bcra.gov.ar/Pdfs/BCRA/jornadas_2011_D_Arista 2.pdf.

D'Avernas, A., Vandeweyer, Q. and Darracq-Pariès, M. (2020). The Growth of Non-Bank Finance and New Monetary Policy Tools. *VOX CEPR Policy Portal.* https://voxeu.org/article/growth-non-bank-finance-and-new-monetary-policy-tools.

EBA (2015). *Guidelines on Limits on Exposures to Shadow Banking Entities.* http://www.eba.europa.eu/documents/10180/1310259/EBA-GL-2015-20+Final+report+on+GL+on+Shadow+Banking+Entities.

Engelen, E. (2017). Shadow Banking after the Crisis: The Dutch Case. *Theory, Culture & Society* 34(5–6): 53–75.

European Systemic Risk Board (ESRB) (2018). *EU Shadow Banking Monitor*, No 3, September.

European Systemic Risk Board (ESRB) (2019). *EU Shadow Banking Monitor*, No 4, June.

Financial Stability Board (2016a). *Implementation and Effects of the G20 Financial Regulatory Reforms.* http://www.fsb.org/wp-content/uploads/Report-on-implementation-and-effects-of-reforms.pdf.

Financial Stability Board (2016b). *Thematic Review on the Implementation of the FSB Policy Framework for Shadow Banking Entities.* http://www.fsb.org/wp-content/uploads/Shadow-banking-peer-review.pdf.

Gorton G. B. (2009). *Slapped by the Invisible Hand: The Panic of 2007.* Federal Reserve Bank of Atlanta's 2009 Financial Markets Conference: Financial Innovation and Crisis. http://www.frbatlanta.org/news/CONFEREN/09fmc/gorton.pdf.

Gorton, G. and Metrick, A. (2012). Getting Up to Speed on the Financial Crisis: A One-Weekend-Reader's Guide. *Journal of Economic Literature* L(1): 128–150.

Hsu, S., Li, J. and Qin, Y. (2013). *Shadow Banking and Systemic Risk in Europe and China.* London: City Political Economy Research Centre (CITYPERC), Department of International Politics, City University. https://openaccess.city.ac.uk/id/eprint/2099/1/CITYPERC-WPS-2013_02.pdf.

Lysandrou, P. and Nevestailova, A. (2014). The Role of Shadow Banking Entities in the Financial Crisis: A Disaggregated View. *Review of International Political Economy.* doi:10.1080/09692290.2014.896269.

Mankiw, G. (2016). *Principles of Macroeconomics.* 8th edition. Boston, MA: Cengage Learning.

Nabilou, H. and Prüm, A. (2017). *Shadow Banking in Europe: Idiosyncrasies and Their Implications for Financial Regulation.* doi:10.2139/ssrn.3035831.

Ordoñez, G. (2018). Sustainable Shadow Banking. *American Economic Journal: Macroeconomics* 10(1): 33–56. doi:10.1257/mac.20150346.

Pozsar, Z., Adrian, T., Ashcraft, A. and Boesky, H. (2012). *Shadow Banking.* Federal Reserve Bank of New York Staff Report N° 458. https://www.newyorkfed.org/medialibrary/media/research/staff_reports/sr458.pdf.

Rose, J. D. (2015). *Old-Fashioned Deposit Runs.* Finance and Economics Discussion Series 2015–2111. Washington: Board of Governors of the Federal Reserve System. doi:10.17016/FEDS.2015.111.

Roubini, N. and Mihm, S. (2010). *Crisis Economics. A Crash Course in the Future of Finance.* New York: Penguin.

Singh, M. (2013). *The Economics of Shadow Banking.* Reserve Bank of Australia. Conference Volume.

Stanley, M. (2015). *The Paradox of Shadow Banking.* http://rooseveltinstitute.org/wp-content/uploads/2015/11/Stanley_Shadow_Banking.pdf.

Tarullo, D. K. (2013). *Shadow Banking and Systemic Risk Regulation.* Remarks at the American for Financial Reform and Economic Policy Institute conference, November 22. https://www.federalreserve.gov/newsevents/speech/tarullo20131122a.htm.

Turner, A. (2012). *Shadow Banking and Financial Stability.* Harvard Law School Forum on Corporate Governance. April 16. https://corpgov.law.harvard.edu/2012/04/16/shadow-banking-and-financial-instability/.

5 Systemic risk and run vulnerability

Systemic risk

Systemic risk has been defined as "the disruption to the flow of financial services that is caused by an impairment of all or parts of the financial system; and has the potential to have serious negative consequences for the real economy" (BIS et al., 2009).

We speak of systemic risk as opposite to idiosyncratic risk. The latter refers to something which may result in damage to a single institution or asset without a significant impact on the rest of the economy. On the contrary, systemic risk has to do with the danger that a certain event or succession of events may result in the collapse of the whole financial system, causing a major downturn in the real economy.

That event may be a natural disaster like a hurricane or an earthquake, a man-made one such as the outbreak of a war or an event created by and within the financial system or the economy at large. In this latter case, it is systemic inasmuch as it has a strong adverse effect on the health of the financial system as a whole. This may happen if the negative shock affects an important constituent of the financial system.

How is systemic risk measured? From a theoretical point of view, Brunnermeier and Oehmk (2012: 62) argue that the ideal would be to have:

> (i) a systemic risk measure for the whole economy and (ii) a logically consistent way to allocate this systemic risk across various financial institutions according to certain axioms. (…) The allocation of this overall systemic risk to each individual financial institution should reflect each institution's total risk contribution to overall systemic risk.

However, the measurement of systemic risk is still in its infancy although it is a fast-growing industry. Bisias et al. (2012) analyzed more than 30 systemic risk measures; Brunnenmeier and Cheridito (2019: 3, 15) criticize previous models because they do not take all channels of contagion into account and propose a practical way of measuring and allocating systemic risk.

Systemically important financial institutions (SIFIs)

One of the practical conclusions drawn from the 2007/2009 financial crisis was the need to identify the so-called SIFIs whose failure could seriously damage the stability of the whole financial system.

An institution may pose a systemic risk due to its size, risk contribution and interconnectedness with the rest of the financial system. A particular institution is systemically important if it has such a size that the expected losses it may generate if it were to fail can have a significant impact on a large customer base. A second condition is that the institution is involved in activities of higher than average risk which makes it a substantial contributor to the overall risk of the financial market. A third condition is that, because of its interconnections, its failure may trigger defaults of other financial institutions and/or substantial losses for its shareholders or institutional and private debt holders to an extent that trust in the stability of the financial system would be endangered, potentially leading to disruptions in financial markets.

Was Lehman Brothers a systemically important financial institution? It was the fourth-largest US investment bank although with $639 billion in assets it was far below Goldman Sachs (over $1 trillion in assets), JP Morgan Chase (over $2 trillion in assets) and Citigroup (over $2 trillion in assets); it was highly involved in the risky subprime mortgage-backed securities and collateral debt obligations businesses although no one knew in the market the exact extent of the bank's exposure to them; finally, it was substantially interconnected with one important money market fund and had a key interconnection with AIG, an insurance company that had insured trillions of dollar worth of mortgage securities and had to be rescued one day after Lehman's failure.

Lehman's bankruptcy precipitated the collapse of the Reserve Primary Fund – a money market mutual fund. The fund had a $785 million allocation to short-term loans issued by Lehman Brothers. These loans, known as commercial paper, became worthless when Lehman filed for bankruptcy, causing the Fund to break the buck. Then, investors became concerned about the value of the fund's other holdings and pulled their money out of the fund, which saw its asset decline by nearly two-thirds in about 24 hours. Unable to meet redemption requests, the Reserve Primary Fund froze redemptions for up to seven days. When even that was not enough, the fund was forced to suspend operations and commence liquidation. This started a run on the rest of the money market funds.

Lehman's bankruptcy also precipitated the need of bailing out AIG, a major seller of credit default swaps. If AIG went bankrupt, it would have triggered the bankruptcy of many of the financial institutions that had bought these swaps. For this reason, the near failure of AIG initially created fear in the financial sector and such fear had a contagion effect in the market resulting in the failure or near failure of related financial institutions.

Box 5.1 American International Group (AIG)

For decades, AIG was a global powerhouse in the business of selling insurance. But in September 2008, the company was on the brink of collapse.

A new financial product known as a collateralized debt obligation (CDO) became the darling of investment banks and other large institutions. CDOs lump various types of debt from the very safe to the very risky into one bundle for sale to investors. The various types of debt are known as tranches. Many large institutions holding mortgage-backed securities created CDOs. These included tranches filled with subprime loans. That is, they were mortgages issued during the housing bubble to people who were ill-qualified to repay them.

A division of the company called AIG Financial Products (AIGFP) sold insurance against investment losses (see Chapter 3). At the end of the 1990s it started insuring CDOs against default through a financial product known as a credit default swap. The chances of having to pay out on this insurance seemed highly unlikely.

A big chunk of the insured CDOs came in the form of bundled mortgages, with the lowest-rated tranches comprised of subprime loans. When foreclosures on home loans rose to high levels, AIG had to pay out on what it had promised to cover. The AIGFP division ended up incurring about $25 billion in losses.

It was clear that AIG was in danger of insolvency. To prevent that, the federal government stepped in. Investment banks that had CDOs insured by AIG were at risk of losing billions of dollars. A huge number of mutual funds, pension funds and hedge funds had invested in AIG or were insured by it, or both.

If AIG went down, it would have sent shockwaves through the already shaky money markets as millions lost money in investments that were supposed to be safe.

Source: Investopedia

These were the main *direct* effects of Lehman's failure. The *indirect* effects were still worse.

The decision not to rescue Lehman sent a message to the market: no further bailouts could be expected. The underlying concerns about counterparty risk came suddenly to the fore, and every large financial institution had to look at their counterparties much more carefully than before.

It was interpreted, after Lehman's failure, that in case a financial institution became insolvent its only alternative would be to file for Chapter 11 with serious consequences for its creditors – mostly other financial institutions. Individual institutions were induced to be extremely prudent. But, as underlined by the Paradox of Prudence, the micro-prudent behavior by individual institutions turned out into macro-imprudent results. The natural outcome was a hoarding of cash, a shortening of loan terms, a dramatic rise in rates where lending did occur, and the deepening of the financial crisis. All financial institutions were in need of cash and had to sell assets to get it. So, the prices of all assets plummeted. The crisis spread from one kind of assets to the others.

The uncertainty on who held what implied that any financial institution was under suspicion. As creditors did not know where their investments stood, they ran to dump them as soon as possible. This indiscriminate run of short-term creditors of financial institutions affected insolvent and solvent institutions as well.

However important Lehman's interconnection with AIG was, the decisive issue for the financial market stability was the lack of transparency as to the holding and valuation of securities, in particular of subprime mortgage-backed securities. This opacity greatly inhibited the ability of investors to evaluate the risks incurred by institutions that held or were suspected of holding these products. It was hard to distinguish illiquid from insolvent institutions. Fear of infected financial markets and generalized panic was the outcome.

Where are we now, a decade after the global financial crisis as far as SIFIs are concerned? Despite the promises to address too-big-to-fail issues after the crisis, the fact is that large banks have continued to become larger and more complex, and systemically important banks' share of global banking assets has increased in recent years (World Bank, 2019).

Interconnectedness, contagion and panic

The description of events that followed Lehman's failure leads us to distinguish between three different channels of transmission of a certain shock to the rest of the financial system: interconnectedness, contagion and panic.

Connectedness between Lehman Brothers and the Reserve Primary Fund, on one hand, and between Lehman Brothers and AIG on the other, explain how the first wave of financial stress started.

A second wave was set in motion by contagion[1] when any financial institution holding or suspected of holding subprime mortgage-related securities became under suspicion and suffered a huge withdrawal of funds even if they had no relationship with the failed institution.

As Anderson et al. (2018: 19) rightly remark, information about the causes and magnitude of any shock and the risky exposures of each bank are often not easily available, because all involved parties have a strong incentive for guarded self-interest. This makes it hard to distinguish solvent parties from insolvent in periods of high uncertainty.

Finally, a third wave was unleashed by panic: runs affected then indiscriminately any financial institution, whatever their assets, their size or their solvency.

Policies to reduce interconnectedness

After the experience of the 2007/2009 financial crisis, extensive interconnections in the financial system were considered as potential sources of systemic risk.

The Dodd-Frank Act tries to reduce the magnitude of asset interconnectedness. On one hand, as we saw in Chapter 3, the Act limits banks' credit exposure to their affiliates and to other financial institutions and provides an expanded definition of credit exposures.

On the other hand, by limiting the amount of credit that may be extended to a single borrower as well as giving regulators the possibility of capping the institution's exposure to a single significant funding the Dodd-Frank Act reduces the consequences of an eventual failure of a large financial institution.[2]

It also mandates central clearing of derivatives and other financial contracts in certain cases. In such a case, the central clearing counterparty "stands between over-the-counter (OTC) derivatives counterparties, insulating them from each other's default. Effective clearing mitigates systemic risk by lowering the risk that defaults propagate from counterparty to counterparty" (Duffie and Zhu, 2010: 2).

Interconnectedness and contagion in economic theory

The literature on banking crises and panics goes back to the seminal paper by Diamond and Dybvig (1983). In their model,

> contracts have multiple equilibria. If confidence is maintained, there can be efficient risk sharing, because in that equilibrium a withdrawal will indicate that a depositor should withdraw under optimal risk sharing. If agents panic, there is a bank run and incentives are distorted. In that equilibrium, everyone rushes in to withdraw their deposits before the bank gives out all of its assets. The bank must liquidate all its assets, even if not all depositors withdraw, because liquidated assets are sold at a loss.
>
> (Diamond and Dybvig, 1983: 403)

In their model, a bank run is caused by a shift in expectations, which could depend on almost anything, consistent with the apparently irrational observed behavior of people running on banks.

Scott (2016a) emphasizes the distinction between interconnectedness and contagion. He argues that interconnectedness was not a major cause of the last financial crisis as no large financial firms failed as a direct result of their exposures to Lehman Brothers. Instead, he goes on to argue, in 2008 systemic risk existed due to contagion.

The role of interconnectedness among financial institutions in transmitting financial stress has been modeled in economic theory by different authors. For instance, Allen and Gale (2000) focus on linkages among financial institutions. They center attention on the overlapping claims that different sectors of the banking activity have on one another. This can have a domino effect, causing a problem at one bank to spread to others.

In the same way as in Allen and Gale, in a paper by Gai et al. (2010) there is no distinction between contagion and interconnectedness. As a matter of fact, their transmission mechanism is based on connectedness between banks although they speak of contagion. In their model, the decision by any one bank to hoard liquidity makes it harder for the banks which were previously borrowing from it to meet their own liquidity condition without resorting to hoarding themselves. The hoarding behavior of one institution has the potential to trigger liquidity stress at any of the banks to which it is connected via an interbank lending relationship. They count as systemic those episodes in which at least 10% of banks are forced into hoarding liquidity.

The truth is that the term contagion was rarely used in economics before 1995, after which it occasionally appeared in articles discussing the impact of the Mexican Peso crisis on other countries in Latin America (Forbes, 2012: 4).

This should not be a surprise. Mainstream economic theory has difficulties in modeling pure contagion, let alone panic. Neoclassical economics was built under the assumption that information is complete, perfect and symmetric. Information is complete when the same knowledge is available to all market participants. Perfect information means that everybody knows everything they need to make the best choice. Information is symmetric if all participants have the same information. Under these assumptions, contagion is ruled out. For contagion to exist some information failure is necessary.

In the real world, information is in most cases incomplete, imperfect and asymmetric. To deal with these cases, economics had to develop the branch of information economics. This development has allowed studying information failures which are associated with other market failures, including incomplete risk markets and imperfect capital markets, providing thus a better framework for looking at the economy than the older perfect markets competitive paradigm. Stiglitz (2017) provides insights into the contribution done by this branch of economic theory.

Specifically, the literature on financial contagion tries to explain why, in financial markets, co-movements across asset prices are observed that cannot be explained in terms of linkages among financial institutions.

A first precedent in this respect is Keynes's "beauty contest" model of market behavior which maintains that asset prices may become unmoored from economic fundamentals due to people allocating their wealth based on what they think other investors think, rather than what they themselves do. For Keynes (2008: 142), speculation is "the activity of forecasting the psychology of the market." Economic agents act according to what they expect the rest of the agents will do. Even professional investment managers have a strong incentive to follow the herd because "it is better to fail conventionally than to succeed unconventionally" (Keynes, 2008: 141).

Scott (2016a) characterizes contagion in financial markets as a liquidity-driven phenomenon in which short-term creditors in response to informational constraints withdraw from institutions preemptively, as happened to money market funds with no exposure to Lehman during the financial crisis.

Chen (1999) builds a model with multiple banks with interim revelation of information about the performance of some banks. A certain number of interim bank failures results in pessimistic expectations about the general state of the economy, and leads to runs on the remaining banks.

Calvo and Mendoza (1999) emphasize the role of imperfect information. Contagion takes place when investors optimally choose to mimic arbitrary market portfolios instead of paying for information that would be relevant for their portfolio decision. When a rumor favors a change of portfolio, all investors "follow the herd."

Gorton (2008) underlines the role of asymmetric information in the events which led to the 2007/2009 financial crisis. Asymmetric information refers to a situation where one side of a transaction knows more relevant information than the other side. Investors bought different kinds of structured products having little knowledge of what they were really purchasing. He argues that for CDO investors and investors in other instruments that had CDO tranches in their portfolios, it was not possible to penetrate the chain backwards and value the chain based on the underlying mortgages. Therefore, when the run started, it triggered a generalized fear of suffering losses on subprime and subprime-related securities and subprime-linked derivatives.

Heider et al. (2009) resort also to asymmetric information to show how the attempt by suppliers of liquidity to protect themselves from lending to "bad" borrowers may result in a market breakdown. In this model, the lack of information about the real counterparty risk results in liquidity hoarding.

Lagunof and Schreft (1999) show how contagion can occur even within a rational expectations framework. Investors initially hold portfolios that are linked in the sense that an investor's expected and actual portfolio returns depend on the portfolio choices of other investors. Realized project failures break some portfolio linkages, which causes some investors to incur losses and reallocate their portfolios, thereby breaking additional linkages. Investors who foresee that the crisis may lower their returns may protect themselves by preemptively shifting to a portfolio that is safer in that it reduces their exposure to any ongoing contagion. Since all investors are identical, if one takes such preemptive action, then they all do, causing the instantaneous collapse of all remaining portfolio linkages. An economy is considered more fragile the earlier this total financial collapse occurs.

The paper arrives at a couple of surprising conclusions. The first one is that the distinction between rational and irrational behavior is absolutely irrelevant. What does matter is the distinction between exuberant and apprehensive investors. Provided there is at least one apprehensive investor in the economy, total financial collapse can occur, regardless of the fundamentals and the rationality of investors. Apprehensive investors perceive a contagious financial crisis as more likely than it actually is. Given this misperception, they believe they benefit from reallocating their portfolios to preempt experiencing portfolio losses. It is this behavior that by itself initiates a contagious financial crisis. Even if the rationally exuberant investors in this economy correctly forecast that the fundamentals make financial crises unlikely, they must respond strategically to the portfolio reallocations they expect by the apprehensive investors. They choose to reallocate their own portfolios to protect themselves against losses due to the contagion the apprehensive investors initiate.

The second unexpected conclusion is that "a financial crisis that looks as if it were initiated by real shocks to the economy instead could have been caused solely by the presence of rational, but unjustifiably apprehensive, investors" (Lagunof and Schreft, 1999: 4).

These results coincide with conclusions arrived at in empirical works on financial crises (see, e.g., Kaminsky et al., 2003) in the sense that crises may occur despite the fundamentals being sound or may not occur despite the fundamentals being weak.

One policy conclusion Lagunof and Schreft draw from their model is about the key role that a lender of last resort may play to stop ongoing contagion by providing loans to investors who actually incur losses and are about to reallocate their portfolios initiating the first round of contagion.

A second policy conclusion is the need for monitoring lenders' portfolios in order to stimulate greater diversification and thus increase the number of shock-induced project failures needed to initiate a crisis. It is worth remarking that this was proposed almost 10 years before the great concentration of the financial system in mortgage-backed securities operations brought it close to collapse.

Allen et al. (2011) argue that when bank debt is short term, banks are informationally linked; investors respond to the arrival of interim information in a way that depends on the composition of the banks' asset structures. Let us suppose there is a "clustered" asset structure meaning that within each cluster all banks hold the same portfolio. At an intermediate date, investors receive a signal concerning banks' future solvency. The signal indicates whether all banks will be solvent in the final period or whether at least one of them will default. As banks' assets are opaque, the market receives information on banks' overall solvency rather than on any individual bank. Upon observing the signal, investors update the probability that their bank will be solvent at the final date and roll over the debt only if they expect to be able to recover their opportunity cost. Allen et al. show that, upon the arrival of bad news, rollover occurs less often in the clustered than in the unclustered asset structure. In the clustered structure, upon the arrival of negative information, if investors infer that the conditional default probability is high, they decide not to roll over. When rollover does not occur, all banks in the cluster are forced into early liquidation. The market failure in this model is that banks are unable to coordinate on a particular composition of asset structure. In the unclustered structure defaults are less concentrated, neighboring banks do not hold identical portfolios and the arrival of the bad signal indicates a lower probability of a rash of bank defaults.

Panic

Panic occurs when there is an indiscriminate run in which investors withdraw their funds from any institution or market even though they have not invested in the same risks and are not subject to the same original shocks. Of course, in a world of rationality, absolute transparency and perfect information panic is quite unconceivable. But such a world is not the real world.

As President Franklin D. Roosevelt famously observed in his first inaugural address: "The only thing we have to fear is fear itself."

Panic characterized the last stage of the 2007/2009 financial crisis. In former Chairman Bernanke's (2009) words:

> Falling asset prices and the collapse of lender confidence may create financial contagion, even between firms without significant counterparty relationships. In such an environment, the line between insolvency and illiquidity may be quite blurry.
>
> Panic-like phenomena occurred in other contexts as well. Structured investment vehicles and other asset-backed programs that relied heavily on the commercial paper market began to have difficulty rolling over their short-term funding very early in the crisis, forcing them to look to bank sponsors for liquidity or to sell assets.
>
> Following the Lehman collapse, panic gripped the money market mutual funds and the commercial paper market, as I have discussed. More generally, during the crisis runs of uninsured creditors have created severe funding problems for a number of financial firms. In some cases, runs by creditors were augmented by other types of "runs" – for example, by prime brokerage customers of investment banks concerned about the funds they held in margin accounts. Overall, the role played by panic helps to explain the remarkably sharp and sudden intensification of the financial crisis last fall, its rapid global spread, and the fact that the abrupt deterioration in financial conditions was largely unforecasted by standard market indicators.

However important in the real world, panic has received little attention in the economics literature.

One rare exception is Kindleberger and Aliber (2011: 33) who refer to panic as equivalent to the German expression *Torchlusspanik*, "door-shut-panic": investors crowd for fear not to be able to get through the door before it slams shut. Scott (2016a), who – as seen above – emphasizes the role of contagion in the last financial crisis, makes no difference between panic and contagion.

Mishkin and Eakins (2015: 210) refer to it just as a situation where "multiple banks fail simultaneously."

Gorton (2012: 32–42) gives an account of the panics which affected the US economy in 1819, 1837, 1857, 1873, 1907, 1930 and 2007/2009. However, it is a description of events, not an economic analysis.

Some contributions to the subject come from authors outside the field of economics.

Wang et al. (2016) model panic as the result of interactions using complex network theory. Although they have in mind emergency situations such as fires, the model could be extended to model financial panic. They argue that when someone gives up their own views and takes actions consistent with most of the surrounding people, "herding behavior" may emerge. They build a dynamic complex network composed of three types of people, namely calm people, herding people and panic people. The evolution of herding people to panic people – from simple contagion to panic – is interpreted by a specific concept of "herding–panic threshold." When the total utility exceeds the herding–panic threshold specified for herding people, they become panicked.

Lee et al. (2018) is one of the scarce papers devoted to the study of panic in financial markets. The authors analyze periods of financial crisis and try to identify herd behavior in the stock exchange of different continents. They measure herd behavior by the degree of comovement in stock markets. They estimate a revised herd behavior index using historical stock price data. They show that during the global financial crisis in 2007/2009 and the European sovereign debt crisis the index hit the upper limit, which the authors interpret as the measure of panic level attained.

Kleinnijenhuis et al. (2013) undertake a research on the role of financial news in a market panic and conclude that news may have a relevant role in this respect. They recommend a more sober, policy-oriented style of reporting supported by proactive news sources in order to prevent panic escalation.

Policy response to systemic risk

According to Scott (2014: 10), "since the 2008 crisis, regulators have focused primarily on three policy responses to the problem of systemic risk: (i) capital requirements, (ii) liquidity requirements, and (iii) insolvent bank resolution procedures."

At the height of the 2007/2009 financial crisis, the large financial institutions had too little capital to maintain market confidence in their solvency. For this reason, the Emergency Economic Stabilization Act passed in October 2008 instituted the $700 billion Troubled Assets Relief Program (TARP) of which $250 billion were allocated to inject capital into troubled but viable financial institutions. The Treasury received preferred stock or debt securities in exchange for these investments.

The international Basel III agreement, the Financial Stability Board and Section 171 – the Collins Amendment – of the Dodd-Frank Act have increased the amount of bank capital with the purpose of ensuring that banks will be able to withstand future downturns. At the same time, higher bank capital requirements are one way of making shareholders have more skin in the game with the expectation that this would induce them to avoid excessive risk taking.

Capital requirements are tailored according to the level of market risk an institution is exposed to. In particular, it is supposed to be a sort of insurance against what Scott calls "correlation risk," that is, the risk of a common external shock with simultaneous, adverse consequences on many financial institutions (e.g., the fall of housing prices in the period prior to the 2007/2009 financial crisis). The unexpected collapse of asset prices due to an exogenous event can result in a fire sale of bad assets with serious effects on bank profitability. The increased capital requirements are meant to prevent the insolvency of multiple banks caused by actual large losses.

However, it is always difficult to *a priori* know what amount of capital is necessary to absorb the eventual losses from fire sales. Moreover, as Aikman et al. (2019: 164) argue, "a key question is whether risks in the financial system can be known with sufficient certainty to be estimated accurately." Capital requirements are just a first line of defense aimed at assuring creditors that financial institutions are strong enough to survive an economic shock and have capital buffers against unexpected losses.

In the case of the Eurozone and Japan, standing capital injection facilities for future bailout needs have been enacted. Under the European Stability Mechanism, the ECB has the authority to recapitalize banks. In Japan, the Deposit Insurance Corporation of Japan is authorized to extend assistance to financial institutions that purchase assets or merge with failed financial institutions in order to facilitate the transaction or to prevent financial institutions from failing. On the contrary, in the United States there is nothing equivalent now that TARP has expired.

Moreover, as D'Arista (2011: 8) rightly points out,

> the crisis made clear just how strongly capital requirements pushed institutions and the system as a whole in a pro-cyclical direction. It is not only that markets will supply capital in a boom and withhold it in a downturn, but that the impact on capital of changes in the value of assets has the same pro-cyclical effects. The downward spiral set in motion by falling prices and charges against capital in the fall of 2008 argues for a view of capital as a threat to solvency, not a cushion. There is simply not enough capital available in a downturn to safeguard individual institutions let alone a financial system.

This authorizes us to take a skeptical point of view on how capital requirements may function to prevent or moderate the effects of financial dislocations.

For the time being one apparent result of the provisions on risk-weighted capital requirements has been that many banks have offloaded complex assets that attracted higher capital requirements; this allowed their assets to look much less risky to their internal models.

Liquidity is the second line of defense. While capital requirements attempt to warrant solvency, minimum liquidity requirements are supposed to assure that financial institutions hold a permanent pool of high-quality liquid assets that can be sold (or pledged as collateral) to face any sudden surge of withdrawals by depositors and other short-term debt holders. As a matter of fact, bank failures are usually triggered by liquidity shortages.

In Chapter 7, the liquidity requirements implemented after the crisis will be analyzed in more detail. Nonetheless, let me anticipate that I agree with some of the objections pointed out by Scott (2016a) on this subject. First of all, persistent disruption to short-term borrowing markets could eventually overrun even the strongest portfolio of liquid assets. Therefore, short-term creditors of a financial institution would still have an incentive to exit sooner, while that portfolio is still intact, rather than later, after waves of outflow have exhausted it. Second, as happens with several regulatory reforms implemented after the financial crisis, liquidity requirements apply mainly to traditional banks while, as it happened in the 2007/2009 crisis, contagion may spread far beyond the traditional banking sector.

It has been argued that private liquidity requirements will make it less necessary to resort to public liquidity through the use of central bank lender-of-last-resort authority. Consequently, the role of the Fed as lender of last resort has been restricted by the regulatory reform in the hope that private liquidity might be a close substitute for the public one.

In fact, in the post-crisis anti-bailout environment the scope of the Fed's authority to lend has been severely restricted while simultaneously strengthening collateral requirements for any emergency lending.

As has already being said, one of the predominant ideas behind the financial legal reform was to contain moral hazard: the existence of a lender of last resort potentially creates moral hazard on a massive scale inducing bankers to take reckless risks, it was argued. Therefore – the argument went on – the more restricted the banks' access to it the better.

However, what experience tells is that banks are far from being eager to borrow from the central bank because of the stigma associated with that borrowing. During the last financial crisis, banks were reportedly concerned that market participants might learn about their borrowing and view it as a sign of a weak financial condition. That's why the Fed had to create new anonymous lending programs during the financial crisis (the Term Securities Lending Facility, the Primary Dealers Credit Facility and Term Auction Facility) which were designed to use auctions to make loans without publicly revealing borrowers' identities.[3] During the COVID-19 crisis, eight big banks agreed to borrow from that source of funds in order to counter that stigma.

On the other hand, a strong lender of last resort helps prevent panics from occurring. Policy responses in a crisis are fundamentally about managing expectations. If the role of the central bank as lender of last resort is not clear enough any serious disruption may trigger a race among unsecured short-term creditors to get out as soon as possible. Private liquidity buffers might not be enough to contain such hemorrhage.

Thus, the financial legislation enacted after the 2007/2009 crisis may not be able to contain the damage to the economy from an extreme crisis or to break a classic financial panic, as Geithner (2019) warns. According to Geithner's own experience, overwhelming force is needed to change expectations and restore confidence. And overwhelming force requires backing policies with a large amount of money, large enough to be credible. A typical example is Mario Draghi's statement that the ECB was "ready to do whatever it takes to preserve the

Euro." Although the program known as Outright Monetary Transactions was never used, its mere existence served to calm the storm. In the same vein, the famous speech of March 12 1933 by President Roosevelt was followed the next day by queues of depositors lined up to redeposit their money.

Box 5.2 Excerpts from Franklin D. Roosevelt's Fireside Chat 1: On the Banking Crisis

By the afternoon of March 3 scarcely a bank in the country was open to do business. Proclamations temporarily closing them in whole or in part had been issued by the Governors in almost all the states.

It was then that I issued the proclamation providing for the nation-wide bank holiday, and this was the first step in the Government's reconstruction of our financial and economic fabric.

[...]

I do not promise you that every bank will be reopened or that individual losses will not be suffered, but there will be no losses that possibly could be avoided; and there would have been more and greater losses had we continued to drift. I can even promise you salvation for some at least of the sorely pressed banks. We shall be engaged not merely in reopening sound banks but in the creation of sound banks through reorganization. It has been wonderful to me to catch the note of confidence from all over the country. I can never be sufficiently grateful to the people for the loyal support they have given me in their acceptance of the judgment that has dictated our course, even though all of our processes may not have seemed clear to them.

After all there is an element in the readjustment of our financial system more important than currency, more important than gold, and that is the confidence of the people. Confidence and courage are the essentials of success in carrying out our plan. You people must have faith; you must not be stampeded by rumors or guesses. Let us unite in banishing fear. We have provided the machinery to restore our financial system; it is up to you to support and make it work.

It is your problem no less than it is mine. Together we cannot fail.

Source: University of Virginia, Miller Center

Another issue the new legislation had to tackle was the too-big-to-fail issue. As stated in Chapter 3, it has been dealt with the creation of an Orderly Liquidation Authority (OLA). Under the OLA, the FDIC and Fed are provided tools to help resolve failing firms safely outside bankruptcy proceedings. In order to be placed into receivership under OLA, the financial company must be designated as posing systemic risk in the event of failure, and it must be in default or in danger of default. The determination is made on the eve of bankruptcy by the Federal Reserve and FDIC with final approval by the Treasury Secretary upon consultation with the President. The aim is to provide a restructuring of financial institutions in a way that ensures continuation of essential business lines, with minimum disruption and the preservation of franchise value and low cost to the public. The new resolution mechanism helps restrain the damage caused by the failure of a large complex financial institution, by limiting the scope of default to the obligations of the parent, allowing the operating subsidiaries, such as the banks and broker dealers underneath the parent, to continue to operate, and ensuring funding for the resolution would be available. However, as Scott (2014: 13) warns, "given the uncertainties of how resolution procedures will actually affect short-term creditors, good resolution procedures cannot by themselves prevent contagion." And if contagion does occur the curtailed lender of last resort authority may find it difficult to address it and prevent it to turn into panic.

Lender of last resort and deposit insurance

The fact that only a fraction of bank deposits is backed by actual cash available for withdrawal implies they are vulnerable to sharp increases in the demand for currency. Such sharp increases in demand for currency can bring about a widespread call-in of loans and a dramatic fall of asset prices.

Whenever demand for reserve money abruptly increases only the central bank can meet the need. Central banks act as lenders of last resort providing reserve money (and other forms of liquidity) to the banking system.

In the aftermath of the 1930s crisis two main institutions emerged: the lender of last resort and deposit insurance. After the Great Depression there was a consensus that a lender of last resort is necessary to prevent financial panic. Although the Federal Reserve System was created in 1913, its structure and powers were circumscribed by restrictive legislation. It was only after the 1930s crisis that it was accepted that in periods of financial turmoil, when banks have doubts about lending to each other and lots of people may suddenly want to withdraw their money from their bank account, the lender of last resort may be the only source where they can get the funding they badly need for their daily business. Despite the arguments that bank failures are simply a logical punishment resulting from imprudent risk taking and that banks should be allowed to fail in order to prevent moral hazard, the truth is that only in a contagion-proof world can the government and regulators credibly commit to a policy of allowing any bank to fail regardless of its size. This is what mainstream macroeconomics does not understand and why it devoted so much effort to conceptualizing the case for central bank independence, while its role as lender of last resort was widely regarded as either unnecessary or counterproductive.

As runs are fundamentally liquidity-driven, a lender of last resort may prevent panic by supplying cash to liquidity-thirsty banks. According to Bagehot's doctrine – which dates back to 1873 – monetary authorities should lend only to illiquid but solvent banks. If so, a by-product of the central bank's decision to lend will be a positive signal that the recipient is fundamentally sound. However, it is very difficult in practice to distinguish in real time between illiquidity and insolvency.

As a matter of fact, during the latest financial crisis, central banks in some cases lent to systemically critical institutions against sufficient but illiquid and risky assets. This required some special institutional arrangements. For example, in the case of

> the protection provided to Citi and Bank of America, the extension of credit to AIG and the TALF, the Treasury absorbed the lion's share of the credit risk with the Federal Reserve either latently or actually providing most of the funding.
>
> (Domanski et al., 2014: 60)

As Bernanke (2013: 5) pointed out,

> the Fed lent not only to banks, but, seeking to stem the panic in wholesale funding markets, it also extended its lender-of-last-resort facilities to support nonbank institutions, such as investment banks and money market funds, and key financial markets, such as those for commercial paper and asset-backed securities.

In fact, during the latest financial crisis, the interbank lending largely dried up because no financial institution had confidence in the solvency of other players. Even banks that enjoyed a liquidity surplus preferred to hoard it rather than making it available to others on the interbank market.

The Federal Reserve, the ECB and the Bank of England have each assisted banks with special loans and asset purchases designed to bolster banks' positions, expand the supply of liquidity and reduce the risk of deposit withdrawals extending their intervention even beyond the provisions of the traditional notion of lender of last resort.[4] "From mid-2007 until early 2009, central banks extended the equivalent of about $4 trillion in major currencies in liquidity support to banks and non-banks, to individual institutions and markets, and in domestic and foreign currency" (Domanski et al., 2014: 44).

Nevertheless, as stated above, the Dodd-Frank Act placed significant constraints on the Fed's lending authority.

One of them is that the Fed can make emergency loans only under a "broad" program. A Fed regulation implementing this provision requires that at least five institutions must be "eligible" for any Fed program. As Scott (2016b) rightly points out, this means that the Fed might have to wait for five institutions to be under attack before being able to act.

Although the Fed can now lend to non-bank institutions, they should be solvent institutions, a requirement not imposed on lending to banks. Who is in charge of assuring the aided institution is solvent? In a bill passed by the House but not enacted into law it was required that federal regulators of the potential borrower would have to certify that the borrower is not insolvent.

The second institution which emerged from the 1930s crisis is the deposit insurance. It originated when in 1934 the Federal Deposit Insurance Corporation (FDIC) was created guaranteeing depositors the first $100,000 of their accounts; in October 2008 this amount was increased to $250,000.

The rationale behind the creation of the FDIC was that banks were vulnerable to liquidity shocks usually linked to their main funding source at that time – deposits. But although deposit insurance protects banks from runs driven by depositors, it does not guard them from other liquidity shocks. As banks increasingly relied for their funding on the wholesale capital markets, deposit insurance did not protect them from a run originated in the shadow banking system as was the case during the latest financial crisis. That is why in September 2008, following the breakout of the run on the money market funds, the Treasury had to use its Exchange Stabilization Fund authority to guarantee the money market funds. The same happened during the COVID-19 crisis.

Taking into consideration the increasing role they play in funding the financial system, Scott (2014: 107) proposes a system of universal insurance for short-term financial liabilities whether held by banks or non-bank financial institutions. He provides some figures to support his proposal: non-deposit financial liabilities (all uninsured) totaled $14.7 trillion at the end of 2012 while deposits totaled only about $9.5 trillion. At the end of 2012, only 49% of all short-term liabilities, including deposits outstanding, were insured. This is roughly equivalent to the percent of deposits that were insured in the early 1940s, he remarks. His main concern is with money market mutual funds given their vulnerability to contagious runs and the fact that their shares represent around 50% of short-term non-deposit liabilities. However, he admits that "it would be politically difficult if not impossible to propose expansion of deposit insurance in the context of the anti-bailout Washington consensus. Not only is lender-of-last resort demonized as a bailout, deposit insurance is as well" (Scott, 2014: 119). But he warns: "neither the Federal Reserve (as lender of last resort) nor the FDIC (as insurer), acting in the current scope of their powers, is capable of providing an adequate public guarantee that will protect the financial system from contagion in the future" (Scott, 2014: 121).

The Fed intervention during the 2007/2009 crisis was a matter of three stages: first came monetary easing before Bear Stearns, then came the lender of last resort stage as the Fed liquidated its holdings of Treasury bills and lent the proceeds to a wide variety of counterparties against a wide variety of collateral, and finally, after Lehman and AIG, came a stage that Mehrling (2011) called dealer of last resort. In this third stage, the Fed intervened, on the one hand, as market-maker in the money market where it served as the central counterparty standing between borrowers and lenders and, on the other hand, in the market for mortgage-backed securities where the Fed was for a while purchasing 90% of all new issues (Mehrling, 2014: 110).

The central bank as dealer of last resort

In theory, in order to halt runs, central banks, acting as lenders of last resort, are supposed to lend to solvent institutions against illiquid but high-quality collateral to provide the necessary funds to pay out debts in a crisis. However, in practice, it is not easy to know whether the supposedly "safe assets" being used as collateral are indeed safe. A central bank does not always have the expertise to fully understand, value and manage the assets against which it is lending. For this reason, it may be important for central banks – as contingent lenders – to undertake robust planning focused on crisis preparedness. Having banks being able to preposition collateral may be helpful for central banks, as it gives them time to evaluate the assets which can be rapidly called upon if the need arises. With good planning, responses to extreme events are likely to be more robust and resilient. In particular, central banks should consider, in normal times, what constitutes a suitable inventory of assets for use in collateral transformation activities in times of financial stress. Examining collateral outside of those assets currently eligible for use as collateral in lending operations can serve to provide better flexibility to the central bank in times of stress.

Besides, it is a difficult issue to determine when a bank is solvent, but illiquid, and when the illiquidity is simply a symptom of an insolvent bank. The main difficulty has to do with the way in which assets are valued. For purposes of lender of last resort functions, assets should be valued based on their worth under normal market conditions. In principle, book values probably come closer to this ideal than market values, since accounting rules are designed to reflect changes in underlying, long-term value, while muting the effects of market swings. Anyway, haircuts are generally applied to the stated valuations, so that the central bank lends less than the calculated value of the collateral to protect itself from potential losses.

Just at the start of the 2007/2009 financial crisis, Buiter and Sibert (2007) warned that:

> now that financial markets (and non-bank financial institutions) have increasingly taken over the function of providing credit and all forms of finance to deficit spending units, a credit crunch or liquidity crunch manifests itself in a different way from the world described by Walter Bagehot's lender of last resort.

They went on to argue that the failure to match willing buyers and sellers at prices acceptable to both in the financial instruments markets demands the central bank to become the market-maker of last resort.

The Great Recession revealed the limitations of monetary stimulus alone to overcome a severe recession. The Fed doubled the monetary base between September and December of 2008 but that money didn't reach the people: it only increased bank reserves. The federal funds rate was cut from about 5% in mid-2007 to nearly 0% in late 2008, yet the economy continued to suffer from inadequate aggregate demand for goods and services. Most of the cash was simply parked at the Fed as banks' extra reserve money. As Samuelson very graphically said more than 70 years ago:

> "You can lead a horse to water, but you can't make him drink." You can force money on the system in exchange for government bonds [...] but you can't make the money circulate against new goods and new jobs [...] You can tempt businessmen with cheap rates of borrowing, but you can't make them borrow and spend on new investment goods.
>
> (Samuelson, 1948: 354)

This situation is called a "Supply-Side Liquidity Trap": a point may be reached where printing money increases real monetary balances but has little effect on real liquidity (Calvo, 2016: 33). As Galbraith (2012) points out:

> Banks don't lend reserves, and they don't need reserves in order to lend. Banks create money by lending. They need a client willing to borrow, a project worth lending to, and collateral to protect against risk. If these are lacking, no amount of reserves will turn the trick.

As Koo (2016: 24) rightly points out, when "private-sector borrowers sustain huge losses and are forced to rebuild savings or pay down debt to restore their financial health," they have no choice but to pay down debt or increase savings regardless of the level of interest rates in order to restore their financial health. We are here in the presence of an economy in which everyone wants to save but no one wants to borrow, even at near-zero interest rates. Under these circumstances, "there is very little that monetary policy, the favorite of traditional economists, can do to prop up the real economy" (Koo, 2016: 34).

When the lender of last resort function revealed to be insufficient, the Fed intervened as market-maker in the money market. In the same vein, the European Central Bank, using Long-term Refinancing Operation and Outright Monetary Transactions, either swapped illiquid securities of European banks with cash or pledged to purchase assets that were otherwise illiquid in markets. This type of interventions has prompted a debate about the role of central banks as market-makers of last resort.

It is important to bear in mind that "market-maker of last resort (MMLR) is not an extension of the lender of last resort (LOLR) function; it is a completely new role for the central bank" (Dooley, 2014: 128) This role is brought to the fore by the fact that credit markets are driven by trust in collateral rather than trust in banks (or non-banks). The central bank intervenes supplying its own liabilities to replace those assets whose value is under suspicion.

This may be necessary when market participants become radically uncertain about how to value the underlying instruments used as collateral. The authorities entering the market as bidders could signal that fears about an asset class are misplaced. This is OK if they know something the market does not. However, it may happen that they face the same problem as the market – they really just don't know. But as Buiter and Sibert (2007) argued,

> dealing with a liquidity crisis and credit crunch is hard. Inevitably, it exposes the central bank to significant financial and reputational risk. The central banks will be asked to take credit risk (of unknown) magnitude onto their balance sheets and they will have to make explicit judgments about the creditworthiness of various counterparties. But without taking these risks the central banks will be financially and reputationally safe, but poor servants of the public interest.

Li and Ma (2019) argue that in times of crisis central banks should boost the market liquidity of bank assets rather than directly lend to "solvent-but-illiquid" banks, among other things, because of the already mentioned difficulty of distinguishing illiquid banks from insolvent ones. The authors emphasize that a dealer of last resort should not concern itself with the solvency of individual institutions but should focus on maintaining a "fair price" of banks' assets which can be based on the long-run fundamentals.

Li and Ma remark that, from an operational point of view, a bank that fails because of illiquidity cannot be distinguished from one that fails because of fundamental insolvency, which leaves regulators informationally constrained. Whereas in practicing market-makers policies, instead of assessing the solvency of a bank, regulators only need to estimate the value of assets to be purchased, which can be much less informationally demanding.

Mehrling (2011) argues that the Fed must maintain its role of dealer of last resort if it wants to play a role in stabilizing the economy in a future financial crisis. It should set a price floor for key assets, which in normal times should be some distance below from the market price.

As a matter of fact, the Fed played an active role as dealer of last resort during the COVID-19 crisis, as explained in the Epilogue of this book.

The experience of the 2007/2009 crisis showed that injecting liquidity may be necessary but not sufficient to save the financial system and avoid a major downturn in the economy. The fact that central banks can help by creating money reflects the fact that financial crises are in the first place a matter of liquidity. However, they may not be only a matter of liquidity. Market-maker policies may be a necessary complement. When a solvency issue is at play, capital injection may also be required. This was the role played by TARP in the US during the latest financial crisis. Now it is expected that this role may be played by the required capital buffers (see Chapter 7).

In spite of the pessimistic warning by Geithner (2019: 27) that "many of the tools that were essential to resolve this crisis have been eliminated or curtailed" by the Dodd-Frank Act, during the COVID-19 crisis US authorities were able to resort to section 13(3) for emergency lending, as detailed in the Epilogue.

Run vulnerability

Measurement of aggregate run vulnerability and its composition is a critical component in evaluating and regulating systemic risk.

Runs are a possibility every time illiquid assets are turned into liquid assets. But this is precisely the main function that banks and other financial institutions fulfill and that is why they are exposed to deposit runs or, in general, to an inability to access the debt markets for new funding. The inability to roll over debt through new securities issuances has a similar effect for non-banks to deposit withdrawals for banks.

That's why Cochrane (2014) proposes a run-free financial system by eliminating run-prone securities from it. In his view, demand deposits, fixed-value money market funds or overnight debt must be backed entirely by short-term government debts. Banks should be 100% equity-financed which means they cannot fail because they have no debt. Of course, these banks don't have money to lend but, according to Cochrane, today's technology makes sure this can't be a problem.

But in today's real world there is still a plethora of run-prone assets.

Bao et al. (2015) define "runnables" as "pay-on-demand" transactions which embed defaultable promises made by private agents or state and local governments without explicit insurance from the federal government.

> In general, the pay-on-demand feature implies that in the event of stress – caused by credit-risk concerns, large swings in short-term interest rates, or deteriorations in market liquidity – investors may exhibit bank-run-like behavior by redeeming their shares, unwinding their transactions, or deciding not to roll over their positions.
>
> (Bao et al., 2015)

The ultimate reason for runs is liquidity mismatch between assets and liabilities. This is a necessary but not a sufficient condition. The other feature which makes runnable a contract is that it promises fixed values payable in full on demand on a first-come first-served basis (Cochrane, 2014: 197). For example, if I know that the withdrawal of my non-insured deposits depends on the liquidity of long-term assets held by the bank and I hear that some people are withdrawing their deposits I will rush to withdraw my money before the bank's assets become completely illiquid. Other people will do the same and this will set in motion a bank run. Notice that the bank's ability to pay back deposits depends in the first place on the liquidity, not only the value, of its assets. A bank can be solvent, holding assets exceeding its liabilities under normal economic circumstances, but illiquid and therefore unable to pay back its deposits. That is why bank runs may be self-fulfilling prophecies and even "healthy" banks can fail.

Bao et al. (2015) identify a number of liabilities that fit their definition of runnables: uninsured bank deposits, money market mutual funds shares, repos and securities lending, commercial paper, variable-rate demand obligations, federal funds borrowed and funding agreement backed securities. They estimate both the composition and the total size of runnables from the second quarter of 1985 to the first quarter of 2015. Prior to the mid-1990s, the amount of runnable liabilities outstanding was steady at approximately 40% of US GDP. At the beginning of 2015 they represented 60% of GDP, after reaching more than 80% of GDP at the beginning of 2008. While repos were the largest component before the financial crisis, uninsured deposits are now the main component. As the authors point out, it is still an issue to have a quantitative framework to determine the optimal level of runnables that trades-off the social cost of amplifying shocks in crises and the benefits of financing.

The opposite of "runnables" is "safe assets." In this respect, it has been suggested to discuss if for the prevention of crises,

> a comprehensive regulatory approach to shadow banking need to include mechanisms – involving the government directly or indirectly – for the creation of more genuinely safe assets, as well as limitations on the runnable varieties that can precipitate or exacerbate financial stress.
>
> (Tarullo, 2016: 4)

Let's go to this subject.

The "safe assets" issue

Starting with Caballero et al. (2014, 2016) a growing literature has developed which instead of explaining the financial crisis pointing out to the supply side (the financial system) places the emphasis on the asset demand side. The crisis would have had its origin in a situation of excess demand for safe assets which the finance industry – with the invaluable help of the credit rating industry – tried to satisfy by manufacturing in large scale private AAA-rated assets.

In the same vein, Lysandrou (2011/12: 242) points out that it was the mass demand for CDOs that called for their mass production.

According to Caballero et al. (2017: 29), "a safe asset is a simple debt instrument that is expected to preserve its value during adverse systemic events." They go on to explain that before the crisis, the collective growth rate of the advanced economies that produce safe assets has been lower than the world's growth rate. The main reason has been the disproportionately high growth rate of high-saving emerging economies such as China. This excess demand for safe assets was the reason for an explosion of the supply of AAA-rated securitized instruments manufactured by the financial industry. Unfortunately, a lot of these instruments turned out to be just pseudo-safe assets as the subprime mortgage crisis finally put clearly in evidence.

Is there anything like an absolutely riskless asset? In order to be riskless, it should be an asset easily convertible into the same amount of real resources at any time. In a world without inflation, money fulfills that function. US government debt as well as insured demand deposits do it too. In a world with inflation these two still fulfill that role provided the rate of interest is not lower than the rate of inflation. The rest of the so-called "safe" assets (commercial paper, money market funds, repurchase agreements, private label AAA asset-backed securities and so on) entail a certain degree of risk; the purchaser of them is insured against that risk by being paid a rate of interest above the risk-free rate. If that risk is underestimated, as it happens when an AAA label is bestowed to a quasi-junk bond, the investor is not duly insured and sooner or later will suffer the consequences in the same way as happens when a person is a victim of burglary without being fully insured against it.

All risky assets are information sensitive: news can change the perception people have with respect to their safety. For this reason, they may be subject to runs in case they become under suspicion about their value stability and/or their liquidity. They are runnables.

One obvious solution to a shortage of safe assets is for countries that produce safe assets to issue more of them. As Caballero et al. (2017) recall, the experience of Japan over recent decades suggests that the capacity of a core economy to issue debt may be extremely large.

The alternative of privately creating safe assets faces the difficulty that the private sector's ability to insure against a truly systemic event is limited. Public and private safe assets are not perfect substitutes. For this reason, public debt to fund infrastructure investment becomes particularly attractive, as the debt is formally backed by the state and public works boosts growth in the asset-producing countries and helps to recover economies from a slowdown. Thus, infrastructure investment generates the cash flow to service debt payments.

Notes

1 I use contagion in a different way from, for instance, Scott (2016a). While Scott includes in contagion any transmission mechanism apart from connectedness, I reserve the concept only to the run-like behavior from one financial institution to other institutions that have something in common with it which makes the latter suspicious of being in risk of following the path of the first one.
2 Dodd-Frank Act §164 and §165.
3 Gorton and Ordoñez (2020) argue that opacity in emergency lending is indeed optimal.
4 See Jeffers (2010) for an account of the way central banks acted during the 2007/2009 financial crisis.

References

Aikman, D., Haldane, A. G., Hinterschweiger, M. and Kapadia, S. (2019). Rethinking Financial Stability. In O. Blanchard and L. H. Summers (ed.), *Evolution or Revolution? Rethinking Macroeconomic Policy after the Great Recession*. Cambridge, MA: MIT and Peterson Institute for International Economics, pp. 143–192.

Allen, F. and Gale, D. (2000). Financial Contagion. *Journal of Political Economy* 108(1): 1–33.

Allen, F., Babus, A. and Carletti, E. (2011). Asset Commonality, Debt Maturity and Systemic Risk, November 4. doi:10.2139/ssrn.1954810.

Anderson, R., Danielsson, J., Baba, C., Das, U. S., Kang, H. and Segoviano M. A. (2018). *Macro-Prudential Stress Tests and Policies: Searching for Robust and Implementable Frameworks.* IMF Working Paper. WP/18/197.

Bao, J., David, J. and Han, S. (2015). The Runnables. *FEDS Notes*, September 3. https://www.federalreserve.gov/econresdata/notes/feds-notes/2015/the-runnables-20150903.html#f2.

Bernanke, B. S. (2009). *Reflections on a Year of Crisis.* Speech at the Federal Reserve Bank of Kansas City's Annual Economic Symposium, Jackson Hole, Wyoming, August 21. https://www.federalreserve.gov/newsevents/speech/bernanke20090821a.htm.

Bernanke, B. S. (2013). Remarks at Fourteenth Jacques Polak Annual Research Conference, IMF, November 8.

BIS, FSB, and IMF (2009). *Guidance to Assess the Systemic Importance of Financial Institutions, Markets and Instruments: Initial Considerations.* https://www.imf.org/external/np/g20/pdf/100109.pdf.

Bisias, D., Flood, M., Lo, A. W. and Valavanis, S. (2012). *A Survey of Systemic Risk Analytics.* Office of Financial Research Working Paper #0001.

Brunnenmeier, M. K. and Cheridito, P. (2019). Measuring and Allocating Systemic Risk. *Risks* 7(2): 46. doi:10.3390/risks7020046.

Brunnenmeier, M. K. and Oehmk, M. (2012). *Bubbles, Financial Crises, and Systemic Risk.* http://citeseerx.ist.psu.edu/viewdoc/download?doi=10.1.1.640.39&rep=rep1&type=pdf.

Buiter, W. and Sibert, A. (2007). The Central Bank as the Market Maker of last Resort: From lender of last resort to market maker of last resort. *VOX CEPR Policy Portal.* August. https://voxeu.org/article/subprime-crisis-what-central-bankers-should-do-and-why.

Caballero, R. J. and Farhi, E. (2014). *The Safety Trap.* National Bureau of Economic Research Working Paper 19927.

Caballero, R. J., Farhi, E. and Gourinchas, P. O. (2016). Safe Asset Scarcity and Aggregate Demand. *American Economic Review* 106(5): 513–518.

Caballero, R. J., Farhi, E. and Gourinchas, P. O. (2017). The Safe Assets Shortage Conundrum. *Journal of Economic Perspectives* 31(3): 29–46.

Calvo, G. A. (2016). *From Chronic Inflation to Chronic Deflation: Focusing on Expectations and Liquidity Disarray since WWII.* NBER Working Paper 22535.

Calvo, G. A. and Mendoza, E. G. (1999). *Rational Contagion and the Globalization of Securities Markets.* NBER Working Papers. WP 7153. https://www.nber.org/papers/w7153.pdf.

Chen, Y. (1999). Banking Panics: The Role of the First-Come, First-Served Rule and Information Externalities. *Journal of Political Economy* 107: 946–968.

Cochrane, J. H. (2014). *Toward a Run-Free Financial System.* https://faculty.chicagobooth.edu/john.cochrane/research/papers/across-the-great-divide-ch10.pdf.

D´Arista, J. (2011). *Reregulating and Restructuring the Financial System: Some Critical Provisions of the Dodd-Frank Act Presentation.* Central Bank of the Argentine Republic. Money and Banking Conferences. http://www.bcra.gov.ar/Pdfs/BCRA/jornadas_2011_D_Arista2.pdf.

Diamond, D. W. and Dybvig, P. H. (1983). Bank Runs, Insurance Deposit and Liquidity. *The Journal of Political Economy* 91(3): 401–419.

Domanski, D., Moessner, R. and Nelson, W. (2014). Central Banks as Lenders of Last Resort: Experiences During the 2007–10 Crisis and Lessons for the Future. In BIS, *Rethinking the Lender of Last Resort.* BIS Papers No 79. https://www.bis.org/publ/bppdf/bispap79.pdf.

Dooley, M. (2014). *Can Emerging Economy Central Banks Be Market-Makers of Last Resort?* BIS workshop, Rethinking the Lender of Last Resort, Basel, May 15. https://www.bis.org/publ/bppdf/bispap79k.pdf.

Duffie, D. and Zhu, H. (2010). *Does a Central Clearing Counterparty Reduce Counterparty Risk?* http://www.stanford.edu/~duffie/DuffieZhu.pdf.

Forbes, K. (2012). *The "Big C": Identifying Contagion.* NBER Working Paper Series. Working Paper 18465. http://www.nber.org/papers/w18465.pdf.

Gai, P., Haldane, A. and Kapadia, S. (2010). *Complexity, Concentration and Contagion.* https://www.cmu.edu/tepper/faculty-and-research/seminars-and-conferences/assets/docs/CR-Docs/CR-2010-Gai-Haldane-Kapadia.pdf.

Galbraith, J. K. (2012). Don't Put Faith in the Fed: Quantitative Easing Isn't Magic. We Need a Dose of Realism about What Central Banks Can Achieve. *The Guardian (London)*, September 21.

Geithner, T. F. (2019). The Early Phases of the Financial Crisis: Reflections on the Lender of Last Resort. *Journal of Financial Crises* 1(1): 1–38. https://elischolar.library.yale.edu/journal-of-financial-crises/vol1/iss1/1.

Gorton, G. B. (2008). *The Panic of 2007.* NBER Working Paper No. 14358.September.

Gorton, G. B. (2012). *Misunderstanding Financial Crises.* New York: Oxford University Press.

Gorton, G. B. and Ordoñez, G. (2020). Fighting Crises with Secrecy. *American Economic Journal: Macroeconomics* 12(4): 218–245. doi:10.1257/mac.20190169.

Heider F., Hoerova, M. and Holthausen, C. (2009). *Liquidity Hoarding and Interbank Market Spreads. The Role of Counterparty Risk.* European Central Bank. Working Paper Series. No. 1126. https://www.ecb.europa.eu/pub/pdf/scpwps/ecbwp1126.pdf.

Jeffers, E. (2010). The Lender of Last Resort Concept: From Bagehot to the Crisis of 2007. *Revue de la Régulation.* Autumn. https://journals.openedition.org/regulation/8903.

Kaminsky, G. L., Reinhart, C. M. and Vegh, C. A. (2003). *The Unholy Trinity of Financial Contagion.* George Washington University Working Papers. https://home.gwu.edu/~graciela/home-page/research-work/working-papers/unholy.pdf.

Kleinnijenhuis, J., Schultz, F., Oegema, D., and van Atteveldt, W. (2013). Financial news and market panics in the age of high frequency sentiment trading algorithms. *Journalism* 14(2): 271–291. doi:10.1177/1464884912468375.

Keynes, J. M. (2008 [1936]). *The General Theory of Employment, Interest and Money.* New Delhi: Atlantic.

Kindleberger, C. P. and Aliber, R. Z. (2011). *Manias, Panics and Crashes: A History of Financial Crises.* 6th edn. New York: Palgrave Macmillan.

Koo, R. C. (2016). The Other Half of Macroeconomics and the Fate of Globalization and Three Stages of Economic Development. In G. P. Lima and M. A. Madi (eds.), *Capital and Justice.* London: World Economics Association Book Series Vol. 4.

Lagunof, R. and Schreft, S. L. (1999). Financial Fragility with Rational and Irrational Exuberance. *Journal of Money, Credit and Banking* 31: 351/60.

Lysandrou, P. (2011/12). The Primacy of Hedge Funds in the Subprime Crisis. *Journal of Post Keynesian Economics* 34(2): 225–253.

Lee, W., Choi, Y. H., Kim, C. and Ahn, J. Y. (2018). A Case Study for Intercontinental Comparison of Herd Behavior in Global Stock Markets. *Communications for Statistical Applications and Methods* 25(2): 185–197. doi:10.29220/CSAM.2018.25.2.185.

Li, Z. and Ma, K. (2019). *Contagious Bank Runs and Buyer of Last Resort.* https://www.zhaoli.org/uploads/2/3/3/6/23368752/bank_run_20190525.pdf.

Mehrling, P. (2011). *The New Lombard Street. How the Fed became the Dealer of Last Resort.* Princeton, NJ: Princeton University Press.

Mehrling, P. (2014). Why Central Banking Should Be Re-Imagined? In BIS, *Re-thinking the Lender of Last Resort.* BIS Papers No 79.

Mishkin, F. and Eakins, S. (2015). *Financial Markets and Institutions.* 8th Edition. Harlow: Pearson.

Samuelson, P. A. (1948). *Economics: An Introductory Analysis.* New York: McGraw-Hill.

Scott, H. S. (2014). *Interconnectedness and Contagion – Financial Panics and the Crisis of 2008.* doi:10.2139/ssrn.2178475.

Scott, H. S. (2016a). *Connectedness and Contagion. Protecting the Financial Systems from Panics.* Massachusetts: The MIT Press.

Scott, H. S. (2016b). *Connectedness and Contagion: A Global Perspective.* Address to the International Monetary Fund.

Stiglitz, J. E. (2017). *The Revolution of Information Economics: The Past and the Future.* NBER Working Paper No. 23780.

Tarullo, D. K. (2016). Speech at the Center for American Progress and Americans for Financial Reform Conference, Washington DC, July 12.

Wang, J., Chen, M., Yan, W., Zhi, Y. and Wang, Z. (2016). A Utility Threshold Model of Herding–Panic Behavior in Evacuation Under Emergencies Based on Complex Network Theory. *SIMULATION* 93(2): 123–133. doi:10.1177/0037549716678659.

World Bank (2019). *Global Financial Development Report 2019/2020: Bank Regulation and Supervision a Decade after the Global Financial Crisis.* Washington, DC: World Bank.

6 How to prevent a new financial crisis

Bubbles and financial crises in economic history

Bubbles are large, sustained overpricing of financial or real assets. Historically, bubbles appear associated to financial crises.

The Dutch tulip mania is considered the first example of a bubble in economic history. Tulips came from Turkey and were introduced into the Netherlands in the 16th century. Their popularity reached unprecedented heights in the 1630s. Tulips and tulip bulbs were bought and sold frantically; lots of people jumped on the bandwagon buying options they could pay for later, some even putting up their homes as collateral. The market crashed suddenly in February 1637; prices plummeted and many investors were left penniless.

The 1719–1720 South Sea bubble is another example. The South Sea Company was formed in 1711 in London and it was granted exclusive trading rights with Spain's colonies in the South Seas (Southern America) including the supply of slaves for 30 years to the Spanish plantations. The South Sea Company issued stock to investors to help finance its operations. After the resounding success of their first share issue, the company issued even more shares as their prices soared. It was thought that the company "could never fail." Many investors became fabulously wealthy almost overnight as their shares soared. But in 1718 Britain and Spain went to war, stopping all chances for trade. However, shares of the company surged more than eightfold in 1720, from £128 to £1050. The company's directors realized that their company's shares were incredibly overvalued relative to its profits and decided to sell them while other investors were still unaware that the company was barely profitable. At some point investors learned that the South Sea Company's management team had sold all of their shares in the company. Panic selling started and many fortunes were lost in a heartbeat. Finally, the Bank of England stepped in as lender of last resort and helped to prevent a banking crisis.

More recently, Japan experienced a real state and stock market bubble during the 1980s. Japanese stocks and urban land values tripled between 1985 and 1989. The bubble burst in 1991, setting the stage for Japan's subsequent years of price deflation and stagnant economic growth.

At the end of the past century, the increasing popularity of the Internet triggered a massive wave of speculation in the "new economy" businesses. Hundreds of dotcom companies achieved multi-billion dollar valuations as soon as they went public. The NASDAQ Composite Index, home to most of these dotcom company stocks, soared from a level of under 500 at the beginning of 1990 to a peak of over 5,000 in March 2000. The index crashed shortly thereafter, plunging nearly 80% by October 2002 and triggering a US recession.

Finally, we have the US housing bubble whose collapse led to the subprime meltdown, as already detailed in Chapter 2.

Standard neoclassical theory precludes the existence of bubbles based on the argument that they are incompatible with rational behavior. However, it has been shown that even rational agents who know that the market will eventually collapse would like to ride the bubble as it continues to grow and reap high returns, expecting to exit the market before it crashes (Abreu and Brunnermeier, 2002: 174). As Citigroup chairman and CEO Charles Prince said in 2007, "as long as the music is playing, you've got to get up and dance." Just a few weeks after this (in)famous comment the music stopped.

One common element in most bubbles is herd behavior. Once Hamelin's melody gathers a certain number of followers, everybody tries to join the crowd.

Bubbles are not the problem; credit risk concentration is

Bubbles tend to appear in the initial stage of the process which ends in a crisis when the bubble bursts. Brunnermeier and Oehmk describe the process:

> In the typical anatomy of a financial crisis, a period of booming asset prices (potentially an asset price bubble), initially triggered by fundamental or financial innovation, is followed by a crash. This crash usually sets off a number of amplification mechanisms and, ultimately, this often leads to significant reductions in economic activity. The resulting declines in economic activity are often sharp and persistent.
>
> (Brunnermeier and Oehmk, 2012: 7)

The increase in systemic risk is not limited to the turmoil following the burst of a bubble, but exists already during its build-up phase (Brunnermeier et al., 2019). If so, it seems crucial to intervene long before the bubble bursts.

However, it is difficult to identify a bubble in real time and even more difficult to choose the precise moment to bring it down before it damages the whole financial system. In fact, identifying unambiguously the presence of a bubble in an asset price remains an unsolved problem because the fundamental value of an asset is, in general, not directly observable and it is usually difficult to estimate. Further, it is not possible to distinguish between an exponentially growing fundamental price and an exponentially growing bubble price.

Fortunately, the issue is not the bubble itself but the probability that its bursting may disrupt the financial system with a huge impact on economic activity. This may happen if and only if the bubble has been fueled with credit. This is the main difference between the 2007/2009 subprime mortgage crisis and the internet one of the late 1990s. "The severity of the destruction caused by a bursting bubble is determined not by the type of asset that turns 'toxic' but by the degree of leverage employed by the holders of those toxic assets" (Greenspan, 2014: 9).

If so, the real issue is to avoid excessive concentration of loans in any one sector or kind of assets of the economy. The issue is not necessarily to try to identify bubbles and follow their trajectory but to prevent the financial system from being overexposed to some particular sector of the economic activity or some particular kind of asset where a bubble may develop.

The 2007/2009 crash was not caused by the housing bubble in itself but because of the deep involvement of the financial system in it.

With around 10 million mortgage applications for home purchases per year – millions of which were making their way into mortgage-backed securities every year – it was not even remotely feasible to inspect every mortgage. But precisely the huge number of mortgages lent by each institution every month should have been an alert sign that the financial system was becoming overexposed to the risk of default in that specific market. For example, when China's housing markets were overheating in 2012, the authorities prohibited banks from making loans on second or third houses, and prevented banks from lending to foreigners and non-residents for the purpose of house purchases (Shim et al., 2013: 87).

Excessive concentration of loans in any one sector, region or kind of assets exposes lenders to the risk of heavy losses. At the beginning of the century, the US financial system held heavy concentrations in real estate loans. When the real estate market crashed mortgage delinquencies and defaults rose and the value of mortgage-backed assets held by banks and shadow banks dropped accordingly.

This does not mean that a new financial crisis will necessarily have its roots in the real estate market. Quoting Greg Ip of the *Wall Street Journal*: "Squeezing risk out of the economy can be like pressing on a water bed: the risk often re-emerges elsewhere."

It is a useless exercise trying to predict what sector the new financial crisis will come from. New vulnerabilities are likely to appear and financial institutions may very well try to find ways around the new legislation. New risks can develop out of things that do not appear initially to contain that kind of possibility. The risks of the future are unlikely to come from the precise places that they've come in the past. It is well known that predictions are hard, especially about the future.[1]

The only way to avoid a new crisis is to prevent the financial industry from being excessively exposed to *any* particular sector of the economy, region or kind of assets.

In the same way as limits are imposed on banks' exposures to single counterparties, the central bank should impose caps to the exposure of the financial system as a whole to any particular industry, group of countries or kind of assets as well as to the reliance on concentrated funding sources. This will allow restricting the risk from sectoral or geographical concentration of asset exposure or funding sources. As already mentioned in Chapter 5, Allen et al. (2011) show that information contagion is more likely for groups of banks that hold common asset portfolios. The proposed restriction would constrain the amount of risk that the financial system may face of an economic downturn or default in any one specific industry or region or from a particular kind of asset. This approach requires horizontal aggregation of financial institutions' balance-sheets to check that the exposure to any sector, region or type of assets does not exceed a given level.

Central banks have now the raw material for this: for example, in the US, the largest bank holding companies and foreign banking organizations have to report periodically their top exposures; the same happens in Europe under the European Union large exposures regime; in India banks have to report, on a monthly basis, their 20 top exposures. With this information, each central bank can carry out a consolidated analysis of the financial sector exposure. In contrast with the dynamic sector risk-weight adjustment methodology that is employed by some central banks in emerging markets, this approach does not rely on regulatory discretion to identify risk pockets. Moreover, a by-product of this restriction may be a greater flow of credit to the underserved sectors, helping in diversifying banks' credit portfolio and the structure of the economy.

As part of their macro-prudential policy, central banks should establish the acceptable limits of concentration risk and the mechanisms to monitor and control that the system behaves within them. For example, if the composition of banks' portfolios reveals an excessive concentration in mortgages or a high participation of mortgage-backed securities in financial institutions' assets, corrective measures should be triggered. For example, these assets should no longer be considered as save assets for risk-weighted capital ratio[2] (RWCR) purposes and those institutions exceeding the limits be subject to the systemic tax fee suggested in Acharya et al. (2009: 284).

Of course, a necessary condition for the implementation of these credit limits is proper accountability of financial institutions to their regulators. Lack of transparency has been one of the flaws exposed by the financial crisis.

The lack of transparency in the financial industry

There has always been a tension between the right to data privacy and the obligation of transparency. Individual financial institutions emphasize the former while regulators stress the latter. After the recent financial crisis, the pendulum has swung towards privileging transparency over privacy given the negative externalities of bank failures. Financial reform legislation has given new powers and directives to regulatory agencies, demanding from financial institutions greater transparency of prices, volumes and exposures to regulators and in aggregated form to the public.

The US financial meltdown had a direct antecedent in Japan's banking crisis of the 1990s. The boom and bust of real estate prices were the primary reason for that crisis which burst in 1995 when 13 Japanese financial institutions went effectively bankrupt. The banking crisis had been developing for already a couple of years but "Japan's language and culture provided an ideal cloak for secrecy" (White, 2002: 1). The success in hiding the problem served only to magnify the impact once the facts emerged.

The 2007/2009 financial crisis also developed in an environment of great opacity. The financial derivatives markets and the development of the "shadow" banking system allowed the evasion of disclosure requirements and favored regulator passivity due to the build-up of hidden risk. After the crisis, the FSB established in 2012 the Enhanced Disclosure Task Force with a view to set out recommendations to enhance the risk disclosure of banks.

It is supposed that disclosure should allow debt investors to ensure that banks do not take on too much risk.

The Enhanced Disclosure Task Force comprised banks, analysts, investors and auditors. In October 2012 it produced a report containing 32 specific recommendations for enhancing risk disclosure. In December 2015 the FSB published the Task Force third progress report and formally disbanded the Task Force considering its mission had already been accomplished. The report concluded that most progress implementing the Task Force recommendations had been made by Canadian and UK banks. In contrast, where efforts to follow the EDTF recommendations were more recent (e.g. China, Japan), implementation rates were lower and differences between the bank and user assessments were wider. The user group of investors and analysts found that fewer than half of the banks as a whole provided quantitative information about counterparty credit risk from derivatives transactions or details about the composition of collateral held.

A study based on quantitative indices that measures progress on disclosure applied to a sample of 50 major banks from around the world analyzes disclosure of information that is relevant to debt investors and to financial stability (Sowerbutts et al., 2013) They find that, on a global level, there has been an improvement in disclosures over time. However, the authors assert that:

> as well as having information available, investors must have the ability to process this information. Simply disclosing more information is not always helpful to investors. Large amounts of "noisy" data that are not key to understanding the risks banks are taking may make it more difficult for investors to extract the key information.
>
> (Sowerbutts et al., 2013: 332)

They remark that investors have very little – if any – influence on management's decisions while relying on equity holders to discipline management may not be sufficient because debt and equity holders often have different and conflicting interests when it comes to the risk that a firm takes.

Sowerbutts et al. (2013) conclude that the incentive structure encourages the build-up of new types of risks which may not be covered by existing rules and guidance.

The need for a realignment of incentives in the financial industry

The very nature of leverage, which is based on debt contracts and hence involves limited liability on the part of the borrower (or its shareholders), induces excessive risk-taking because it distorts borrowers' incentives. Limited liability implies that very large losses are not borne by the borrower because they lead to default and hence to the transfer of these losses to the lenders. The distribution of returns that borrowers face is tilted towards high payoffs and does not fully represent the underlying payoff risk associated with holding risky assets (Challe, 2012: 41).

Managers who do not have "skin in the game" may be tempted to take excessive risks using other people's money.

Managerial compensation schemes played a key role in the financial crisis. Compensation contracts were too focused on short-term trading profits rather than long-term incentives (Moro, 2016: 71).

As I have asserted in one of the chapters of the volume written with my colleague Beniamino Moro, "excessive risk-taking by financial institutions was a factor that significantly contributed to the incubation of the crisis. Compensation policies can play a useful role in reducing excessive risk-taking" (Beker, 2016: 228).

In the aftermath of the financial crisis it has become widely accepted that, by enabling executives to cash large amounts of equity-based and bonus compensation before the long-term consequences of decisions are realized, pay arrangements have provided them incentives to focus excessively on short-term results and give insufficient weight to the consequences that risk-taking would have for long-term shareholder value. On top of that, bank managers' pay had been tied to highly levered bets on the value of banks' assets, giving executives little incentive to take into account the losses that risk-taking could impose on preferred shareholders, bondholders, depositors and taxpayers (Bebchuk and Spamann, 2009).

Executive compensation has been the subject of several regulatory norms requiring increased disclosure:

> The corporate scandals of the early 2000s, including Enron, Worldcom, Tyco, and others, led to a wave of regulation aimed at improving the corporate governance environment. A common feature of this was the implementation of guidelines concerning the independence of the members of the board of directors.
>
> (Bhagat and Bolton, 2013)

After the financial crisis, legislation focused on the elimination of compensation structures that give executives incentives to take unnecessary and excessive risks.

> In the United States, the Securities and Exchange Commission (SEC) mandated increased disclosure of compensation in 2006, and say-on-pay

> legislation was passed as part of the Dodd-Frank Act in 2010. In 2013, the European Union imposed caps on bankers' bonuses, the SEC mandated disclosure of the ratio of Chief Executive Officer (CEO) pay to median employee pay, and Switzerland held an ultimately unsuccessful referendum to limit CEO pay to twelve times the pay of the lowest worker.
>
> (Edmans and Gabaix, 2016: 1632/33)

In their 2009 meeting, the G-20 leaders "committed to act together to … implement strong international compensation standards aimed at ending practices that lead to excessive risk-taking."

The former President and CEO of the Federal Reserve Bank of New York, William C. Dudley has argued that a well-designed compensation structure can help favorably tip the balance between maximizing benefits and risk-taking by "effectively extending the time horizon of senior management and material risk-takers, and by forcing them to more fully internalize the consequences of their actions" (Dudley, 2014). For example, "as long as deferred compensation is set at a horizon longer than the life of the trade, this can ensure the firm's and the trader's incentives are aligned and the 'trader's option' is effectively mitigated" (Dudley, 2014).

If part of their compensation only becomes available to executives with a lag, this extends the time horizon over which their decisions are taken. Moreover, the executive compensation regime may include provisions that would force managers to return past bonuses if, for example, their decisions cause losses over the longer term.

Usually, the structure of the compensation package combines rewards for short-term profitability and for long-term growth potential and the stability of earnings. Short-term profitability is encouraged with the base salary and a bonus that is tied to the firm's recent performance, while long-term growth and stability are encouraged through restricted stocks, stock options, benefit packages, pension plans and so forth.

From the economic theory point of view, executive compensation regimes have been analyzed as a principal-agent problem within the theory of agency. The principal is the owner of the business and the agent is the manager. Agency models have analyzed how to reach a desirable allocation of risk between the owner (shareholders) and the manager. The incentives in the compensation manager's contract are supposed to guide the manager's behavior to achieve the owner's goals. The literature has showed that stock options which give managers a claim on the upper tail of the outcome distribution offer incentives to managers to invest in high-risk high-return projects. A stock option gives the holder the right to acquire a share at some future date for a prespecified price, the "strike price." In such a case, executives have incentives for risk-taking because they will fully capture stock price gains but will not fully bear stock price declines, as common shareholders would. Following a risky strategy will have a positive expected effect on the executive's payoffs.

Prior to the financial crisis, CEOs in banking holding companies received a substantial share of their compensation not in common shares, but in options on such shares (Bebchuk and Spamann, 2010: 17/18). Executives who get a stock option pay have incentives to engage in risky business beyond what is efficient because they do not internalize the adverse effects that risk-taking has on other stakeholders in the bank.

An exercise analyzing Citigroup and Bank of America's top executives pay at the end of 2006 shows that both banks' executives were heavily invested in their respective company's stock and their options strongly encouraged risk-taking (Bebchuk and Spamann, 2010: 21). Their monetary gain from a given large increase in the value of their firm's assets was greater than their monetary loss from an equally large decline in the value of these assets.

An empirical study examines the relationship between incentive compensation and the default risk in financial institutions domiciled in the United States using data on 117 financial firms from 1995 through 2008 (Balachandran et al., 2010). It concludes that incentives were designed to promote risk-taking and that they actually worked: financial firms did take big risks. The results indicate that the default risk measure is positively correlated with the equity-based incentive compensation. In previous academic research it was already found out that equity-based incentives encourage risk-taking decisions (Rajgopal and Shevlin, 2001).

How to avoid excessive risk-taking

Hugh McCulloch, who was the First Comptroller of the Treasury in 1863–1865, proposed to amend the National Bank Act so that the failure of a national bank be declared *prima facie* fraudulent and that its officers and directors be made personally liable for the debts of the bank and be punished criminally unless they can prove their innocence. It has been recently argued that something in this vein would put a limit to the perverse incentive that managers have to engage in excessive risk-taking using the customers' money. A second best may be the proposal for the creation of a database of banker misconduct. This would avoid "the problem of 'rolling bad apples.' In these cases, employees who are dismissed due to suspicion or proof of misconduct are unwittingly hired by other firms in the industry, where they have the opportunity to repeat their actions" (Dudley, 2018). In the same direction, "putting a greater onus on senior management for the costs incurred from regulatory fines or other legal liabilities, rather than on shareholders alone" (Dudley, 2018) may be a way of making them responsible for costly breakdowns.

Box 6.1 Hugh McCulloch (1808–1895)

By 1860 more than 10,000 different bank notes circulated throughout the United States, each with the name of a bank on it and a number of dollars which the named bank promised to pay in coin if the note were presented to it.

Abraham Lincoln's Union government during the Civil War had to solve the problem of a chaotic currency and at the same time the more pressing problem of how to finance the war.

As comptroller of the currency (1863–1865), Hugh McCulloch successfully implemented the National Bank Act of 1863, authorizing the issuance of national bank notes by national banks. The Comptroller was in charge of organizing and supervising the new banking system through regulations and periodic examinations.

As secretary of the Treasury (1865–1869) under Presidents Abraham Lincoln and Andrew Johnson, McCulloch attempted in vain to return the United States to the gold standard by withdrawing from circulation paper money issued during the Civil War.

He proposed to make officers and directors personally liable for the debts of their bank.

Source: Encyclopaedia Britannica

After the 2007/2009 financial crisis, legislation was passed with the aim of discouraging excessive risk-taking. The implicit assumption has been that this goal can be met by aligning management with shareholders' interests. However, managers might still take on more risks beyond what is efficient if this maximizes both shareholders' and their own expected payoffs (through both stocks and stock options), possibly at the expense of the debtholders. This may increase the probability of insolvency due to more risk-taking.

Bebchuk and Spamann (2009) argue that aligning management with shareholders' interests is not an appropriate solution and may in some cases even make matters worse. According to these authors, shareholders in the financial sector have an interest in taking more risks than is socially desirable. This happens because the capital structures partially insulate shareholders from the effect of declines in the value of bank assets at either the bank level or the bank holding company level. This may stimulate risk-taking by shareholders and executives aligned with them beyond what is efficient because they do not internalize the adverse effects that risk-taking has on other stakeholders in the bank such as creditors and the depositor insurer. Therefore, aligning the interests of executives with those of shareholders could eliminate risk-taking that is excessive from the shareholders' points of view but cannot be expected to prevent risk-taking that, although it serves executives and shareholders, is socially excessive.

Edmans and Gabaix (2016) present an extensive survey of traditional and modern theories of executive compensation. They distinguish between "good" and "bad" risk-taking. Good risk is the one that improves firm value while bad risk is the one that reduces it. They argue that an equity aligned manager may undertake a project even if it has a negative net present value because shareholders benefit from the upside, but have limited downside risk due to limited liability, in coincidence with Bebchuk and Spamann's argument. In this respect, Edmans and Liu (2011) show that a potential solution to such risk shifting is to compensate the manager with debt as well as with equity. They argue that a debt aligned manager will contemplate the creditors' interests. Creditors are concerned with not only the probability of default, but also recovery values in default. Debt renders the manager sensitive to the firm's value in bankruptcy, and not just the incidence of bankruptcy – exactly as desired by creditors. Tying compensation to the bank's default risk may help prevent managers and shareholders from making too risky bets. A mix of equity and debt in managers' compensation may correct the existent asymmetry between expected managers' share in profits and in losses.

The same reasoning leads us to consider that boards should represent not only the interests of shareholders but also those of the creditors of the bank, for instance certain types of bond holders.

Broadly speaking, risk-taking ventures may have a positive expected value for shareholders but a negative expected value to the public. Most of the systemic harm from a bank's failure may hurt the public, including creditors, depositors, taxpayers and ordinary citizens impacted by an economic collapse, causing widespread poverty and unemployment.

> This misalignment between corporate risk-taking and the public interest is created by corporate governance law, which requires managers of a firm to view the consequences of their firm's actions, and thus the expected value of corporate risk-taking, only from the standpoint of the firm and its investors.
>
> (Schwarcz and Peihani, 2018: 3)

On the other hand, as Schwarcz and Peihani rightly argue, only SIFIs, by definition, could engage in risk-taking that leads to systemic externalities. Therefore, a special regime should apply to managers of those firms to prevent them from socially excessive risk-taking. In this respect, the authors argue for a "public governance duty," requiring managers of SIFIs to assess the impact of risk-taking on the public as well as on investors. Governments by default should have the right to enforce the public duty.

As mentioned above, former President and CEO of the Federal Reserve Bank of New York, William C. Dudley argued in favor of a deferred compensation that does not begin to vest for several years. He added:

> Given recent experience, a decade would seem to be a reasonable timeframe to provide sufficient time and space for any illegal actions or violations of the firm's culture to materialize and fines and legal penalties realized … I also believe that this longer vesting portion of the deferred compensation should be debt as opposed to equity.
>
> (Dudley, 2014)

Dudley adds that in order to prevent an individual's accumulated deferred debt compensation from acting as a friction to job mobility, firms might want to allow this vesting to continue even if an individual leaves the firm.

It has also been suggested that the variable component of compensation to bankers should be granted only after three or five years when the bank knows how much value they have effectively created.

To summarize, although the legislation reforms enacted after the financial crisis may have some beneficial effects about risk-taking incentives that are excessive from the perspective of shareholders they do not eliminate incentives to take risks that would be excessive from a social perspective.

From theory to practice

The ideas on making sure that managers have skin in the game have been put in practice by only very few financial organizations.

For example, as of 2008 Credit Suisse announced it would pay managers a portion of their bonuses in financial instruments whose value depends on the performance of risky assets that the bank is exposed to.

According to this scheme, the bank's staff can reap sizable rewards if the underlying assets do well although they cannot get their money until a couple of years have elapsed. In fact, above a certain threshold, a portion of variable compensation is subject to mandatory deferral. The higher an individual's total compensation, the higher the percentage that is deferred. Deferred compensation elements are typically subject to a vesting period of three years and are subject to negative adjustment in the event of a divisional loss. A portion of the deferred compensation takes the form of Contingent Capital Awards, which have rights and risks similar to certain contingent capital instruments issued by the bank group in the market. There is a prohibition on all staff from entering into transactions to hedge the economic exposure tied to their long-term compensation prior to award vesting.

At the root of this initiative is the idea of trying to align the managers' interests with the long-run bank's interests, discouraging excessive risk-taking.

The 2019 FSB progress report on sound compensation policies comments that in recent years there has been an increased focus on compensation as a tool to address conduct risk. This has been driven by recent instances of misconduct. One of them was the LIBOR scandal, when a small number of banks manipulated LIBOR to their benefit; another one was the Forex scandal, where banks colluded for at least a decade to manipulate exchange rates for their own financial gain; a third one was the creation of millions of unauthorized accounts at Wells Fargo encouraged by a remuneration regime that compensated bank employees on sales volume.

According to the FSB report, since the financial crisis fines and legal costs for misconduct by global banks are estimated to have reached more than $320 billion. It also mentions that risk management processes and internal controls surrounding compensation have changed significantly post-crisis. Risk management and control personnel are engaged in the design and operation of incentive compensation arrangements of employees beyond senior executives to ensure that risk is properly considered.

However, compensation practices that incentivize prudent risk-taking need a push from the regulatory side because most of the banks and other financial institutions are still reluctant to implement them just by their own initiative.

Risk mispricing by credit rating agencies

As stated in Chapter 2, the financial crisis was the result of the combination of four factors: the irrational belief that house prices would rise forever, the colossal edifice of securitization built upon a shaky and highly risky base, the development of an unregulated shadow banking system and the mispricing of risk by credit rating agencies (CRAs). It is time to have a look at this last point.

CRAs played a key role in the subprime meltdown. Without the generous ratings assigned by them to subprime mortgage-backed securities these assets would not have been so highly demanded by investors.

CRAs are paid by issuers, so that their interest is more aligned with that of securities' issuers than with that of investors. The existence of a small number of issuers of structured products gave them considerable market power in the ratings market.

Under-pricing of risk benefits issuers in two ways: one, because unsophisticated investors are thus induced to buy rated-inflated securities; two, because regulation requires institutional investors to invest only in highly rated securities.

On the other hand, opacity in the issuance of structured debt securities acts in the same direction, expanding even more their primary market.

Mispricing of risk is an everyday phenomenon. Each time someone sells some asset at a loss it is because they have mispriced the risk at the time of the investment decision. But even if the mispricing has to do with a great number of people this would not have an impact on the economy as a whole. The problem arises when it is a mispricing of a systemic risk i.e. a risk that may endanger the stability of the financial system as a whole. By mispricing mortgage-related securities risk the credit rating agencies allowed that trillions of dollars were invested in them by most of the financial institutions thus compromising the health of the entire financial system. Inflated credit ratings led to a massive mispricing of risk whose correction later detonated a crisis that put in evidence the failures of the initial ratings of structured debt securities.

Credit rating agencies regulation

According to Professor Andrea Miglionico the main problems in connection with CRAs' *modus operandi* are: "(1) the ´issuer-pays' business model; (2) over-reliance on ratings for regulatory purposes and on the part of investors; (3) limited competition; and (4) lack of accountability" (Miglionico, 2019: X).

In spite of their key role in the financial meltdown, CRAs emerged practically untouched after it. Although the Dodd-Frank Act devotes a whole chapter to the subject, its norms have been only partially implemented.

According to Partnoy (2017),

> these reforms have had little or no impact, and ... therefore the same credit rating-related dangers, market distortions, and inefficient allocations of capital that led to the crisis potentially remain. The major credit rating agencies are still among the most powerful and profitable institutions in the world. The market for credit ratings continues to be a large and impenetrable oligopoly dominated by two firms: Moody's and S&P. And yet credit ratings are still as uninformative as they were before the financial crisis. Simply put, credit ratings remain enormously important but have little or no informational value.

The US Securities and Exchange Commission (SEC) permits financial firms to use for regulatory purposes only those agencies known as nationally recognized statistical rating organizations (NRSRO). This is a regulator barrier to entry to this oligopolistic market. Moreover, there are institutional and regulatory features that make sure there is always demand for their services. Many institutional investors are restricted to invest in assets with certain ratings.

Although Section 939A of Dodd-Frank provided for the removal of NRSRO references to credit ratings from both statutes and rules, regulatory reliance on ratings remains pervasive. Credit ratings continue to play a significant role in federal regulation, in a wide range of areas, and regulators continue to adopt new regulations that depend on ratings.

The regulatory act created a new office within the SEC: the Office of Credit Ratings (OCR), in charge of overseeing NRSROs. This includes annually examining the NRSROs.

Although during these years the OCR reported several transgressions by NRSROs, civil actions based on them have been infrequent.

The SEC is also required by the Dodd-Frank Act to adopt new rules that concern several issues connected with NRSRO s activities.

In this respect, in August 2014, the SEC adopted new requirements which address internal controls, conflicts of interest, disclosure of credit rating performance statistics, procedures to protect the integrity and transparency of rating methodologies, disclosures to promote the transparency of credit ratings, and standards for training, experience and competence of credit analysts.

Nevertheless, the essential problem is that the primary sources of revenue for their ratings continue to come in the form of fees that are paid by the security issuer. When John Moody started his company (and the ratings industry) in 1909, most of its income came from the investors. Since the development of photocopying machines in the early seventies, the cost of reproducing the books of ratings sold to investors decreased dramatically, threatening the viability of the investors-pay model. In fact, there is a "free-rider" problem because non-paying investors could benefit from easy access to the rating lists. From then on, fees are collected from issuers. However, with today's technology, the free-rider problem should no longer be an obstacle to implement the investor-pay model. It is just an issue of stopping document copying by preventing use of copy/paste, screen grabs and printing.

The issuer-pays model raises a potential conflict of interest because the agencies are paid by the organizations whose debt they rate. This incentivizes the NRSRO to offer an unduly favorable rating of the issuers' security so as to keep them as clients. On top of this, it also happens that institutional investors – who need high ratings to buy the securities at all – may have a vested interest in rating agencies awarding high ratings.

From the theoretical point of view, it has been argued that agencies cannot be tempted to provide biased ratings because this would damage the agencies' reputation. Therefore, if they expect to remain in business over a longer term, they would give priority to preserving their long-run reputation as an accurate provider of ratings (White, 2018: 17).

However, as the same author admits, it is clear that "the CRAs' business model – whereby the issuers of the securities paid for the ratings – very likely did encourage the CRAs to accede (or cater) to the RMBS (residential mortgage-backed securities) issuers' desires to obtain higher ratings" (White, 2018: 13). Reputational pressures alone do not create adequate incentives to avoid biased ratings, according to the last financial crisis experience.

After the subprime meltdown, the Dodd-Frank Act required the SEC and the Government Accountability Office to study the issuer-pays model and alternatives to it. It also required the SEC to recommend a business model for the NRSROs. If no business model were recommended, it required the SEC to create a board that randomly assigns credit rating to the NRSROs. However, the SEC has neither endorsed a business model for the NRSROs nor implemented the random assignment model (Rivlin and Soroushian, 2017). The NRSROs business model is still an issue open to discussion.

Another conflict of interest emerges when CRAs offer advisory services to issuers. For instance, an issuer can ask a rating agency how it would rate a financial instrument with certain characteristics, and may even ask how these should be modified to obtain a certain rating. This type of activity facilitates rating shopping, that is, it allows an issuer to identify the rating agency that would provide the most favorable rating to its financial instruments. In this way they can make sure that structured products get an AAA rating. The selection and slicing done in association with a CRA makes sure that each tranche will get the desired rating. For example, investment banks "could adjust their CDO packages to get the desired rating while minimizing the efforts to improve the quality of the package" (Darbellay, 2013: 125). For this reason, it has been argued that the formulation of ratings should be completely separated from ancillary services.

In this respect, in principle, an NRSRO is forbidden from: 1) structuring the same products that it rates, 2) allowing analysts who participate in determining credit ratings from negotiating the fees that issuers pay to be rated, 3) allowing analysts to accept gifts in any amount over $25 from entities that receive ratings from the NRSRO. However, there are several exceptions to this rule; for example, if the NRSRO discloses the existence of that conflict of interest. The SEC also required NRSROs to publish performance statistics for 1, 3 and 10 years within each rating category; to disclose how frequently credit ratings are reviewed; whether different models are used for new issue and surveillance; and whether changes made to models are applied retroactively to existing ratings; and make publicly available in a machine-readable format ratings action histories for all credit ratings.

The SEC has required a more completely separation between the credit analysis function and sales and marketing activities prohibiting an employee who participates in sales or marketing activities to also participate in determining a credit rating or in developing the procedures or methodologies used to produce the credit rating; it also requires a one-year look-back review when a credit analyst leaves the NRSRO to work for an entity rated by the NRSRO or an issuer, underwriter or sponsor of securities being rated by the NRSRO.

As far as CRAs' liability is concerned, it is worth remembering that during the Great Depression, Congress enacted the Securities Act of 1933 to regain investor confidence in the stock market requiring that issuers provide certain disclosures to the investing public. Specifically, under Sections 7 and 11, when an issuer includes statements in a prospectus from experts, the prospectus must also include consent to liability from the expert. However, in 1982, the Securities Act Rule 436(g) exempted credit rating agencies from this requirement; this exemption was removed by the Dodd-Frank Act but this repeal never went into effect because the SEC issued a no-action letter, acknowledging refusal by the credit rating agencies to consent to expert liability. The result is that the CRAs cannot be liable as experts under Section 11, even though Dodd-Frank clearly provides that they should be. This marks a clear difference with other "financial gatekeepers" in the economy such as auditors or financial analysts who are subject to liability as experts.

The Dodd-Frank Act also made amendments to Rule 17g-5 to deal with "rating shopping" –soliciting preliminary ratings from several CRAs and only reveal to investors the most favorable one – and the potential conflict of interest that arises in an arranger-pay model; in particular, these amendments require a rating agency hired by an issuer to disclose the rating assignment and provide information to both hired and certified non-hired NRSROs. The purpose of this amendment has been to increase the number of credit ratings extant for a given structured product promoting the issuance of credit ratings by NRSROs that are not hired by the arranger. In this way, the users of structured credit ratings would be provided with more views on the creditworthiness of the rated products.

However, very few shadow ratings have been produced under this new mechanism. One problem is that non-hired NRSROs are not able to disclose information in the website to investors, which limits their ability to provide rationale for a given shadow rating.

In this respect, Pagano and Volpin (2009: 422) propose the disclosure of the entire set of data available to the arrangers and servicers. This would allow investors and/or specialized information processors to assess the risk of default of a specific product and the change in risk characteristics over time. Another proposal by these authors is that issuers should disclose the magnitude of the tranche that they retain in each issue and in each of its tranches, as well as the fee paid to the CRA who rated the issue, in order to help investors to better gauge the quality of the issue and of its tranches.

The fact is that, in spite of the Dodd-Frank Act provisions, very little has changed neither in respect to the conflicts of interests concerning NRSROs nor to promoting increased competition in this oligopolistic market. More than a decade after the crisis to whose origin they were major contributors, "the major credit rating agencies remain among the powerful and profitable institutions in the world" (Partnoy, 2017: 1414).

Notes

1 However, Frankel (2017) takes the risk and points out to three candidates: a) the bursting of a stock-market bubble; b) the bursting of a bond-market bubble; and c) geopolitical risk.
2 See Chapter 7.

References

Abreu, D. and Brunnermeier, M. K. (2002). Bubbles and Crashes. *Econometrica* 71(1): 173–204.

Acharya V. V., Pedersen, L. H., Philippon, T. and Richardson, M. (2009). Regulating Systemic Risk. In V. V. Acharya and M. Richardson (eds.), *Restoring Financial Stability: How to Repair a Failed System*. New York: New York University, Stern School of Business, pp. 283–304.

Allen, F., Babus, A. and Carletti, E. (2011). *Asset Commonality, Debt Maturity and Systemic Risk*. doi:10.2139/ssrn.1954810.

Balachandran S., Kogut, B. and Harnal, H. (2010). *Did Executive Compensation Encourage Extreme Risk-taking in Financial Institutions*? Manuscript. https://www0.gsb.columbia.edu/mygsb/faculty/research/pubfiles/5388/extreme%20risk%20financial%20services%20compensation%20balachandran%20kogut%20harnal_v2.pdf.

Bebchuk, L. A. and Spamann, H. (2009). Regulating Bankers' Pay. *Georgetown Law Journal* 98(2): 247–287.

Beker, V. A. (2016). Current Issues and Policies. In B. Moro and V. A. Beker, *Modern Financial Crises: Argentina, United States and Europe*. Ch. 11. Financial and Monetary Policy Studies 42. Switzerland: Springer International Publishing. doi:10.1007/978-3-319-20991-3_3.

Bhagat, S. and Bolton, B. (2013). Bank Executive Compensation and Capital Requirements Reform. *Journal of Financial and Quantitative Analysis* 48(1): 1–33.

Brunnenmeir, M. K. and Oehmk, M. (2012). *Bubbles, Financial Crises, and Systemic Risk*. http://citeseerx.ist.psu.edu/viewdoc/download?doi=10.1.1.640.39&rep=rep1&type=pdf.

Brunnermeier, M. K., Rother, S. and Schnabel, I. (2019). *Asset Price Bubbles and Systemic Risk.* Discussions Series Papers – CRC TR 224, Discussion Paper No. 095. https://www.crctr224.de/en/research-output/discussion-papers/discussion-paper-archive/2019/asset-price-bubbles-and-systemic-risk-markus-brunnermeier-simon-rother-isabel-schnabel.

Challe, E. (2012). Leverage, Excessive Risk-Taking, and Financial Instability. *L'actualité de la Recherche en Finance.* January. www.louisbachelier.org/wp-content/uploads/Leverage,%20Excessive%20Risk-Taking_0.pdf.

Darbellay, A. (2013). *Regulating Credit Rating Agencies.* UK: Edward Elgar.

Dudley, W. C. (2014). *Enhancing financial Stability by Improving Culture in the financial Services Industry.* Remarks at the Workshop on Reforming Culture and Behavior in the financial Services Industry, Federal Reserve Bank of New York, New York City. http://www.ny.frb.org/newsevents/speeches/2014/dud141020a.html.

Dudley, W. C. (2018). *The Importance of Incentives in Ensuring a Resilient and Robust Financial System.* Remarks at the US Chamber of Commerce, Washington, DC. https://www.newyorkfed.org/newsevents/speeches/2018/dud180326.

Edmans, A. and Gabaix, X. (2016). Executive Compensation: A Modern Primer. *Journal of Economic Literature* 54(4): 1232–1287. doi:10.1257/jel.20161153.

Edmans, A. and Liu, Q. (2011). Inside Debt. *Review of Finance* 15(1): 75–102.

Frankel, J. (2017). Why Financial Markets Underestimate Risk. *Project Syndicate.* September 25. https://www.project-syndicate.org/commentary/financial-markets-crisis-risk-by-jeffrey-frankel-2017-09.

Greenspan, A. (2014). *The Map and the Territory 2.0. Risk, Human Nature and the Future of Forecasting.* London: Penguin Books.

Miglionico, A. (2019). *The Governance of Credit Rating Agencies: Regulatory Regimes and Liability Issues.* Cheltenham: Elgar Financial Law and Practice.

Moro, B. (2016). The Run on Repo and the Policy Interventions to Struggle the Great Crisis. In B. Moro and V. A. Beker, *Modern Financial Crises: Argentina, United States and Europe*, Ch. 4. Financial and Monetary Policy Studies 42. Switzerland: Springer International Publishing. doi:10.1007/978-3-319-20991-3_3.

Pagano, M. and Volpin, P. F. (2009). Credit Ratings Failures and Policy Options (November). CEPR Discussion Paper No. DP7556. Available at SSRN: https://ssrn.com/abstract=1533162.

Partnoy, F. (2017). What's (Still) Wrong with Credit Ratings. *Harvard Law School Forum on Corporate Governance.* https://corpgov.law.harvard.edu/2017/05/31/whats-still-wrong-with-credit-ratings/.

Rajgopal, S. and Shevlin, T. J. (2001). Empirical Evidence on the Relation between Stock Option Compensation and Risk Taking. *EFA 0217.* doi:10.2139/ssrn.172689.

Rivlin, A. M. and Soroushian, J. B. (2017). *The NRSROs Business Model Is Still An Issue Open to discussion. Brookings. Credit Rating Agency Reform Is Incomplete.* https://www.brookings.edu/research/credit-rating-agency-reform-is-incomplete/.

Schwarcz, S. L. and Peihani, M. (2018). *Addressing Excessive Risk Taking in the Financial Sector: A Corporate Governance Approach.* Policy Brief No. 139, September. Centre for International Governance Innovation. https://www.cigionline.org/sites/default/files/documents/PB%20no.139_1.pdf.

Shim, I., Bogdanova, B., Shek, J. and Subelyte, A. (2013). Database for Policy Actions on Housing Markets. *BIS Quarterly Review*, September.

Sowerbutts, R., Zimmerman, P. and Zer, I. (2013). Banks' Disclosure and Financial Stability. *Bank of England Quarterly Bulletin* 53(4): 326–335.

White, L. S. (2018). The Credit Rating Agencies and Their Role in the Financial System. Stern School of Business. Reprinted in E. Brousseau, J. Glachant and J. Sgarded (eds.), *Oxford Handbook on Institutions, International Economic Governance, and Market Regulation*. Oxford: Oxford University Press.

White, S. S. (2002). *Banking Crisis in Japan: Prediction of Non-Performing Loans.* https://theses.lib.vt.edu/theses/available/etd-07172002-210604/unrestricted/thesischapters1to4.pdf.

7 Micro- and macro-prudential regulation

Changes in prudential regulation after the Great Recession

While before the global financial crisis central banks focused mainly on monetary policy and less on financial stability, they are now highly focused on the latter.

In this context, macro-prudential policy has become established as a new policy area. It does not replace the traditional regulation, often called micro-prudential; it complements it after the global financial crisis demonstrated micro-prudential regulation was insufficient to guarantee the health of the financial system as a whole. Macro-prudential policy is defined as the use of primarily prudential tools to limit systemic risk (IMF-FSB-BIS, 2016: 4).

While micro-prudential supervision focuses on safeguarding individual financial institutions from idiosyncratic risks and preventing them from taking too much risk, macro-prudential regulation has to do with the fact that financial institutions may not internalize the adverse externalities which their risk-taking behavior may generate on the economy as a whole. Macro-prudential supervision aims to internalizing those externalities.

As the former General Manager of the Bank for International Settlements Andrew D. Crockett suggested, one can think of the whole financial system as a portfolio of securities, with each institution representing a security. The overall risk of the portfolio is not just the sum of the risk of individual institutions but depends fundamentally on the correlation between them. Limiting the risk of the system as a whole is quite a different thing to limiting the risk of each institution separately, as was usually the case. From the macro-prudential point of view, actions that may seem desirable or reasonable from the perspective of individual institutions may result in unwelcome system outcomes (Crockett, 2000).

The Basel III accords have significantly changed prudential supervision, with a view to improving micro-prudential supervision as well as complementing it with a macro-prudential dimension designed to address systemic risk.[1]

In the EU, the new prudential rules for its banking system that came into force on January 1, 2014 provide Member States with a common legal framework that includes a set of macro-prudential instruments.

Micro-prudential regulatory reform

"Under the umbrella of Basel III, international reform of micro-prudential regulation has focused on four key areas: capital, leverage, liquidity, and resolution" (Aikman et al., 2019a: 144). Let us have a look at these four areas.

Capital

With respect to capital standards, the reforms have been implemented by nearly all countries internationally. They are focused on increasing – quantitatively and qualitatively – the capital maintained by banks against their risk-weighted assets exposures.

The idea is that a well-capitalized bank will be able to handle major write-downs of its assets without defaulting on its creditors and depositors. Banks are required to hold a larger portion of their liabilities in the form of equity so that they can absorb losses from a very severe shock without being forced to sell off their assets at fire-sale prices and trigger the sort of contagion that threatened the global financial system in 2007/2009. However, available research suggests that instead of raising capital, banks prefer to reduce their lending because issuing equity is costly. Given the expected adverse impact of issuances on share prices., bank executives generally prefer to limit the growth of assets over the issuance of new equity. This may imply a reduction in credit supply. Other studies argue that substantially higher equity capital requirements in the long run will not affect the loan supply adversely, but curb excessive risk-taking (World Bank, 2019: 14).

Leverage

In order to constrain excess leverage Basel III has implemented a leverage ratio which is set at a minimum level of 3%. This means that the ratio of the bank's core capital to its total assets should be equal or above 3%. Its purpose is to reinforce the risk-based capital requirements with a simple, non-risk-based "backstop."[2]

Banks are required to fully disclose to the markets their financial leverage. In April 2016, the Basel Committee introduced an additional leverage ratio requirement for global systemically important banks.

Liquidity

In the Basel III rules, regulators have also designed global standards for the minimum liquidity levels to be held by banks. They rely on two minimum ratios. The first is a "Liquidity Coverage Ratio" which is a kind of stylized stress test to ensure that a bank would have the necessary sources of high-quality liquid assets (HQLA) to survive a 30-day market crisis. HQLA means assets that can be easily and immediately converted to cash at little or no loss of value.

The second is the Net Stable Funding Ratio (NSFR) which relates the bank's available stable funding to its required stable funding. The NSFR is expressed as a ratio and must equal or exceed 100%. "Stable funding" is defined as the portion of those types and amounts of equity and liability financing expected to be reliable sources of funds over a one-year time horizon under conditions of stress. The NSFR aims to limiting over-reliance on short-term wholesale funding to finance medium to long-term assets and activities.

In this respect, Brunnermeier et al. (2011, 2014) suggested an alternative liquidity measure – Liquidity Mismatch Index (LMI) – which has been implemented in an exercise by Bai et al. (2017). The purpose is to measure the mismatch between the funding liquidity of liabilities and the market liquidity of assets. As LMI can be aggregated across banks it is not only informative regarding individual bank liquidity but it also provides a macro-prudential liquidity parameter, measuring the liquidity mismatch for the whole financial system, offering thus an early indicator of eventual crises. Bai et al. construct the LMI for 2882 bank holding companies during 2002–2014 and investigate its time-series and cross-sectional patterns. The empirical results show that, had the LMI been computed in 2007, it would have been a good predictor of the need of liquidity the Fed had to inject to mitigate the liquidity-run aspect of the financial crisis. Compared with the Basel standards, the LMI performs better in both macro- and micro-dimensions. However, as the authors recognize, the LMI measures are not yet a finished product, but they are a promising tool which has still to be improved to serve as a macro-prudential barometer.

Resolution

The new resolution and restructuring regimes designed after the crisis try to make sure that the winding up of financial institutions will be an orderly process with minimum disruption of the financial markets. The FSB has established standards of total loss absorbing capacity (TLAC) for globally systematically important banks to make sure they can be bailed-in in case of failure without the need for bail-out by public funds.

As already mentioned in Chapter 3, the Dodd-Frank Act tries to reduce taxpayer exposure to loss from support in case of resolution of financial institutions. With this purpose, bank holding companies with total consolidated assets of $50 billion or more and nonbank financial companies designated as SIFIs by the FSOC have to periodically submit resolution plans – commonly known as living wills – that must describe the company's strategy for rapid and orderly resolution under the US Bankruptcy Code in the event of material financial distress or failure of the company. In the case of Europe, ensuring the orderly resolution of failing banks with minimum impact on the real economy and the public finances is the main purpose of the single resolution mechanism instituted as one of the pillars of the European Banking Union. The Single Supervisory Mechanism (SSM), a new arm of the European Central Bank, directly supervises more than 100 "significant" banks, with the remainder supervised by national authorities, subject to the final authority of the SSM.

Macro-prudential regulatory reform

The set of most significant macro-prudential measures have to do with capital buffers, stress testing, lending standards and the shadow banking system. We have already dealt with the latter in Chapter 4. Let us have a look at the other three groups of instruments.

Capital buffers

When a solvency issue is at play, liquidity backstop is not sufficient and capital injection is required. Building and releasing capital buffers can help maintain the ability of the financial system to function effectively, even under adverse conditions. Basel III included the gradual introduction, starting from 2016, of the so-called capital conservation buffer – equal to 2.5% of the risk-weighted assets – aimed at ensuring that banks keep a capital cushion to absorb the losses associated to periods of economic and financial stress. This is an automatic mechanism which allows a bank to accumulate high-quality capital during good times that will be eroded by losses during bad times without limiting the normal bank's activities.

This dynamic capital buffer recognizes that risks to the financial system vary over the credit cycle. Thus, additional capital is required during the upswing which can be released during the downswing.

The same idea inspired the additional countercyclical capital buffer – also introduced as part of Basel III but subject to national supervisory authorities' approval – which rises when the credit supply is above its trend and falls during phases of credit contractions. This requirement is not automatic but can be imposed on a discretionary basis by the individual national supervisors in case of excessive credit growth and according to the aggregate risk environment.

Aikman et al. (2019b) estimate what size of the countercyclical capital buffer would have allowed banks to continue lending in line with historical credit growth rates during the last financial crisis. The result is that had a countercyclical capital buffer of 4.7% been built-up in the run-up to the crisis, it would have ensured that banks would have had sufficient capital to avoid applying for TARP and to continue growing their balance sheets in line with the long-run average growth rate. However, the authors recognize that macro-prudential policy frameworks should be calibrated with some built-in "slack" to account for the inherent difficulty of risk assessment, particularly in real time (Aikman et al., 2019b: 115–116).

Basel III also imposed higher capital requirements on systemically important firms. "These capital add-ons apply to the 30 designated global systemically important banks (G-SIBs) and the roughly 160 domestic systemically important banks (D-SIBs), to be phased-in between 2016 and 2019" (Aikman et al., 2019a: 146).

The new rules place a greater focus on Common Equity Tier 1, which includes those instruments (common shares, stock surplus, retained earnings) that have no maturity date and have no obligation to distribute dividends. This high-quality capital can absorb losses without the need of bank liquidation and therefore allows the bank to continue its activities.

Finally, Basel III requires that total capital must be equal to at least 8% of the bank's risk-weighted assets.

Stress tests

Macro-prudential stress tests aim at helping to assess the ability of the system to continue to function under a range of adverse economic and financial conditions, thereby complementing the use of early warning indicators.

Stress testing started in the early 1990s just as an instrument for banks' internal risk management purposes. While some European regulatory authorities did conduct stress tests in the early 2000s – before the financial crisis – these tended to be simple exercises with little direct impact on policy. During the financial crisis, stress tests for large banks were used to estimate how much capital each bank would have to raise. But it was only after the crisis that they have taken on a much more prominent role within the regulatory toolkit.

In fact, after the financial meltdown, regulatory stress tests moved from being small-scale, isolated exercises, to large-scale, comprehensive risk-assessment programs. Their purpose is analyzing how financial institutions would cope with hypothetical adverse scenarios, such as severe recessions or financial crises.

The US Supervisory Capital Assessment Program (SCAP) conducted by the Federal Reserve in early 2009 was the first prominent example of this new wave of stress tests. In a marked departure from the past, the results of the SCAP were publicly disclosed on a bank-by-bank basis. SCAP was followed by a proliferation of frameworks for regular concurrent stress testing across central banks and supervisory authorities.[3]

The Dodd-Frank Act requires the Federal Reserve to conduct an annual supervisory stress test on SIFIs. The Dodd-Frank Act also requires these same firms to conduct their own stress tests and report the results to the Federal Reserve twice a year.

These instruments provide forward-looking information to help gauge the potential effect of stressful conditions on the ability of those organizations to absorb losses and continue to lend. The Fed-conducted annual assessment includes a Comprehensive Capital Analysis and Review which evaluates a firm's capital adequacy and planned capital distributions.

Firms strongly depend on this assessment in order to go on with some key decisions, such as any dividend payments and common stock repurchases. If the Federal Reserve objects to a firm's capital plan, the firm may only make capital distributions that the Federal Reserve has not objected to.

Section 401 of the Dodd-Frank Act stipulates that any bank holding company, regardless of asset size, that has been identified as a "global systemically important" bank holding company ("G-SIB") shall be treated as a bank holding company with $250 billion or more in total consolidated assets.

On the other hand, no non-bank financial company is currently subject to the capital planning or stress test requirements.

As the financial crisis demonstrated, interconnections and contagion between different parts of the financial system can serve to transmit stresses originating in a particular market segment across the broader financial system, amplifying the effects of the initial shock. As Brazier (2017: 4) remarks, "the core principle behind bank stress testing – the need to assess whether the system could respond to severe economic shocks in ways that make them worse – needs to be applied to the wider financial system."

The aim of the macro-prudential stress testing is to assess not just the health of a particular institution however big and interconnected it is but the resilience of the financial system as a whole.[4] However, most macro-prudential stress tests only cover banks and their creditors, and therefore fail to capture interactions with non-banks that make up a substantial part of the financial system nowadays. In fact, non-bank components of the financial system are playing an increasing role as banking regulation induces a migration of financial activities to funds and investment vehicles of various types.

On the other hand, a key issue is whether stress tests results actually provide reliable information on the resilience of banks. In this respect the case of Banco Popular, Spain's fifth-largest bank, seems to give a negative answer. It passed the European Central Bank's Asset Quality Review in 2014 and the European Banking Authority's stress test in 2016; only six months after this last stress test, it collapsed. As a matter of fact, Banco Santander bought it for the nominal sum of one euro after depositors withdrew money *en masse* from the failing institution.

Is this just a failure of the EU stress tests? It does not seem to be the case. Goldstein (2017) argues that stress tests currently conducted in both the United States and the European Union fall short of what is needed to promote financial stability; in particular he warns that the metrics used in the stress tests are not good enough to discriminate between healthy and sick banks.

Lending standards

Other macro-prudential instruments include those aimed at influencing lending standards – for example, through setting loan to value limits (LTV), loan to income limits (LTI) or margin requirements on collateralized borrowing in financial markets. As a matter of fact, the majority of macro-prudential actions since 2010 have fallen into these lending standards category (Aikman et al., 2018: 33). They are particularly aimed at the housing sector with the purpose of addressing the build-up of systemic risk due to excess credit to this sector.

Proposals to improve macro-prudential supervision

He and Krishnamurthy (2019: 34) argue that most stress tests "miss the general equilibrium feedback effect of the stress on aggregate bank balance sheets to the real sector and back to bank balance sheets." They present a general equilibrium model which allows computing the fixed point of this feedback mechanism.

Cortes et al. (2018) propose a Systemic Risk and Interconnectedness framework, to measure systemic risk accounting for interconnectedness across banks and non-banks, including insurance companies, pension funds, investment funds and hedge funds.

For this purpose, they characterize financial systems as portfolios of financial entities/sectors.

The authors identify two different types of interlinkages: direct and indirect. Direct interlinkages primarily stem from contractual obligations between financial entities. Indirect interlinkages can be caused by exposures to common risk factors and market price channels, including asset fire sales (triggered by stressed entities) and asset sell-offs (due to information asymmetries across agents). Cortes et al. describe the generic characteristics of relevant sectors in financial systems, comment on key structural changes in these sectors and describe direct and indirect channels of interconnectedness and spillovers across sectors.

According to the authors, the Systemic Risk and Interconnectedness framework can be increasingly relevant, as structural changes in financial intermediation are shifting the locus of risk to the non-financial sector, and involve increasing interlinkages across sectors.

In this respect, as already mentioned in Chapter 3, central counterparties may become new too-big-to-fail entities which should also be stress-tested and their resolution plans agreed to.

Broadly speaking, the lack of appropriate data remains a basic difficulty to move forward in the macro-prudential stress testing field. One of the vital pending issues is to agree what data should be made available and collected for financial stability purposes.

For this reason, Anderson et al. (2018) propose the development of "encompassing frameworks" aimed at integrating a diverse collection of data and of modeling frameworks with different characteristics as a way to maximize the information content of heterogeneous data sources and minimize potential model error.[5]

Anderson et al. remark that macro-prudential stress tests may offer a quantitative, forward-looking assessment of the resilience of individual banks and of the whole financial system. By simultaneously subjecting a number of institutions to the same scenario, stress tests allow for an assessment of the system as a whole after losses from an adverse shock have materialized. Discussion has also started about the potential uses of macro-prudential stress tests to support macro-prudential policy.

Adrian and Brunnermeier (2016) argue that the build-up of systemic risk typically occurs in seemingly tranquil times. That is why they propose a forward-looking systemic risk measure – *forward-ΔCoVaR* – that can be used in a time-series application of macro-prudential policy.

Aikman et al. (2015) collected forty-four indicators of financial and balance sheet conditions, cutting across measures of valuation pressures, nonfinancial borrowing and financial-sector health to provide a framework for assessing the build-up of vulnerabilities to the US financial system. However, although their approach would have signaled heightened vulnerabilities in the mid-2000s, it would have also signaled elevated risks during the late 1990s. Therefore, it seems that the instrument needs to be improved in order to distinguish between events of a more limited nature and those that can lead to a global financial crisis.

Scenario stress testing may be a particularly appropriate tool for developing forward-looking approaches. Introducing views on potential financial market and economic evolutions into the system's risk measurement methods and translating these views in terms of risks may help detecting vulnerabilities.

I have argued in Chapter 6 that to prevent financial crises central banks should establish the acceptable levels of sectoral, regional or asset concentration risk as well as the mechanisms to monitor and control that the system behaves within them. In the same way, the central bank should also set concentration risk ceilings for exposures to funding sources.

Holistic stress tests looking at the risks being faced by the financial system as a whole may be especially useful in the identification of concentration risk. The aim is identifying exposures with the potential to produce losses large enough to threaten the financial system's health.

The new financial regulatory architecture: pros and cons

To sum up, the new financial regulatory architecture includes risk-weighted capital requirements (RWCR), the leverage ratio (LR), the liquidity coverage ratio (LCR) and the net stable funding ratio (NSFR). This system of multipolar regulation – as Aikman et al. (2019a: 163) call it – is, for some authors, over-identified. Aikman et al. defend the multiple constraint approach arguing that any individual constraint creates incentives for banks to engage in avoidance or arbitrage. A multipronged approach mitigates this risk.

It has been argued that RWCR is better suited than the LR to guard against solvency risk (Gordy, 2003; Sironi, 2018), in which case LR may be redundant. But, as Aikman et al. remind us, this is true if and only if risks in the financial system can be known with sufficient certainty to be estimated accurately. In a world of radical uncertainty, we are very far from that. Radical uncertainty means the kind of uncertainty statistics cannot deal with. And this is particularly true when you need to forecast adverse tail events.

As the former Governor of the Bank of England Mervin King (2017: 138) argues, in a world subject to radical uncertainty "it is better to be roughly right than precisely wrong."

This logic is one rationale for the use of a risk-unweighted LR in capturing solvency risks, which is simpler, more transparent and less subject to strong assumptions than RWCR.

On the other hand, studies of bank capital during the global financial crisis suggest that investors paid much less attention to risk-weighted capital ratios. In fact, results reveal that higher capital was linked with higher stock returns during the crisis and that this relationship is stronger when capital is measured as a simple leverage ratio rather than a risk-weighted ratio, particularly for large banks (World Bank, 2019: 13).

Finally, risk weights should not depend exclusively on past behavior of assets but they should be periodically adjusted to dis-incentivize excessive concentration of assets in some kind of them.

For the time being, as already noticed in Chapter 5, one apparent result of the provisions on risk-weighted capital requirements has been that many banks have offloaded complex assets that attracted higher capital requirements; this allowed their assets to look much less risky to their internal models.

Financial institutions' Achilles heel has always been a sudden withdrawal of funding. LCR tries to ensure an available buffer of liquid assets to meet banks' 30-day liquidity needs. However, maturity transformation can also create risks over longer horizons. For this reason, NSFR complements LCR to ensure banks are resilient to a medium-term funding run. The goal is to reduce the probability that shocks affecting a bank's usual funding sources might erode its liquidity position, as it happened during the last financial crisis when wholesale markets closed for an extended period. NFSR seeks that banks reduce their dependency on short-term wholesale markets.

As of January 1, 2019, the minimum LCR required for internationally active banks is 100%. In other words, the stock of liquid assets must be at least as large as the expected total net cash outflows over the 30-day stress period.

With respect to NSFR, Basel III requires it to be equal to at least 100% on an ongoing basis. In other words, the amounts of available stable funding and required stable funding must be equal. That is:

$$\text{Available amount of stable funding} / \text{Required amount of stable funding} \geq 100\%$$

As mentioned before, available stable funding is defined as the portion of capital and liabilities expected to be reliable over the time horizon considered by the NSFR, which extends to one year.

Aikman et al. (2019a: 165) used a data set on the pre-crisis balance sheet characteristics of global banks to compute RWCR, LR and NFSR for those banks at that time. They divided the sample into banks that "survived" and banks that "failed" between 2007 and 2009 and analyzed how successful various combinations of regulatory constraints might have been in identifying failed and surviving banks.

Concerning LR, they found that a 4% leverage ratio requirement would not have been met by around 70% of banks that subsequently ended up failing. That means that most failing banks had a leverage ratio below 4%. It might have served as a decent signal of subsequent failure. However, there was a 30% of those that failed whose leverage ratio was above 4%. If the leverage ratio requirement would have been 5.66%, the hit rate jumped from 70% to 90% although the false alarm rate increased substantially.

The authors also report results as far as RWCR and NFSR performance, which in balancing hit and false alarm rates are relatively inferior to the ones got for LR. They conclude that "it is possible to achieve lower false alarm rates for the same hit rate when multiple metrics are used" (Aikman et al. 2019a: 170), an argument which favors the use of multiple metrics.

Box 7.1 A counterfactual exercise

To illustrate the meaning of their results when trying to identify failing banks, Aikman et al. (2019a) compare two failing bank cases: the American bank Countrywide and the Belgian bank KBC Group. They explain:

> At the end of 2006, Countrywide had a leverage ratio of 7.7% and a risk-weighted capital ratio of 11.6%. Even if capital regulation had been more stringent in 2006, Countrywide may not have been required to raise capital. But its NSFR was just 0.76, indicative of the structural liquidity risk it was undertaking. By including the NSFR in the suite of regulatory metrics, it would have been possible to capture the risks that Countrywide was undertaking without resorting to materially more stringent capital regulation. By contrast, KBC Group had an NSFR of 1.12, well above the current indicative regulatory standard. It also had a reasonable risk-weighted capital ratio of 8.7%, well above the median capital ratio in the sample. But its leverage ratio was 3.5%. A system of regulation excluding the leverage ratio would have been unable to capture risks of the type KBC Group was undertaking prior to the crisis.

The main conclusion the authors draw from this counterfactual exercise is that multiple regulatory metrics would have helped in capturing those banks' fragility before the crisis.

The other side of the coin is, as Greenwood et al. (2017) argue, that multiple regulatory constraints may reduce diversity in the financial system; excessive homogeneity of the financial system can create systemic risks (Haldane, 2009).

Last but not least, in the 2018 round of the Financial Development Barometer – an informal poll of policy makers undertaken for the World Bank's Global Financial Development Report – 38% of respondents think that risk-weighted capital requirements are too low to ensure financial stability, suggesting that the debate regarding the optimal level of bank capital is far from over (World Bank, 2019).

Regulatory arbitrage

Any financial regulation induces changes in the behavior of the institutions subject to it. Regulatory arbitrage is the way by which banks structure activities to reduce the impact of regulation minimizing its negative effects on profits. For this purpose, they seek to hold less capital and liquidity for a given level of risk. If a leverage ratio is the binding constraint, banks will seek higher risk assets rather than expanding balance sheets. On the contrary, if the binding constraint is risk-based capital standards, they will expand balance sheets and reduce their exposure to risk.

Banks as well as the rest of financial institutions will always try the way to be subject to the most relaxed rules. They would constantly jump fences in order to be where the grass is greenest.

What should be done to minimize regulatory arbitrage? First of all, harmonize the rules. Arbitrage exists whenever a national, sectoral or any other kind of difference occurs. In this respect, Basel III can contribute to prevent cross-jurisdiction arbitrage setting a common suite of standards once the process of transposing it into national law is completed.

However, there is still another area for regulatory arbitrage where much work has to be done; it has to do with the links between banks and shadow banks. Although the Basel Committee on Banking Supervision already produced a document containing guidelines on identification and management of step-in risk, they have not yet been implemented by member states. Step-in risk refers to the risk that a bank provides financial support to an entity beyond, or in the absence of, its contractual obligations should the entity experience financial stress.

In the meantime, increased regulation of banks has been inducing a migration of banking activities toward the mainly unregulated shadow banking system. This happens as the gap between capital and liquidity requirements on traditional institutions and non-regulated institutions has increased. Irani et al. (2018: 4) find that relatively low-capital banks use loan sales to reduce risk-weighted assets and enhance regulatory capital ratios. The funding gaps created by these loan sales are filled by non-bank financial institutions.

This transfer of risks to non-banks could increase overall risk, especially if these financial intermediaries are outside of the regulatory perimeter but are highly interconnected with SIFIs.

Finally, closing loopholes in existing regulation is a complementary way of tackling regulatory arbitrage.

Regulation places a burden on banks. As complying with them is costly, banks are always tempted to work around rules. Any regulation means a restriction on the expected rate of return by lowering the level of risk investors or banks are allowed to take. However, this does not necessarily mean a lower *ex post* average rate of return; it only means that the riskier bets are excluded or restricted, precisely those that may result in huge losses for individual institutions as well as for society. Excessive risk-taking by financial institutions was a factor that significantly contributed to the incubation of the last financial crisis.

Anyway, regulatory arbitrage will always exist. Regulated institutions will always try to offload their riskier assets to non-regulated financial institutions. In principle, this should not be a big problem. Broadly speaking, casinos are not prohibited; this is because at their entrance there is usually a neon sign stating "casino." So, anyone entering it knows this is a casino, not an insurance company nor a bank. The problem emerges when there is no sign at the entrance and people do not know that they may be risking their money. For this reason, it should be strictly required from any financial institution to state clearly and unequivocally whether its activities are within or outside the regulatory perimeter.

Prudential regulation of SIFIs

As already mentioned, the fact that the failure of large financial firms could trigger financial instability led to establishing a prudential regulatory regime that applies to large banks and to non-bank financial institutions designated as SIFIs.

As stated in Chapter 4, in the US banking companies with over $250 billion in assets are automatically considered SIFIs. The Federal Reserve is required to apply a number of safety and soundness requirements to them that are more stringent than those applied to smaller banks. Some of these requirements related to capital and liquidity overlap with parts of the Basel III international agreement. With respect to other large financial organizations, the Dodd-Frank Act empowers the FSOC to designate non-bank financial institutions as SIFIs.

At the international level, the Financial Stability Board has identified global systemically important banks (G-SIBs); the list is updated annually each November. The 2019 list includes 30 institutions, eight of which are headquartered in the United States.

The FSB has established that G-SIBs should be subject to: higher capital buffer requirements, meet the Total Loss Absorbing Capacity (TLAC) requirement, resolution planning and regular resolvability assessments, and higher supervisory expectations. In addition, the interconnectedness of G-SIBs is actively supervised.

The higher capital requirements on systemically important financial firms are those imposed by Basel III. G-SIBs are required to hold relatively more capital than other banks in the form of a common equity surcharge of at least 1% to "reflect the greater risks that they pose to the financial system."

TLAC is an international standard intended to ensure that G-SIBS have enough equity and bail-in debt to pass losses to investors and minimize the risk of a government bailout.

The TLAC standard is the cornerstone of the new regulatory regime. It sets a minimum level of loss absorbing capacity to be held by all G-SIBs: as from January 1, 2019, G-SIBs have to comply with a minimum TLAC requirement equal to the higher of 16% of RWA or 6% of leverage ratio exposure (LR). As from 2022, the minimum thresholds will be set at 18% and 6.75% respectively.

The TLAC standard has not been implemented into EU law. Instead, the EU resolution framework defines a similar loss absorbing capacity requirement: the Minimum Requirement for own funds and Eligible Liabilities (MREL). Contrary to the TLAC, the MREL is set on a case-by-case basis, and for all banking institutions in the European Union, although G-SIBs are subject to stricter rules.

In the US, the TLAC was implemented by a rule issued by the Fed in December 2016 effective at the beginning of 2019.

As already mentioned above, the Dodd-Frank Act requires the Federal Reserve to conduct an annual supervisory stress test on SIFIs.

This implies that 35 banks are subject to stress testing requirements; however, as a number of less complex banks with total assets of less than $250 billion were granted relief for the 2019 cycle, only 18 firms were tested in 2019 (12 US bank holding companies and 6 foreign banks US subsidiaries).

Banks in the US with more than $250 billion in assets are subject to enhanced capital requirements that are tied to stress test results. They must submit a capital plan to the Fed annually which must demonstrate that the bank will remain in compliance with capital requirements under the stress tests. The Fed evaluates the plan on quantitative and qualitative grounds. If the Fed rejects the bank's capital plan, the bank will not be allowed to make any capital distributions, including dividend payments, until a revised capital plan is resubmitted and approved by the Fed.

As already mentioned, G-SIBs are subject to an additional leverage ratio requirement. In the US, banks with more than $250 billion in assets or more than $10 billion in foreign exposure must meet a 3% additional leverage ratio. In April 2014, US bank regulators adopted a joint rule that requires the G-SIBs to meet an enhanced additional leverage ratio of 5% at the holding company level.

With respect to SIFIs that are not banks, in 2013 the FSB, in consultation with the International Association of Insurance Supervisors, identified an initial list of nine multinational insurance groups considered to be global systemically important insurers (G-SIIs). The list was annually updated until 2016. In 2017 and 2018 the FSB decided not to engage in an identification of G-SIIs. In November 2022, the FSB will review the need to either discontinue or re-establish an annual identification of G-SIIs, after evaluating a holistic framework for the assessment and mitigation of systemic risk in the insurance sector prepared by the International Association of Insurance Supervisors.

Thus, only banks and insurance companies have up to now been considered as G-SIFIs. However, the FSB monitors a set of non-bank financial entities or activities that may pose bank-like financial stability risks and/or regulatory arbitrage and publishes an annual report on them as part of its Global Monitoring Report on Non-Bank Financial Intermediation.

Is the present financial system less risky?

Sarin and Summers (2016) carried out a study to test whether changes in financial regulation have led to substantial declines in financial market measures of risk. For major institutions in the United States and around the world and mid-sized institutions in the United States, they measure the perceived default risk of these institutions. Surprisingly, they find that financial market information provides little support for the view that major institutions are significantly safer than they were before the crisis and some support for the notion that risks have actually increased. The authors attribute this result to a dramatic decline in the franchise value of major financial institutions, caused at least in part by new regulations. The post-crisis legal reforms imply lower returns on banks' activities leaving them a riskier proposition than before 2007 for equity investors, although improved solvency standards may have reduced risk for bondholders and depositors in banks, Aikman et al. (2019a: 150) remark.

So, although equity investors may consider their investments riskier because of lower returns, bondholders and depositors may find the system safer. However, the 2019 IMF Global Stability Financial Report points out to the following financial vulnerabilities: rising corporate debt burdens, increasing holdings of riskier and more illiquid securities by institutional investors and increased reliance on external borrowing by emerging and frontier market economies. The conclusion is that "medium-term risks to global growth and financial stability continue to be firmly skewed to the downside" (IMF, 2019: X).

A new institutional economics criticism to present financial governance

The present macroeconomic perspective on financial stability focused on the importance of macro-prudential policy has been criticized from an institutional economics point of view. Salter and Tarko (2018) invoke for this purpose the Nobel laurate Elinor Ostrom contribution on the "design principles" for robust governance institutions.

According to these authors,

> it makes sense to view financial crises as essentially an information problem. They would not exist if accurate common knowledge was available to depositors, investors and insurers. The common knowledge (stored in interest rates and the prices of various assets, stocks and bonds) is imperfect in the sense that various assets, stocks and bonds are often mispriced.
>
> (Salter and Tarko, 2018: 12)

For them, the question is to design a system that can discover those system-wide errors and provide the incentives to correct them. The authors argue that a polycentric system of self-regulation can do this quicker than the present monocentric regulatory authorities.

The argument runs as follows. The only way in which a complex system can be made resilient is by giving up the goal of maximum short-term efficiency, keeping the scale low and implementing redundancies. The short-term efficiency gains in monocentric systems are eventually undermined by their long-term fragility. On the contrary, polycentric systems tend to have higher absorption capacities because shocks do not affect simultaneously the whole system. They are less vulnerable to the problem of putting all the eggs in one basket. Preserving a redundant variety of institutional devices rather than adopting a one-size-fits-all solution is the best way to cope with uncertainty.

In essence, the function of the financial system is to bring together those in want of funds and those offering funds, and to provide credible assurances that loans are going to be repaid. The latter is the awkward part of the job. However, under normal circumstances, this system works smoothly. Of course, there are errors – some investment projects fail – but they are compensated. The smooth operation of this system is governed by prices – interest rates, insurance premiums, stock prices, asset prices, and so on. From this point of view, financial crises are essentially an information problem. They would not exist if accurate common knowledge was available to depositors, investors and insurers. However, the common knowledge is imperfect in the sense that various assets, stocks and bonds are often mispriced. The financial crisis occurs when some substantial fraction of these prices is suddenly revealed to be inaccurate.

Salter and Tarko raise substantial doubts whether top-down regulatory solutions can be successful to avoid a crisis. For them, the alternative is to think about the possibilities for self-governance in a polycentric financial system. According to the authors, the key feature of any polycentric system is that the constituent organizations are governed by an overarching set of rules, which are more or less successful in aligning the information and incentives of individual actors with broader social goals such as financial stability. These rules punish behavior that is privately beneficial but socially costly. A polycentric financial system is not one without regulations, but one in which the regulations are created endogenously by the actors, rather than exogenously by a government regulator. The authors argue that the most interesting and important institution in this regard is the interbank clearinghouse.

They go on maintaining that the interbank clearinghouse can be viewed as an evolved mechanism for governing financial organizations' behavior. The main benefit of a clearinghouse is to prevent the perceived insolvency from growing into a crisis – even in the case of a large and interconnected bank. Unfortunately, their main example in this respect is the 18th century Scottish banking system which was far simpler than the present global financial system.

They conclude that a better system would almost certainly include a move in a more polycentric direction although they admit that some elements of top-down management are perhaps still desirable.

Some issues on the US financial regulatory system

The activity-based character of the US financial regulatory system implies that a host of regulators are in charge of overseeing the financial industry; at the federal level we have:

1 The depository regulators are the Office of the Comptroller of the Currency (OCC), the Federal Deposit Insurance Corporation (FDIC), and the Federal Reserve Board for banks; and the National Credit Union Administration (NCUA) for credit unions.
2 The securities markets regulators are the Securities and Exchange Commission (SEC) and the Commodity Futures Trading Commission (CFTC).

3 The Government-sponsored enterprise (GSE) regulators are the Federal Housing Finance Agency (FHFA) and the Farm Credit Administration (FCA).
4 The consumer protection regulator is the Consumer Financial Protection Bureau (CFPB), created by the Dodd-Frank Act.

In the list is not included the Financial Stability Oversight Council (FSOC) because, although it is nominally in charge of overseeing financial stability, it has no macro-prudential levers under its direct control, and not all of its members have mandates to protect financial stability.

Besides the agencies at the federal level, there are the state bank regulatory agencies, the state insurance regulators and the state securities regulators. Too many hands in the pot!

This system is in sharp contrast with those in Canada, Japan, Australia and in most countries of Europe. It has been argued that the high degree of fragmentation in the US with multiple overlapping regulators and a dual state-federal regulatory system may lead to the existence of numerous gaps whose results are products and markets operating in the shadows.

As Scott pointed out, "when more than one agency is in charge, no single agency is responsible or accountable" (Committee on Capital Markets Regulation, 2009).

Although nominally the FSOC has been empowered to address a systemic crisis, its available instruments are so limited that "its only choice in a liquidity crisis may be to put all the systematically important firm through the OLA process, which, given the uncertainty about this process, could initiate a full-blown systemic crisis" (Acharya et al., 2010: 11).

As a matter of fact, FSOC's only binding tool is the power to designate non-bank financial institutions deemed to be systemically important. It has no other macro-prudential powers. For other policy interventions, it can only issue recommendations to regulators.

It seems advisable to build a unified regulatory system where lines of accountability are clear and transparency is improved across all products.

On the other hand, as the former FDIC's Chairman Sheila Bair (2011) warned, the tools provided by the Dodd-Frank Act will be effective only if regulators show the courage to fully exercise their authorities under the law. Unfortunately, past experience shows that regulators acted too late, or with too little conviction, when they failed to use authorities they already had or failed to ask for the authorities they needed to fulfill their mission (Bair, 2011).

As memories of the global financial crisis fade away, the determination of regulators and reform momentum may tend to decline.

The fintech challenge to financial regulation

The technological revolution since the crisis has already greatly increased the pace of financial innovation, making it ever more difficult for regulators to catch up with the industry. Fintech, high frequency trading and digital currencies all present opportunities but also stability challenges (World Bank, 2019).

The way how financial products and services are produced, delivered and consumed has experienced a rapid advance in recent years thanks to the role played by financial technology (fintech).

The wide use of big data together with advances in artificial intelligence and machine learning, cloud storage, cloud computing and so forth are changing the way business is done in the financial industry.

Fintech activities have been penetrating all areas of the financial system. Traditional financial firms that are increasing investments in technology, tech startups and BigTech firms – like Amazon, Alibaba and PayPal – are the main players in this market.

Technological innovations have allowed for the rapid adoption of mobile payment and fast payment systems around the globe.

The rapid growth of bank-like services provided by fintech firms has raised potential concerns among bank supervisors.

> The goals in fintech regulation has been to design a policy framework that would encourage and support disruptive innovation to enhance financial inclusion and economic growth while at the same time provide protection to the safety and soundness of the banking system and financial stability overall.
>
> (Allen et al., 2020: 40)

Regulation of financial innovation faces what has been called the Innovation Trilemma as pointed out by Brummer and Yadav (2019). Regulators seek to provide clear rules, maintain market integrity and encourage fintech innovations but only two of these three objectives can be achieved simultaneously. For example, if regulators prioritize market safety and simple and transparent rule-making, the rules would likely impose broad prohibitions, which can largely inhibit fintech innovations. The same happens with any other pair of goals: they will inhibit the third one.

For the time being, few authorities have issued specific regulations for fintech products or specialized firms. One reason may be the relatively small size and lack of material impact of fintech, as seen by regulators. Another one, the perception by a majority of authorities that new fintech products and service providers can be accommodated within the current regulatory framework. Most authorities follow the "technology-neutrality" principle according to which the same activity should be subject to the same regulation irrespective of the way the service is delivered.

In what follows we will have a look at various aspects of fintech and the regulatory response to them.

Blockchain, cryptocurrencies and HFT

Blockchain is the technology underlying bitcoin transactions. Blockchain and other digital ledger technologies have been used in creating various cryptocurrencies, leading to the idea that blockchain has the potential to become the mainstream financial technology of the future.

However, extreme volatility of cryptocurrencies has been their Achilles' heel. For this reason, stable-coins have been developed in the crypto world. One of them was announced by Facebook in 2019, the Libra, which would be backed 1:1 by a basket of fiat currency bank deposits. A modified version of the project known as Libra 2.0 was released in 2020. Although it tried to take into consideration the objections from the international regulatory community, financial regulators still have concerns, particularly the risk that unknown participants may take control of the system and remove key compliance provisions.

Blockchain technology is also used in initial coin offerings (ICOs) which are mechanisms to raise funds by selling coins or tokens. They operate similarly to initial public offerings (IPOs) but typically evade the usual regulations and restrictions on IPOs. Particular risks of an ICO include potential fraudulent ICOs and sketchy coins.

In the US, the SEC has classified nearly all ICOs as securities, within their competency and authority.

The sudden rise of cryptocurrencies may pose challenges to central banks, particularly with respect to finding appropriate intermediate targets for the monetary policy.

A possibility open for central banks is to issue their own digital currencies. It has been argued that this has the advantage that it would open up a direct channel by which monetary policy could be transmitted to the public. Critics, however, raise concerns about the risk of a bank run as people would prefer holding a bank account with the central bank directly rather than with private banks.

High frequency trading (HFT) allows transacting a large number of orders in fractions of a second using complex algorithms. It is also called high-speed trading because it involves a high velocity of portfolio turnover. Computer algorithms automatically make trading decisions, submit orders and manage these afterwards, even in milliseconds.

During 2009–2010, more than 60% of US trading was attributed to HFT, though that percentage has declined in the last few years.

Regulators in the US and Europe have investigated certain HFT strategies suspected of manipulating prices. Placing and immediately cancelling thousands of orders per second, which is a common HFT strategy, has been blamed as one of the reasons behind the May 6, 2010 Flash Crash. On that day, in only 20 minutes the broad US securities markets were down almost a trillion dollars, losing at their lowest point more than 9% of their value. It was just a simple algorithm that was responsible for starting this domino effect.

Such a market crash was made possible by the combination of two factors: the growing interconnectivity of the securities markets and the proliferation of high frequency trading.

The astonishing speed and interconnectivity of the markets has allowed the multiplication of complicated automated trading strategies, such as cross-market or index arbitrage, where a program will buy or sell a derivative security while taking an opposite position in the underlying security – profiting when their values merge. Such trades can be done within a few millionths of a second, for a near-zero marginal cost.

As a result of powerful artificial intelligence programs, a large portion of the trading volume in the US is done without a single human knowing why. The consequence is a market in which massively destructive price movements can occur before any human being can even begin to react.

After the 2010 flash crash some regulatory changes were implemented filling some of the loopholes previously exploited by HFT firms. Some others are under study.

It has been argued that speed bumps are necessary to slow down trades coming into the markets, giving the slower trading firms the chance to cancel an order before a faster trader can execute it. On the opposite side, the argument is that faster traders are now a vital element of modern markets as banks have retreated in their role as market makers after the financial crisis.

A fintech regulatory sandbox is a mechanism for firms to conduct tests of new fintech products and services in a live environment under close scrutiny of the supervisor. The innovators can experiment and try out their new ideas under a more relaxed regulatory environment without causing harm to the general population or the financial system. The benefits of regulatory sandboxes include not only signaling a friendly general regulatory approach to fintech innovations but also reducing fintech regulatory uncertainty and increasing regulatory and supervisory capacity (Allen et al., 2020: 41).

On May 16, 2013, the CFTC approved a final rule that sets out interpretive guidance on disruptive trade practices, which includes practices that violate bids or offers, demonstrate intentional or reckless disregard for orderly execution, or constitutes what is commonly known as "spoofing" (bidding or offering with the intent to cancel the bid or offer before execution).

Summarizing, regulators are confronting a digital disintermediation of traditional financial services providers that results in more and qualitatively different forms of data as well as automation and machine learning. These developments exacerbate longstanding trade-offs they face when tasked with exercising oversight over changing markets. The COVID-19 pandemic has expedited the economy toward a more fully digital and cashless lifestyle, with digital banks seeing increased traffic and people embracing digital and contactless technologies. However, these advanced technologies come with a new set of risks. Regulators have to deal with new challenges in order to protect consumers and financial systems while continuing to promote responsible fintech innovations.

Notes

1 A summarized account of the international banking regulation reform undertaken over the past decade can be found in Aikman et al. (2018) and in Sironi (2018).
2 Starting from 2022, banks will have to apply the updated Basel IV leverage ratio, which was introduced in December 2017.
3 Concurrent bank stress test is a simultaneous stress test of several banks carried out under the direction of a stress-testing authority, such as a central bank or banking system regulator.

4 As Brazier (2017: 3) recalls, referring to the last financial crisis, "actions taken by each bank in their own interest turned the system as a whole into an amplifier of the initial shock. The system was not the sum of its parts." Therefore, the system´s health is what really matters.

5 Duffie (2011) proposes an alternative simpler approach based on "n-cubed" reports focused on the largest banks, the largest asset classes and the largest counter-parties.

References

Acharya, V. V., Cooley, T. F., Richardson, M. P. and Walter, I. (2010). *Regulating Wall Street.* Hoboken, NJ: Wiley Finance.

Adrian, T. and Brunnermeier, M. K. (2016). CoVaR. *American Economic Review* 106(7): 1705–1741.

Aikman, D., Bridges, J., Kashyap, A. and Siegert, C. (2019b). Would Macroprudential Regulation Have Prevented the Last Crisis? *Journal of Economic Perspectives* 33(1): 107–130.

Aikman, D., Haldane, A. G., Hinterschweiger, M. and Kapadia, S. (2018). *Rethinking financial stability.* Bank of England. Staff Working Paper No. 712.

Aikman, D., Haldane, A. G., Hinterschweiger, M. and Kapadia, S. (2019a). Rethinking financial stability. In O. Blanchard and L. H. Summers (ed.). *Evolution or Revolution? Rethinking Macroeconomic Policy after the Great Recession.* Cambridge, MA: MIT and Peterson Institute for International Economics, pp. 143–192.

Aikman, D., Kiley, M. T., Lee, S. J., Palumbo, M. G. and Warusawitharana, M. N. (2015). *Mapping Heat in the U.S. Financial System.* Finance and Economics Discussion Series 2015–2059. Washington: Board of Governors of the Federal Reserve System. doi:10.17016/FEDS.2015.059.

Allen, F., Gu, X. and Jagtiani, J. (2020). *A Survey of Fintech Research and Policy Discussion.* https://www.philadelphiafed.org/-/media/research-and-data/publications/working-papers/2020/wp20-21.pdf.

Anderson, R., Danielsson, J., Baba, C., Das, U. S., Kang, H. and Segoviano, M. A. (2018). *Macroprudential Stress Tests and Policies: Searching for Robust and Implementable Frameworks.* IMF Working Papers. https://www.imf.org/en/Publications/WP/Issues/2018/09/11/Macroprudential-Stress-Tests-and-Policies-Searching-for-Robust-and-Implementable-Frameworks-46218.

Bai, J., Krishnamurthy, A. and Weymuller, C. H. (2017). *Measuring Liquidity Mismatch in the Banking Sector.* https://www.gsb.stanford.edu/sites/gsb/files/publication-pdf/lmi-jf.pdf.

Bair, S. (2011). *Examining and Evaluating the Role of the Regulator during the Financial Crisis and Today.* Statement before the House Subcommittee on Financial Institutions and Consumer Credit. https://www.fdic.gov/news/news/speeches/archives/2011/spmay2611.html.

Brazier, A. (2017). Foreword. In Y. Baranova, J. Coen, P. Lowe, J. Noss and L. Silvestri, *Simulating Stress Across the Financial System: The Resilience of Corporate Bond Markets and the Role of Investment Funds.* Bank of England Financial Stability Paper No. 42, July, pp. 3–6. https://www.bankofengland.co.uk/-/media/boe/files/financial-stability-paper/2017/simulating-stress-across-the-financial-system-resilience-of-corporate-bond-markets.

Brummer, C., and Yadav, Y. (2019). Fintech and the Innovation Trilemma. *Georgetown Law Journal* 107: 235–307. https://scholarship.law.vanderbilt.edu/cgi/viewcontent.cgi?article=2112&context=faculty-publications.

Brunnermeier, M. K., Gorton, G. and Krishnamurthy, A. (2011). Risk Topography. *NBER Macroeconomics Annual*. https://www.nber.org/chapters/c12412.

Brunnermeier, M. K., Gorton, G. and Krishnamurthy, A. (2014). Liquidity Mismatch Measurement. In M. Brunnermeier and A. Krishnamurthy (eds.), *Risk Topography: Systemic Risk and Macro Modeling*. Chicago, IL: University of Chicago Press.

Committee On Capital Markets Regulation Releases (2009). The Global Financial Crisis: A Plan for Regulatory Reform. May 16. https://www.capmktsreg.org/2009/05/26/the-global-financial-crisis-a-plan-for-regulatory-reform/.

Cortes, F., Lindner, P., Malik, S. and Segoviano, M. A. (2018). *A Comprehensive Multi-Sector Tool for Analysis of Systemic Risk and Interconnectedness (SyRIN)*. IMF Working Paper. WP/18/14.

Crockett, A. (2000). *Marrying the Micro- and Macro-Prudential Dimensions of Financial Stability*. BIS Speech. https://www.bis.org/speeches/sp000921.htm.

Duffie, D. (2011). Systemic Risk Exposures A 10-by-10-by-10 Approach. In M. Brunnermeier and A. Krishnamurthy (eds.), *Risk Topography: Systemic Risk and Macro Modeling*. Chicago, IL: University of Chicago Press, pp. 47–56.

Goldstein, M. (2017). *Banking's Final Exam: Stress Testing and Bank-Capital Reform*. Washington, DC: Peterson Institute for International Economics.

Gordy, M. B. (2003). A Risk-Factor Model Foundation for Ratings-Based Bank Capital Rules. *Journal of Financial Intermediation* 12: 199–232.

Greenwood, R., Hanson, S. G., Stein, J. C. and Sunderam, A. (2017). Strengthening and Streamlining Bank Capital Regulation. *Brookings Papers on Economic Activity*. BPEA Conference Drafts, September 7–8.

Haldane, A. G. (2009). *Rethinking the Financial Network*. Speech at the Financial Student Association. Amsterdam. https://www.bankofengland.co.uk/speech/2009/rethinking-the-financial-network.

He, Z. and Krishnamurthy, A. (2019). Systemic Risk and the Macroeconomy. *American Economic Journal: Macroeconomics* 11(4): 1–37. doi:10.1257/mac.20180011.

Irani, R. M., Iyer, R., Meisenzahl, R. R. and Pedró, J. L. (2018). *The Rise of Shadow Banking: Evidence from Capital Regulation*. https://www.bis.org/events/confresearchnetwork1809/peydro.pdf.

IMF-FSB-BIS (2016). *Elements of Effective Macroprudential Policies. Lessons from International Experience*. https://www.imf.org/external/np/g20/pdf/2016/083116.pdf.

International Monetary Fund (2019). *Global Financial Stability Report: Lower for Longer*. October. Washington, DC: IMF.

King, M. (2017). *The End of Alchemy: Money, Banking, and the Future of the Global Economy*. London: Little, Brown.

Salter, A. W. and Tarko, V. (2018). Governing the Banking System: An Assessment of Resilience Based on Elinor Ostrom's Design Principles. *Journal of Institutional Economics*: 1–15. doi:10.2139/ssrn.3235752.

Sarin, N. and Summers, L. H. (2016). *Understanding Bank Risk Through Market Measures*. Brookings Papers on Economic Activity. https://ssrn.com/abstract=3230766.

Sironi, A. (2018). *The Evolution of Banking Regulation Since the Financial Crisis: A Critical Assessment*. Università Bocconi. Working Paper 103.December. doi:10.2139/ssrn.3304672.

World Bank (2019). *Global Financial Development Report 2019/2020. Overview*. Washington, DC: World Bank.

8 The reform of the international monetary regime

The international dimension of the last financial crisis

A striking feature of the last financial crisis has been its international dimension. Although controversy remains about the precise connection between global imbalances and the global financial meltdown,[1] it is a fact that the high savings of China, oil exporters and other surplus countries provided a cheap source of external funding that finally ended up fueling the demand for US assets that turned out to be toxic. Once the crisis started, shocks were transmitted across market segments and countries in a relatively synchronized manner. A flight to safety and liquidity – which essentially meant a flight to US treasuries – became the dominant strategy of investors all around the world. The subprime meltdown was followed by the European debt crisis: the southern European nations had been receiving a vast flow of capital mostly from Germany and France and at the end of 2009, the US financial crisis triggered the emergence of serious doubts with respect to the repayment capacity of those highly indebted countries.[2] Between 2010 and 2014, Europe was the focus of turbulence as the continent faced a severe economic and financial crisis.[3] Developing countries with large exposure to international banks, bond and equity markets faced acute challenges to roll over their external debt. These countries faced plunging asset prices, higher cost of borrowing, a massive capital flight and a decrease in exports. Even countries with weak financial linkages with the international capital market were victims of the secondary effects of the crisis.

These linkages between countries appeared as a surprising challenge to the world financial system which, before the crisis, displayed a curious dichotomy, with finance being increasingly global but supervision and regulation largely remaining national in scope and only loosely coordinated internationally.

As the crisis deepened, it became increasingly clear that, as a result of globalization, firms were experiencing funding shortages not only in domestic currencies, but in foreign currencies as well. In particular, dollar funding shortages appeared not just in the United States but in different countries around the world, which, in turn, exacerbated pressures in US funding markets. In response, the Federal Reserve ultimately approved bilateral currency swap arrangements with 14 foreign central banks. Under these swap arrangements, in exchange for their own currencies, foreign central banks obtained dollars from the Federal Reserve to lend to financial institutions in their jurisdictions. These swaps had, in several cases, just a preventive role. In fact, some of the central banks that participated in these arrangements did not end up drawing on the facilities, but the mere existence of these lines helped prevent stresses that could have otherwise developed.

In the context of a global financial system, domestic central banks are unable to address regulation and coordination issues entirely on their own, as they learnt the hard way during the financial meltdown. After the crisis, several initiatives attempted to address the previous lack of coordination in regulation and supervision issues. In this respect, the crisis highlighted shortcomings in capital and liquidity requirements. The Basel III accords already detailed in the previous chapter aim at improving prudential regulation to address these shortcomings at an international level. The Financial Stability Board is another example of international cooperation on the regulatory front imposed by the crisis experience. It has also been understood that international coordination is required for supervision and regulation because of the substantial cross-border operations of many financial firms. Supervisory colleges – multilateral standing working groups of supervisors – provide an instance to enhance information-sharing among supervisors, help the development of a shared agenda for addressing risks and vulnerabilities and provide a platform for communicating key messages among college members.

A report prepared by IMF staff (IMF, 2016) argues that reforms of the international monetary system could focus on three possible areas: i) mechanisms for crisis prevention and adjustment; ii) rules and institutions for enhanced global cooperation on issues and policies affecting global stability; and iii) building a more coherent global financial safety net.

In particular, the staff report admits that measures to ensure an equitable burden of adjustment across countries (e.g., surplus/deficit, source/recipient of capital flows) are critical. In addition, it warns of the rapidly growing intermediation through shadow banking, which has become a major vehicle of large capital flows, and the need to continue strengthening the prudential regulation and supervision of systemic risks. The report points out also the need to consider ensuring liquidity support during systemic events and to limit the potential for contagion. In this respect it argues that the IMF could facilitate such cooperation, allowing creditors to rely on the Fund's expertise in this area.

An international lender of last resort

As already mentioned in Chapter 5, wherever there is a sharp increase in demand for currency, only the central bank can meet the need. National central banks act as lenders of last resort in their respective countries providing reserve money (and other forms of liquidity) to the banking system.

However, the process of globalization has led finance to become a world-wide activity. As has already been mentioned, during and after the 2007/2009 financial crisis, central banks in different countries resorted to swaps in order to obtain foreign currency to boost their reserves and lend on to domestic banks. The decision in October 2013 to establish permanent unlimited swap lines between the C6 – the Fed, the European Central Bank, the Bank of Japan, the Bank of England, the Swiss National Bank and the Bank of Canada – can be seen as a first step in the direction of creating a global lender of last resort.

Why do we need an international lender of last resort? The think tank of academics and financiers known as the Group of Thirty (2018: 23) warns:

> One of the most significant challenges in responding to systemic shock may occur in the face of cross-border failures. We believe there is a significant weakness in the collective ability to manage the cross-border failure of a large multinational institution (let alone several large multinational institutions).
>
> More generally, the crisis-fighting framework is not robust to international contagion, and lacks clear lines of authority, decision making, and accountability for an international lender of last resort.

It adds that "in general, we believe it is less than ideal to have the Federal Reserve, or any central bank, as the de facto international lender of last resort" (Group of Thirty, 2018: 23).

Although the subject has been present in high level discussions, there is still no formal system for a global lender of last resort.

A first thing to notice is that, as happens with central banks in the domestic case, an organization to function as international lender of last resort would have to be able to create world money.

During the last financial crisis, the Federal Reserve acted *de facto* as an international lender of last resort. In fact, it expanded the temporary swap lines that had been established earlier with the European Central Bank (ECB) and the Swiss National Bank, and established new temporary swap lines with other central banks, as has been mentioned above. This allowed central banks to face the heavy demand for US dollar funding coming from foreign commercial banks.

In case of a new financial crisis, should we just rely on this sort of mechanism or is it necessary something else? Landau (2014: 119) remarks that "a novel priority is to avoid liquidity disruptions in the global financial system, where private financial institutions engage into cross-border maturity transformation, with flows denominated mainly in a few major currencies."

According to this author, the main answer to this new requirement has been up to now self-insurance: most countries have increased their foreign exchange reserves at a broadly constant rate of 13–15% a year.

However, during the 2007/2009 financial crisis, even countries with very high levels of reserves entered into foreign currency swaps with the Federal Reserve. Although high levels of reserves may be a useful protection against idiosyncratic risk, they seem to be insufficient in the presence of a systemic shock. On the other hand, over-accumulation of reserves does not come without a cost (see Landau, 2014: 121). An international lender of last resort seems to be a more efficient way of avoiding liquidity disruptions in the global financial system.

Something to have in mind is that we are talking here of an international lender of last resort meant to act in the presence of a systemic shock in order to prevent panic contagion from one country to the other. This is quite different from the task of limited lender of last resort to help a particular country facing balance of payments difficulties or a speculative attack against its currency, tasks the IMF is already in charge of.

In his seminal paper on the subject, Fischer (1999) argued that the IMF could play the role of international lender of last resort. His main argument was that the IMF is able to assemble a sizable financial package in response to a crisis. However, he admits that without the ability to create unlimited amounts of money, the would-be lender of last resort lacks credibility and thus cannot stabilize a panic.

Following Fischer´s ideas, if the IMF is to take the role of global lender of last resort it should be provided with a fast mechanism of creation of Special Drawing Rights (SDRs) in such circumstances.

Furthermore, the IMF should set up a specific area in charge of monitoring systemic risk – in close connection with the FSB. This is necessary because systemic risk is a different issue and needs a different approach from the one used to help individual countries facing balance of payments difficulties or a capital flight.

A second alternative may be to enhance the mechanisms developed during the last financial crisis. This means establishing a global safety net based on central bank swap lines.[4]

The argument in favor of this option is that only central banks – given their ability to create money – have the resources to perform the global lender of last resort function and that they did it successfully during the financial crisis. Moreover, they can adjust swap limits quicker than an international institution like the IMF can do. On the other hand, the difficulty is that these institutions have no legal mandate to perform that function. Some central banks, particularly the Fed, face now more legal restrictions than before the crisis to act as lender of last resort, be it at the domestic or at the international level.

To institutionalize this alternative, it would be necessary to establish a permanent multilateral network of swap agreements. These agreements should make sure that swap lines could be established quickly and safely when necessary. The triggering mechanism is a key issue to be clearly agreed.

It should be noticed that during the COVID 19 crisis, funding stresses quickly eased for banks in jurisdictions with standing swap lines with the Federal Reserve, who expanded the swap line network to additional central banks during the pandemic. US dollar auctions by foreign central banks saw immediate and widespread take-up, especially by Japanese and European banks, which took advantage of the cheap pricing to replenish their dollar funding and did not have to shed US dollar assets at fire-sale prices.

Anyway, besides the legal restrictions that central banks face, there is also a fiscal dimension which has to be taken into consideration. As Landau (2014: 125) points out, "a global safety net would mean that issuers of reserve assets would potentially accept ex ante a significant expansion of their balance sheet for the benefit of other central banks, with the possibility of quasi-fiscal losses down the road." In fact, while a central bank acting as a domestic lender of last resort minimizes risk through demanding the provision of collateral, swaps between central banks are usually unsecured. Therefore, it involves some *ex ante* risk-taking for the lender. However, experience teaches that the risk is minimum as, in many cases, it was the mere signaling effect of the establishment of a dollar swap line that played a major role in confidence-building.

A third alternative would be the creation of a new global institution to act as international lender of last resort. However, it is difficult to discuss this proposal without implying the creation of a world central bank.

Towards a global central bank and currency?

Arestis et al. (2005) argue that financial globalization needs a single currency and an international monetary authority to manage it.

The existence of different currencies implies different possibilities of access to the international loan market. Countries with a hard currency can raise loans in their own currency while countries with soft currencies cannot. The inability to borrow from foreigners in domestic currency is conventionally referred to as "original sin." Even dollarization or currency board regimes do not totally eliminate this restriction. As Arestis et al. exemplify, although Ecuador use the dollar as the domestic currency its inhabitants cannot readily borrow from the international financial market.

Arestis et al. (2005) underline the difference between the countries that can issue their international debts in their own domestic currency as opposed to those who cannot. For the latter, their ability to borrow from the international market is severely restricted by their export performance. This asymmetry can be solved with the introduction of a single world currency. The authors remark that this would allow unifying the borrowing terms and conditions for all countries across the globe. They consider that "under current international institutional arrangements, the IMF has the capability to undertake this function" (Arestis et al., 2005: 21).

In the same direction, the Report of the UN Commission of Experts chaired by Nobel Laurate Joseph Stiglitz has called for the adoption of a truly global reserve currency.

Before going on let us recall Keynes's proposal for the postwar monetary system. His main concern was to solve the problem of maintaining equilibrium in the balance of payments between countries.

For this purpose, he proposed the creation of an International Clearing Union conceived as a bank with the task of financing temporary disequilibria in the balance of trade between countries. Unlike the IMF, member countries would not be required to commit any amount of money in any form to the International Clearing Union. Each country would be simply assigned a current account denominated in an international unit of account called "bancor." Not having deposited anything into its account, the initial balance of each country would be equal to zero. Each member country would have the possibility of financing a trade deficit simply by entering a negative balance on its account. Conversely, a country with a trade surplus would have a positive balance credited to its account. Both would be subject to maximum levels of imbalance, so that it would be impossible to increase a country's debt indefinitely, but also to indefinitely accumulate credits. In fact, a credit balance unused for a certain period of time would be canceled automatically.

Therefore, the burden of readjustment would be shared between both debtor and creditor countries; moreover, not only debtors would have to pay an interest on their debts, but also creditors would have to pay an interest on their credits.[5] The purpose of this mechanism is putting surplus and deficit countries on an equal footing, demanding a symmetric effort to reabsorb imbalances. The ideal situation is one in which all bancor balances have returned to zero. Thus, the International Clearing Union would be financing only temporary disequilibria in the balance of trade.

However, if a country runs a persistent imbalance, its currency would be devalued or revalued accordingly, in order to restore the equilibrium of its foreign trade.

As is well known, Keynes's plan was not adopted at the Bretton Woods Conference. Why? Because, by the end of World War II, the United States were by far the leading industrial power of the world, they had accumulated massive credits towards their European allies and they were the owners of almost all the official gold reserves of the entire world. Why should they have been willing to enter a plan on a level of parity with all the other countries? There was no reason at all to induce the Americans to enter the International Clearing Union (Fantacci, 2012). Instead, a highly asymmetric system was approved in which the burden of adjustment rests on the deficit countries. It contributed to the perpetuation of global imbalances along all these years since 1944.

Keynes's proposal has been rescued after the global crisis in a speech by the governor of the People's Bank of China on the reform of the international monetary system. On that occasion he mentioned that "the creation of an international currency unit, based on the Keynesian proposal, is a bold initiative that requires extraordinary political vision and courage" (Xiaochuan, 2009: 2).

The Chinese proposal consists of adopting an international currency through extending the use of SDRs issued by the IMF, as a means of international settlement and as a reserve asset.

This would require transforming the SDR into a currency. In fact, the SDR is not a currency; it is an international reserve asset.

For the time being, when facing difficulties in their balance of payments, individual countries have no other option than to use the IMF as a sort of central bank. However, the IMF does not have sufficient resources to rescue all country members; it only acts as guarantor to help them raise loans from the international financial market. The IMF does not have reserve-creating powers and, strictly speaking, cannot function as international lender of last resort.

A well-known mainstream economist, Robert Mundell, has long ago argued that although under the present circumstances the Fed is the *de facto* international lender of last resort as the dollar serves as the international reserve currency, it would be far better to have a formal international lender of last resort with well-specified objectives. He contends that the other "four fifths of the world economy does not want a world monetary system based solely on the U.S. dollar, subject to the vicissitudes of U.S. politics and arbitrary management" (Mundell, 1983: 287).

In the same line of thought, Harvard Professor Richard Cooper brought up the idea of a global central bank and currency at a 1984 Federal Reserve conference in Bretton Woods, New Hampshire, celebrated in commemoration of the fortieth anniversary of that one where financial arrangements for the postwar world were made. Although he admitted at the time that "the idea is so far from being politically feasible at present – in its call for a real pooling of monetary sovereignty – that it will require many years of consideration before people become accustomed to the idea."

Inspired in Keynes´s ideas, Davidson argued for an international institutional agreement that "does not require surrendering national control of local banking systems and fiscal policies" (Davidson, 1992/93: 158), implying there is no need for an international central bank. He envisages just a "double-entry book-keeping clearing institution," in line with the Keynesian proposal for an International Clearing Union.

Box 8.1 If a global central bank had existed ...

If a global central bank had existed before today's financial crisis, it could have sounded a shrill warning about irresponsible financial transactions much earlier; and if it had been set up with the enforcement teeth it deserves, it would have had the clout to demand, perhaps as early as 2005, that banks and other financial institutions start building reserves when times were booming, rather than allow them to maintain lower reserves precisely because profits were soaring. It would have seen that financial institutions were accumulating debt that was 30 times their capital and imposed – or caused national central banks to impose – more sober leverage ratios. A global central bank worth its salt would have reined in not just commercial banks but also loosely-regulated investment banks, because all such institutions would have been obligated to adhere to the global banks' regulatory standards or else be blacklisted in global markets. It would have intervened to deal with Lehman Brothers and AIG, both with truly global reach, and thereby put the burden not just on American taxpayers but also taxpayers of other countries who used these institutions' services. Had it existed, a global central bank would have acted without the air of panic that has been exhibited by national central banks and finance ministries in this meltdown. Ideally, it would have gathered its governing board well in advance of a financial blowup to execute a coordinated rescue and global-stimulus plan, part of what should be its ongoing role of preparing for crises. It would be hard to overestimate the political pushback that any official proposal for a global central bank would draw from various constituencies, most especially within the United States. Among their many charges, critics will protest the establishment of "world government." But we have a World Trade Organization with legally binding powers over trade disputes. We have a World Health Organization for communicable disease with the ability to quarantine entire countries. And a World Court functions today that has considerable legal and moral clout.

Source: Jeffrey E. Garten. We Need a Bank of the World. *Newsweek*. November 3, 2008

Farhi et al. (2011) propose a multipolar system based on the issuance of mutually guaranteed European bonds as an alternative to US Treasuries, establishing a foreign exchange reserve pooling mechanism with the IMF and a star-shaped structure of swap lines centered on the IMF. The authors recognize the need, in some specific cases, for temporary controls on capital inflows. They also recommend extending the mandate of the IMF to the financial account and strengthening international cooperation in terms of financial regulation. They assert that it is only a matter of time before the world becomes multipolar and consider it desirable to accelerate the transition to such a world. That requires devising concrete measures to develop a stable and liquid market for Treasury bonds denominated in euros and the renminbi. In particular, they favor the issuance by each European country of a certain amount of bonds corresponding to a predetermined fraction of its GDP. These euro bonds would benefit from the collective guarantee of all issuing countries, and they would be senior to the rest of the country's debt.

Farhi et al. argue in favor of a network of bilateral swap agreements between central banks as an alternative to the need to self-insure by accumulating reserves. They favor reinforcing the role of the IMF including an expansion of its existing financing mechanisms – notably, the New Arrangements to Borrow (NAB) – and an authorization to borrow from financial markets. Even more, the authors assert that the IMF could perform a liquidity transformation function similar to that of a conventional bank, by receiving liquid deposit accounts denominated in reserve currencies and investing them in different assets. The argument in favor of this initiative is that this scheme would offer higher financial returns relative to those obtained from reserves used as self-insurance.

The authors oppose an increasing role for SDRs arguing that it is difficult to envision the creation of an international reserve currency that is not issued by any nation. This is so because fundamental aspects of any reserve currency are the fiscal capacity of the issuing country and the liquidity and market reliability of its treasury bonds. They argue that the factors causing instability in the international monetary system are due mainly to the shortage of reserve assets, in which case the solution cannot be linked to the emergence of an international currency.

Their proposals aim at improving the provision of international liquidity which – the authors remark – is the main problem a reform of the international monetary system should address.

Finally, the authors recognize that a large country – or a country that plays a key role in the global intermediation process – can cause systemic externalities by allowing the formation of significant external imbalances. However, the only recommendation put forward to address this problem is a temporary coordination of policies accomplished through negotiations.

For Padoa-Schioppa (2010), the deep causes of the last crisis include the dollar policy and the monetary regime that has been in force in the world for almost 40 years. The fundamental flaw in the present international monetary "order" lays in its failure to meet the global economy's vital need to be grounded in a degree of macro-economic discipline. For this author, it is an illusion to think that a flexible exchange rate would effectively enforce discipline on national economic policies and ensure the rapid correction of imbalances. He adds that the foreign exchange market is incapable either of eliminating or of governing interdependence because it is too slow in detecting the imbalances that require correction, and when it does detect them, it is incapable of enforcing decisions on the public players who are responsible for those imbalances. For this reason, he evaluates the possibility that SDR may fulfill the role of a global currency. In this respect, he recalls the European experience with the ECU – the European unit of account – which developed successfully into the euro. He argues that the SDR could play a role as a store of value and unit of account for exchange rate policies, intervention and the management of official reserves.

In the case there is an agreement to adopt Padoa-Schioppa´s proposal of making SDR a single international currency, there is an additional question. How should extra SDRs be distributed among countries? Would SDRs issued in excess of what countries hold under the current arrangement be distributed in proportion to the country's IMF quota – as is the present arrangement – or should developing countries receive a larger proportion of them?

There is a paradox with respect to SDR distribution. Developed countries hold the largest proportion of them while the low-income countries are their main users. For this reason, there were several proposals in the 1970s to use the issuance of SDR as a wealth-redistributive tool (Grubel, 1972; Maynard, 1973; Helleiner, 1974; Bird and Maynard, 1975; Bird, 1979). After the last financial crisis and given the renewed interest in SDRs, Alessandrini and Presbitero (2012) updated those proposals aimed at using SDR to help developing countries.

In sum, the financial crisis highlighted the shortcomings and flaws of the present international financial architecture. As we have seen, several proposals have been advanced to address them.

The main divide is between those who think that a network of bilateral swap agreements between central banks together with strengthening the IMF lending toolkit is enough to face a new global financial crisis and those who argue in favor of the creation of a single international currency and an international monetary authority to manage it.

For the time being the first alternative has a majoritarian consensus; the second one has to wait until a new global financial crisis puts the dominant approach to the test. If it turns out that it is not capable of dealing with a global crisis – as probably will happen – the proposed deeper reforms will be then inevitable.

The main contradiction in the present monetary (dis)order

As Mundell pointed out, in the present monetary regime there is a flagrant contradiction: a purely national currency as the dollar is the global anchor currency. This implies that the global monetary policy stance is set by the Federal Reserve who is in charge of promoting domestic objectives, not to keep the global economy on a sustainable course.

This is the old "Triffin dilemma": the contradiction between the issuing country's internal domestic requirements and the external requirements of the world using its currency in the international arena. In Padoa-Schioppa's words, "the stability requirements of the system as a whole are inconsistent with the pursuit of economic and monetary policy forged solely on the basis of domestic rationales in all monetary regimes devoid of some form of supra-nationality" (Padoa-Schioppa, 2010: 11).

The result is an asymmetric financial system in which "it costs only a few cents for the Bureau of Engraving and Printing to produce a $100 bill, but other countries had to pony up $100 of actual goods in order to obtain one" (Eichengreen, 2010: 3).

Moreover, the fact that the bulk of global reserves is in dollars implies that if reserve holders try to switch out of dollar assets simultaneously because they become concerned about the currency's value, they could precipitate a disorderly adjustment.

The issue is how to build a new more balanced monetary order. In this respect, the European experience can be seen as an experimental workshop for a future global order. Europe has shown how to achieve the goal of a single currency and a single central bank. The European case provides the world with a vast collection of experiences, experiments, mistakes and solutions the world should not waste if it wants to forge a resilient international monetary system. The rich experience of Europe's road to build a monetary union from the Rome Treaty signed in 1957 until the creation of the second most important currency in the present world is full of right and wrong decisions the world can learn from.

However, it should be noticed that, contrary to the European experience, the creation of a world currency does not require the suppression of domestic currencies: they are supposed to coexist with it. Hence it does not imply the removal of essential tools of national policy making as the exchange rate management and monetary policy.

It does require the establishment of an international lender of last resort capable of addressing systemic crises.

It does also require removing the "exorbitant privilege" that allows the United States to run large external deficits while financing them with its own currency.

These are the two minimum requisites to build a new global monetary order.

In the Report of the UN Commission of Experts (2009), one of the alternatives proposed is the creation of a new institution, a "Global Reserve Bank." In one version of this proposal, the contributions of all members in their own currencies would serve as backing for the global currency. In another version, the international agency would issue the global currency to member countries like the IMF issues SDRs with the commitment of member countries to accept it in exchange for their own currencies. A third version suggests designating these issues of the global currency as deposits in the Global Reserve Bank that would use them to buy government securities or lend them.

In order to make a non-national currency reserve asset effective, the institution that issues the asset must be a monetary agency (D'Arista and Erturk, 2010: 21). An outline of a modified SDR-type plan that might be effective as a transition vehicle toward the new system is offered in D'Arista and Erturk.

Of course, we should not be naive. The success of any proposal of reform depends on the agreement of the major players in the international economic arena. Previous proposals of reform were never implemented mainly because the major economies – most notably the US – opposed them. A more balanced global system depends on a more balanced relation of forces in the world economy to be implemented as well as on the demonstration that the present regime is incapable of dealing with a global crisis. But when this happens there will be no time to start studying what course to choose. Now is the right time to do it.

Notes

1 See Moro and Beker (2016: Chapter 3) for a discussion of this issue.
2 For the extension of the Great Crisis to European countries sovereign debts see Moro and Beker (2016: Chapter 5).
3 See Moro and Beker (2016: Chapters 5, 6 and 7).
4 Allen and Moessner (2010: 26–34) provide a detailed description of the central banks swap networks developed during the financial crisis.
5 The argument for this is that surplus countries are allowed to sell goods that they would have otherwise not have been able to sell.

References

Alessandrini, P. and Presbitero, A. F. (2012). Low-Income Countries and an SDR-based International Monetary System. *Open Economies Review* 23: 129–150.

Allen, W. A. and Moessner, R. (2010). *Central Bank Co-Operation and International Liquidity in the Financial Crisis of 2008–2009.* BIS Working Papers No 310. https://www.bis.org/publ/work310.pdf.

Arestis, P., Basu, S. and Mallick, S. K. (2005). Financial Globalization: The Need for a Single Currency and a Global Central Bank. *Journal of Post Keynesian Economics* 27(3): 507–531.

Bird, G. (1979). The Benefits of Special Drawing Rights for Less Developed Countries. *World Development* 7(3): 281–290.

Bird, G. and Maynard, G. (1975). International Monetary Issues and the Developing Countries: A Survey. *World Development* 3(9): 609–631.

D'Arista, J. and Erturk, K. (2010). *Reforming the International Monetary System.* Manuscript. https://www.un.org/en/development/desa/policy/wess/wess_bg_papers/bp_wess2010_darista.pdf.

Davidson, P. (1992/93). Reforming the World's Money. *Journal of Post Keynesian Economics* 15(2): 153–179.

Eichengreen, B. (2010). *Exorbitant Privilege. The Rise and Fall of the Dollar and the Future of the International Monetary System.* Oxford: Oxford University Press.

Fantacci, L. (2012). *Why Not Bancor? Keynes's Currency Plan as a Solution to Global Imbalances.* Manuscript. Bocconi University.

Farhi, E., Gourinchas, P. and Rey, H. M. (2011). *Reforming the International Monetary System.* International Growth Center. Working Paper. https://www.theigc.org/wp-content/uploads/2011/03/Farhi-Et-Al-2011-Working-Paper.pdf.

Fischer, S. (1999). On the Need for an International Lender of Last Resort. *Journal of Economic Perspectives* 13(4): 85–104.

Grubel, H. G. (1972). Basic Methods for Distributing Special Drawing Rights and the Problem of International Aid. *Journal of Finance* 27(5): 1009–1022.

Group of Thirty (2018). *Managing the Next Financial Crisis.* Washington DC: Group of Thirty. https://group30.org/images/uploads/publications/Managing_the_Next_Financial_Crisis.pdf.

Helleiner, G. K. (1974). The Less Developed Countries and the International Monetary System. *Journal of Development Studies* 10(3–4):347–373.

IMF (2016). *Strengthening the International Monetary System – A Stocktaking.* https://www.imf.org/external/np/pp/eng/2016/022216b.pdf.

Landau, J.-P. (2014). *International Lender of Last Resort: Some Thoughts for the 21st Century.* BIS Paper (791).

Maynard, G. (1973). Special Drawing Rights and Development Aid. *Journal of Development Studies* 9(4): 518–543.

Moro, B. and Beker, V. A. (2016). *Modern Financial Crises: Argentina, United States and Europe.* Financial and Monetary Policy Studies 42. Switzerland: Springer International Publishing.

Mundell, R. A. (1983). International Monetary Reform: The Optimal Mix in Big Countries. In J. Tobin (ed.), *Macroeconomics, Prices, and Quantities: Essays in Memory of Arthur Okun.* Washington, DC: Brookings Institution.

Padoa-Schioppa, T. (2010). *The Ghost of Bancor: The Economic Crisis and Global Monetary Disorder.* Jacques Delors Institute. Speech. https://institutdelors.eu/en/publications/the-ghost-of-bancor-the-economic-crisis-and-global-monetary-disorder-speech-of-tommaso-padoa-schioppa/.

UN Commission of Experts (2009). *Report of the Commission of Experts of the President of the UN General Assembly on Reforms of the International Monetary and Financial System.* https://www.un.org/en/ga/president/63/pdf/calendar/20090325-economiccrisis-commission.pdf.

Xiaochuan, Z. (2009). *Reform the International Monetary System.* Speech by the Governor of the People's Bank of China, March 23. http://www.bis.org/review/r090402c.pdf.

9 Financial crises and economic theory

Pre-Keynesian models of financial crisis

Since the 19th century, economists have developed models to try to explain economic crises. John Steward Mill and Karl Marx, among others, advanced different explanations of these phenomena.

Mill asserted that there are recurring periods of "over-trading" and "harsh speculation" followed by periods when establishments are shut up and people are deprived of their incomes.

According to Marx, crises are the result of the contradiction between the tendency of the rate of profit to fall and the impetus to accumulate capital. Production accelerates to compensate for the decline in the rate of profit; this finally results in overproduction of commodities and the beginning of crisis.

However, financial crises as we know today are essentially a 20th century phenomenon. For this reason, it is perhaps Wicksell the first economist who should be mentioned in connection with the subject of financial crises. In the Wicksellian approach, dynamic economic processes are explained by the interaction of two rates of return, which typically diverge. One is the money interest rate and the other one the natural rate of return which is determined in the real sphere. Whenever banks have an excess of reserves, they will decrease the nominal rate of interest to increase their loans. As soon as the money interest rate is lower than the natural interest rate, a cumulative investment process is triggered; the economy will come into a situation of overheating. A money interest rate below the natural interest rate, however, is a disequilibrium phenomenon, signaling to would-be investors a greater willingness than in fact exists on the part of agents in general to sacrifice current consumption for the sake of increasing it later. The money that banks create as they make loans enables those who borrow from them to outbid others for resources, forcing saving upon them. Finally, the money interest rate rises to its natural level and the imbalance thus created is revealed along with an inability on the part of borrowers to service their debts. A financial crisis marks the end of a period of forced saving brought about by credit creation. A reverse rush for liquidity starts; if the money interest rate rises above the natural interest rate a deflationary contraction process may result. In such a case, a sharp contraction will lead to systemic problems in the financial system.

Wicksell's monetary model of cumulative inflationary and deflationary phases was taken over by several economists during the last century, among them Schumpeter, Hayek, Fisher and, to a certain extent, Keynes.

Although a generation apart and representing different strands, both Schumpeter and Hayek were part of the Austrian tradition. They share a common Wicksellian heritage although their respective accounts of the dynamic economic processes are rather distinct analytical extensions of the original Wicksellian cumulative process.

For Schumpeter, the origin of business cycles lies in discontinuous changes arising from innovations. An increased activity in the investment goods sector pushed by a spurt of innovations triggers the upswing. Banks create credit to finance entrepreneurial ventures that introduce new products or new processes that increase productivity. Once the gestation period for the new goods has come to an end, the economy adjusts downwards to a new equilibrium position, eliminating some older firms.

Following Schumpeter's terminology, in the "primary wave" there are only two phases: prosperity and recession. However, there may be secondary effects which reinforce the primary process. Owing to these secondary effects, the economic process may overshoot the new equilibrium position at the end of a period of prosperity. In the same way, recession may deteriorate into depression.

For Hayek (2012 [1929], 2012 [1931]) the credit volume given by banks does not necessarily reflect the volume of savings. If credit demand increases for investment, for whatever reason, credit will expand independently of the volume of savings; the credit system is elastic. However, sooner or later a credit expansion will come to an end. During the following contraction the artificially increased capital stock will be destroyed. A financial crisis will restore equilibrium. As we can see, in Hayek's model banks start the cycle, whereas for Schumpeter the prime mover is entrepreneurial action. That is why Hayek criticizes Schumpeter for discarding "the monetary causes which start the cyclical fluctuations" (Hayek, 1966: 17).

Irving Fisher developed a monetary theory of economic fluctuations including a debt-deflation model of depressions aimed at explaining the Great Depression. Over-optimistic expectations lead to periods of expansion including asset price bubbles. Easy money stimulates over-indebtedness. Herding and speculative behavior trigger asset price inflations, which are usually combined with huge credit expansion. When the asset price inflation comes to an end an asset price deflation follows. Non-performing loans start to grow. Distress selling of assets in order to service debt leads to sharply falling asset prices. Firms with non-performing loans try to sell everything in an attempt to survive. The combination of goods market deflation and high debt leads to an increase of the real debt burden by all debtors in the domestic currency. "Deflation caused by the debt reacts on the debt. Each dollar of debt still unpaid becomes a bigger dollar" (Fisher, 1933: 344). Economic downturns may lead to a cumulative breakdown of the financial system. Attempts to liquidate debt in the context of over-indebtedness are self-defeating. "Then we have the great paradox which, I submit, is the chief secret of most, if not all, great depressions: The more the debtors pay, the more they owe" (Fisher, 1933: 344).

The Keynesian theory of economic fluctuations

Up to 1930, crises were mainly considered by mainstream economic literature as an adjustment process to correct existing distortions in the economy. It was a sort of punishment for previous sins.

However, the magnitude of the 1930s crisis called for a different approach. With Keynes's General Theory crises started to be considered as an economic illness requiring treatment.

Keynes devotes Chapter 22 of his famous book to the analysis of economic fluctuations.

Keynes (2008) followed Wicksell in modeling economic dynamic as the interaction of two rates of return. One of the two rates is the money interest rate. The other one is the marginal efficiency of capital defined as the *expected* rate of returns from the capital asset. It is determined by the expected future yields an investment project creates. As long as the marginal efficiency of capital is higher than the money interest rate investment will be carried out and – through the multiplier – income will grow by more than the amount of the increase in the investment expenditure. As soon as the marginal efficiency of capital falls below the interest rate investment will decline. The consequence is a fall in income and employment. The interaction between the two rates leads to periods of high investment and high-income creation and periods of low or no investment and shrinking income creation.

Keynes underlines the close dependence of the marginal efficiency of capital on expectations. "It is chiefly this dependence which renders the marginal efficiency of capital subject to the somewhat violent fluctuations which are the explanation of the trade cycle" (Keynes, 2008: 12). For Keynes, the succession of boom and slump can be explained in terms of the fluctuation of the marginal efficiency of capital relatively to the rate of interest.

In particular, he remarks that:

> the later stages of the boom are characterized by optimistic expectations as to the future yield of capital-goods sufficiently strong to offset their growing abundance and their rising costs of production and, probably, a rise in the rate of interest also.
>
> (Keynes, 2008: 287)

However, this market sentiment will change sooner or later and "when disillusion falls upon an over-optimistic and over-bought market, it should fall with sudden and even catastrophic force" (Keynes, 2008: 287). The essence of the situation is to be found, Keynes underlines, in the collapse in the marginal efficiency of capital, particularly in the case of those types of capital which have been contributing most to the previous phase of heavy new investment.

There are two additional factors which may aggravate the slump. One is a rise in the rate of interest due to an increase in the liquidity-preference precipitated by the dismay and uncertainty as to the future which accompanies a collapse in the marginal efficiency of capital. The other one is the fact that a serious fall in the marginal efficiency of capital also tends to affect adversely the propensity to consume because it involves a severe decline in the market value of Stock Exchange equities. These two factors aggravate still further the depressing effect of a decline in the marginal efficiency of capital.

Keynes warns that the marginal efficiency of capital may suffer such a wide fall that it cannot be sufficiently offset by a corresponding decline in the rate of interest. For this reason, he concludes that the duty of ordering the current volume of investment cannot safely be left in private hands.

The economic crisis from a New Classical perspective[1]

The central contribution of Keynes to economic theory was to focus attention on the economic aggregates (income, consumption, investment, savings, etc.). In Keynesian macroeconomics, quantities are related to other quantities, while the role of prices is de-emphasized. This was the quintessence of macroeconomics until Phelps (1970) criticized this approach by arguing that it lacked proper micro-foundations. Lucas (1976) argued in the same direction, and this "Lucas critique" had devastating effects on the then dominant approach in macroeconomics. Macroeconomic theory took a major turn at that point: New Classical rational expectations representative agent models became the acceptable modeling method. The trick is that this approach implies assuming away any agent coordination failure. In a world of unbounded rationality,[2] no coordination failure and perfect foresight it is very difficult to conceive even the existence of a financial crisis. Within this framework, the origins of economic cycles lie in exogenous shocks to the fundamentals. Business cycles are just the optimal response of rational economic agents to unexpected changes in the economic environment. Consequently, there is no room – nor need – for stabilization policies implemented by the government.

Following these ideas, Kydland and Prescott (1980, 1982) developed a framework to analyze business fluctuations based on a representative agent who solves optimization problems to arrive at competitive equilibria that are always Pareto optimal.

Using this framework, Prescott (1986) studied the business cycles in the US during the post-World War II period. His conclusion was that fluctuations mostly resulted from random changes in the growth rate of business sector productivity.

Ohanian (2010) used a general equilibrium business cycle model to analyze the 2007–2009 recession. His main conclusion is that "lower output and income is exclusively due to a large decline in labor input" (Ohanian, 2010: 45). According to Ohanian, "labor input during the 2007–2009 recession in the United States was far below the level consistent with the marginal product of labor." Given the huge level of unemployment the crisis generated, it is not big news to know that the labor input sharply declined during that period. More surprising is the reason for that decline, according to Ohanian: the marginal rate of substitution between consumption and leisure was very low relative to the marginal product of labor. So, it seems that the crisis was caused by a sudden and mysterious increase in the preference for leisure. American workers suddenly decided to stay at home and watch TV instead of going to work. Of course, if you start assuming that the recession is an equilibrium outcome for agents who maximize their utilities, you are forced to reach that conclusion. We are now again in the pre-Keynesian world where unemployment is always a voluntary decision by workers who have an increased preference for leisure compared with work. Worst of all, this does not contribute at all either to our knowledge of the causes, mechanisms and consequences of the Great Recession nor to the knowledge of the policies to prevent a phenomenon like this from happening again. In fact, as Ohanian himself recognized, neoclassical economists know little about the specific sources and nature of the shocks, why labor market deviations were so large, why productivity deviations seem to play such a small role in the United States in this period, how to model real-world financial and policy events in order to determine their impact on the economy, and why macroeconomic weakness continued for so long after the worst of the crisis passed (Ohanian, 2010: 63). In summary, the new classical business cycle model does not contribute at all to the understanding of the last financial crisis.

The vindication of Minsky's theory on financial instability

After the Great Recession there was a worldwide resurgence of the interest in Keynesian economics.

In fact, mainstream economic theory was blamed for not having even considered the possibility of the type of collapse that the subprime mortgage meltdown unleashed. It not only failed to foresee the depth of the crisis; it did not even consider it possible.

On the other hand, Keynes offered a theory of depression economics that asserted that the crisis is possible and that the market mechanism cannot be relied upon to spontaneously recover from a slump.

Together with Keynes's ideas, the crisis brought to prominence the ideas of Hyman Minsky, after a long period of unjust oblivion.

Minsky called himself a "financial Keynesian." While Keynes identified as a fundamental flaw of the capitalist system the possibility of stable unemployment, Minsky added instability as a normal result of modern financial capitalism. He was convinced that leverage is the Achilles' heel of capitalism. His 1987 analysis of securitization was a prescient study of its nature and perils:

> Securitization lowers the weight of that part of the financing structure that the central bank (Federal Reserve in the United States) is committed to protect. A need by holders of securities who are committed to protect the market value of their assets (such as mutual or money market funds, or

> trustees for pension funds) may mean that a rise in interest rates will lead to a need by holders to make position by selling position, which can lead to a drastic fall in the price of the securities.
>
> (Minsky, 2008 [1987]: 3)

He strongly criticized the neoclassical approach: "The neoclassical way of doing economics, which rests upon splitting the financial system off from what is called the real economy, throws no appreciable light on the effect that a financial system has upon the functioning of the economy" (Minsky, 1992b: 15).

He characterized modern capitalism, especially in the United States, as "money manager capitalism."

According to him, capitalist economies show an in-built propensity to boom-bust cycles. He then presents a financially driven model of the business cycle.

Minsky held that during expansions, investors take on more and more risk, until lending exceeds what borrowers can pay off from their incoming revenues. When over-indebted investors are forced to sell even their less-speculative positions to make good on their loans, markets spiral lower and create a severe demand for cash – an event that has come to be known as a "Minsky moment."

Minsky's financial fragility theory classifies the financing of the purchase of large real illiquid investment projects into three categories: hedge finance, speculative finance and Ponzi finance. Ponzi financing is the most fragile financial system and it is the one most likely to lead to a "Minsky moment."

"Over a protracted period of good times, capitalist economies tend to move from a financial structure dominated by hedge finance units to a structure in which there is large weight to units engaged in speculative and Ponzi finance" (Minsky, 1992a: 8).

Palley (2009) argues that besides this short-run cycle, Minsky's financial instability hypothesis involves a theory of long cycles. This long-cycle rests on a process that transforms business institutions, decision-making conventions and the structures of market governance including regulation. In fact, Ferri and Minsky (1992) claim that the observed behavior of the economy is not the result of market mechanisms in isolation but is due to a combination of market behavior and the ability of institutions, conventions and policy interventions to contain and dominate the endogenous economic reactions that breed instability if left alone. In order to explain why frequent bouts of instability are not observed the authors argue that the economy has evolved usages and institutions, including agencies of government, whose economic impact is to thwart the instability generating tendencies of the economy. The thwarting systems are analogous to homeostatic mechanisms which may prevent a system from exploding. Institutional structures and interventions stabilize the dynamics of capitalist economies and constrain their outcomes to viable or acceptable ones.

Following these ideas, Palley (2009) maintains that there is a long swing dimension implicit in Minsky's thinking. These long-term swings are termed "Minsky super-cycles"; it is the super-cycle that ultimately permits financial crisis when the long-cycle has had time to erode the economy's thwarting institutions.

The process of erosion and transformation of thwarting institutions takes several short-run cycles, creating a long phase cycle. The economy undergoes a full-blown financial crisis that threatens its survivability only when the long-cycle has been long enough to erode the thwarting institutions. Once a full scale bust occurs the economy enters a period of renewal of thwarting institutions.

As Minsky did not provide a rigorous formal model, his contributions did not reach the pages of leading mainstream journals, although his analyses were far more illuminating than many of the elegantly mathematical but often useless models that plagued them. Only after the recent crisis has his name been rescued from oblivion.

Post-Keynesian approach to economic crisis

The Australian post-Keynesian academic Steve Keen was one of the few economists who anticipated the last financial crisis.

This post-Keynesian economist asserts that crisis key early warning indicators include the ratio of private debt to GDP, its rate of growth and acceleration, and sustained sectoral imbalances.

He maintains that although an optimal ratio has not yet been defined, a rapid rise in the private debt to GDP ratio could warn of a speculative bubble while a rapid acceleration of private debt is a strong indicator of an approaching financial crisis. In fact, when that ratio reaches a substantial level, a deceleration in the debt rate of growth may be enough to cause a recession.

Keen (2013) mentions Schumpeter and Minsky's arguments that the change in debt adds to aggregate demand from income alone. In a monetary economy in which banks endogenously create money, aggregate demand is income *plus* the change in debt. The change in debt primarily finances both investment goods purchases and net speculation on asset markets. The acceleration of debt is a major factor in causing changes in the level of output – and hence employment – and the rate of change of asset prices. A deceleration may cause a fall in the level of output, employment and asset prices, particularly when, because of its magnitude, debt has become a major component of aggregate demand.

Keen employs Godley´s "three balances" accounting approach to macro analysis, which maintains that when the government sector, the private sector and the international economy are treated as aggregates, the sectoral balances must sum to zero. This implies that if the public sector runs a surplus and the trade account is negative, the private sector must be in deficit – spend more than its income. But if the private sector spends above its income, this means it has to go more and more deeply into debt.

According to Godley and Wray (2000), the private sector deficit was 5.3% of GDP in 2000 in order to offset a government surplus of 2.2% of GDP and a balance of payments deficit of 3.1%.

The increasing ratio of debt to GDP was an indicator of the degree of financial stress on the American economy.

> The potential for a severe economic crisis was implied by the level of private debt (the aggregate of household, nonfinancial business and finance sector debt) compared to GDP, which by early 2000 had exceeded the peak reached during the severe deflation of 1932.
>
> (Keen, 2013: 247)

In his account of the Great Financial Crisis, Keen argues that the economy crashed simply because the rate of growth of the debt slowed down. He endorses Vague's criteria for a serious credit crisis (Keen, 2017). According to the American philanthropist and former banker Richard Vague these criteria are a private debt level exceeding 150% of GDP and growth in debt exceeding 17% of GDP over the preceding five years.

Keen concludes that the ever-rising levels of private debt make another financial crisis almost inevitable.

How mainstream economics tries to recover from failure

Before the crisis, money and credit were seen in many mainstream economic models as veils of no consequence for economy activity.

Part of the reorientation of mainstream economics after the financial crisis consisted of adding a financial-intermediary sector to the real sectors and analyzing the dynamic interactions between that sector and the rest of the economy.

For example, Gertler and Kiyotaki (2010) introduce the assumption that a bank's ability to raise funds depends on its capital. This allows them to show that portfolio losses experienced in a downturn lead to losses of bank capital that are increasing in the degree of leverage. In equilibrium, a contraction of bank capital and bank assets raises the cost of bank credit, slows the economy and depresses asset prices and bank capital further.

The striking point is that had this paper been written before the financial crisis, most mainstream economists – probably even the authors themselves – would have called that assumption as *ad hoc*, something which at that time was enough to disqualify any economic model. For instance, price and wage rigidity assumption in Keynes's General Theory was considered *ad hocery* because of its lack of microfoundations and was a main methodological argument against his theory. Now, the authors accept that "due to financial market frictions, bankers may be constrained in their ability to obtain deposits from households" (Gertler and Kiyotaki, 2010: 2016). Welcome mainstream economics to the real economic world!

The issue is that while in empirical sciences, whenever there is a conflict between theory and empirical evidence, it is theory which is in trouble, for mainstream economics it was just the opposite, as if economics were a branch of applied mathematics and not an empirical science. But reality has shown its ugly face in the shape of a global crisis, and mainstream economic theory was one of its main casualties. Thus, there is no alternative but to get rid of previous self-imposed methodological constraints and to take the real world into consideration and try to introduce some bit of it in mainstream economic models, even with forceps if necessary.

Box 9.1 Debt default in mainstream economic theory

One canonical assumption in the general equilibrium model is that agents keep their promises. What happens if this assumption is relaxed?

Yale Professor John Geanakoplos addressed this question. He is not only Professor of Economics but had a working experience on Wall Street, first as director of a firm that issued mortgage derivatives and later as director of one which invested in them; so, he learned both sides of the business.

Interestingly, he wrote a paper in 1996, long before the financial crisis took place; in that paper he tried to answer the aforementioned question within the framework of a general equilibrium model with incomplete markets and applying his personal business experience.

He argues that, in the modern world, the vast majority of promises are guaranteed by tangible assets called collateral. For example, a residential mortgage is a promise to deliver a specified amount of money in the future that is secured by a house. If the promise is broken, the house can be confiscated and sold, with the proceeds needed to cancel the debt turned over to the lender.

His main argument is that much of Wall Street´s activity is directed to the stretching of collateral to cover as many promises as possible. Making more collateral available makes it possible to make more promises, improving social welfare. How does Wall Street do this "welfare improving" activity?

Until the 1970s, banks that issued mortgages held these promises from homeowners. But after deregulation they could rid themselves of the mortgages by selling them to other investors. This was the "originate and distribute" model.

Here is where Wall Street steps in by buying big mortgage pools and splitting them into different pieces (tranches). These collateral mortgage obligations are promises backed by pools of promises which are backed by individual promises which are backed by physical homes.

In 2007, the value of US residential mortgages alone was roughly $10 trillion and the (notional) value of collateralized credit default swaps was estimated to exceed $50 trillion. Good job, Wall Street!

A default happens when an agent does not deliver what they has promised. In such a case, the lender will seize the collateral. In the case of tranching, the same collateral backs several promises to different lenders. For this reason, tranching usually involves a legal trust which is in charge of dividing up the collateral among the different claims according to some contractual formula.

Geanakoplos (1996: 28) builds a standard general equilibrium model with incomplete markets and demonstrates that once the possibility of defaults is admitted, the free market arranges for the optimal amount of default. Contrary to the intuitive idea that default is suggestive of disequilibrium his model shows that there is an equilibrium amount of default.

Of course, to arrive at such a conclusion some heroic assumptions have been made on the road. For example, although there is infinity of potential scenarios, the modeler assumes that *all* future possible states of the world are included in the model. Agents have perfect conditional foresight i.e. they anticipate today what future prices will be for every possible scenario and there are no informational asymmetries.

These extreme assumptions allow arriving at some other striking conclusions: "even if it is true that defaults on subprime mortgages led to a crash *ex post*, such mortgages might have been Pareto improving *ex ante*" (Geanakoplos and Zame, 2013: 4) and "social welfare is higher after the crash than immediately before, and social welfare is higher after default than immediately before" (Geanakoplos and Zame, 2013: 44). Welcome the financial meltdown!

And finally, the most important policy conclusion: "any valid welfare-based argument for regulation of down-payment requirements would seem to require that regulators could correctly forecast the price changes that would accompany such regulation" (Geanakoplos and Zame, 2013: 4). *Vade retro*, regulators! Do not dare interfere the free market optimal solution!

Source: Geanakoplos (1996) and Geanakoplos and Zame (2013)

The challenge for economic theory

The 2007/2009 financial crisis exposed the shortcomings of mainstream economic theory. The crisis showed that mainstream economics was quite unprepared to deal with it. Mainstream economists did not even consider it possible.

An exhaustive search of early warnings of the crisis in mainstream economic literature between 2000 and mid-2007 proves how far it was from what was going on in economic reality (Imperia and Maffeo, 2011). The authors reflect their main conclusion in the paper's title: "A search in vain for warnings about the current crisis in economic journals with the highest impact factors."

In fact, the authors selected the 16 economic journals with the highest impact factor and after checking the articles published between 2000 and the summer of 2007 they conclude that concerns over the possibility of a wide ranging economic crisis do not seem present in the articles which can be traced back to the mainstream theory.

Paraphrasing Keynes we can say that neoclassical economists resemble Euclidean geometers in a non-Euclidean world. Thus, the first step is to reconcile economic theory with economic reality. This implies to throw over several of the unrealistic neoclassical assumptions (price symmetric flexibility, unbounded rational expectations, no coordination problems, the representative agent, and so on) which automatically rule out the mere possibility of an economic crisis.

It is also imperative to elaborate a new order of priorities for the agenda of economic research. Studying economic pathologies and how to cure them should be more encouraged while fewer resources should be devoted to merely showing why an economy, under certain assumptions, may be in good health.

Economic crises are a recurring phenomenon. As Reinhart and Rogoff (2009) exhaustively show, financial crises and sovereign debt defaults are far from being strange events in economic history, in both less developed as well as developed countries.

A major rethinking of economics seems to be absolutely necessary. As I have proposed elsewhere,

> in order to rebuild economic theory it is necessary to have in mind that economics – and especially macroeconomics – is supposed to be a guide for economic policy as well as a tool to explain and predict real-world economic behavior. For this reason, the departure point has to be the need of studying economic illnesses rather than trying to prove the non-existence of economic problems, as neoclassical economics mainly does. Studying real-world economic pathologies and how to cure them should be the main task of economic science.
>
> (Beker, 2020: 2)

Economic crisis is one of these pathologies economics has yet to study better in order to provide society with an answer about its deep causes and how to prevent their occurrence. This book tries to be a modest contribution to this task.

Notes

1 This section and the following one are based on Beker (2012).

2 As opposed to Simon's bounded rationality where agents are supposed to have a limited access to information and the computational capacities that are actually possessed by organisms, including man.

References

Beker, V. A. (2012). Rethinking Macroeconomics in Light of the U.S. Financial Crisis. *Real-World Economics Review* 60.

Beker, V. A. (2020). *Alternative Approaches to Economic Theory. Complexity, Post Keynesian and Ecological Economics.* Abingdon and New York: Routledge.

Ferri, P. and Minsky, H. P. (1992). Market Processes and Thwarting Systems. *Structural Change and Economic Dynamics* 3: 79–91.

Fisher, I. (1933). The Debt Deflation Theory of Great Depressions. *Econometrica* 1: 337–357.

Geanakoplos, J. (1996). *Promises Promises.* Cowles Foundation for Research in Economics at Yale University. Cowles Foundation Discussion Paper No. 1143.

Geanakoplos, J. and Zame, W. R. (2013). Collateral Equilibrium: A Basic Framework. Cowles Foundation for Research in Economics at Yale University. Cowles Foundation Discussion Paper No. 1906. *Economic Theory* 56: 443–492.

Gertler, M. and Kiyotaki, N. (2010). Banking, Liquidity, and Bank Runs in an Infinite Horizon Economy. *American Economic Review* 105(7): 2011–2043.

Godley, W. and Wray, L. R. (2000). Is Goldilocks Doomed? *Journal of Economic Issues* 34: 201–206.

Hayek, F. A. (1966). *Monetary Theory and the Trade Cycle*. New York: A. M. Kelley Publishers.

Hayek, F. A. (2012 [1929]). Monetary Theory and the Trade Cycle. *Collected Works of F.A. Hayek*, 7. Chicago, IL: University of Chicago Press.

Hayek, F. A. (2012 [1931]). Prices and Production. *Collected Works of F.A. Hayek*, 7. Chicago, IL: University of Chicago Press.

Imperia, A. and Maffeo, V. (2011). As If Nothing Were to Happen: A Search in Vain for Warnings About the Current Crisis in Economic Journals with the Highest Impact Factors. In E. Brancaccio and G. Fontanta (eds.), *The Global Economic Crisis. New perspective on the critique of economic theory and policy*. London and New York: Routledge.

Keen, S. (2013). Predicting the "Global Financial Crisis": Post-Keynesian Macroeconomics. *Economic Record* 89(285): 228–254.

Keen, S. (2017). *Can We Avoid Another Financial Crisis?* Cambridge: Polity Press.

Keynes, J. M. (2008 [1936]). *The General Theory of Employment, Interest and Money*. New Delhi: Atlantic.

Kydland, F. E. and Prescott, E.C. (1980). A Competitive Theory of Fluctuations and the Feasibility and Desirability of Stabilization Policy. In S. Fischer (ed.), *Rational Expectations and Economic Policy*. Chicago, IL: University of Chicago Press, pp. 169–198.

Kydland, F. E. and Prescott, E. C. (1982). Time to Build and Aggregate Fluctuations. *Econometrica* 50(6): 1345–1370.

Lucas, R. E. Jr (1976). Econometric Policy Evaluation: A Critique. *Carnegie-Rochester Conference Series on Public Policy* 1(1): 19–46.

Minsky, H. P. (1992a). *The Financial Instability Hypothesis*. The Jerome Levy Economics Institute of Bard College. Working Paper No. 74. http://www.levyinstitute.org/pubs/wp74.pdf.

Minsky, H. P. (1992b). *The Capital Development of the Economy and the Structure of Financial Institutions*. The Jerome Levy Economics Institute of Bard College. Working Paper No. 72. http://www.levyinstitute.org/pubs/wp72.pdf.

Minsky H. P. (2008 [1987]). *Securitization*. The Jerome Levy Economics Institute of Bard College, Policy Note. http://www.levyinstitute.org/pubs/pn_08_2.pdf.

Ohanian, L. (2010). The Economic Crisis from a Neoclassical Perspective. *Journal of Economic Perspectives* 24(4): 45–66.

Palley, T. I. (2009). *A Theory of Minsky Super-Cycles and Financial Crises*. Hans Böckler Stiftung. Macroeconomic Policy Institute. Working Paper. June. https://www.boeckler.de/pdf/p_imk_wp_5_2009.pdf.

Phelps, E. (1970). *Microeconomic Foundations of Employment and Inflation Theory*. New York: W. W. Norton & Company, Inc.

Prescott, E. C. (1986). Theory Ahead of Business Cycle Measurement. *Quarterly Review*, Federal Reserve Bank of Minneapolis, pp. 9–22.

Reinhart C. M. and Rogoff, K. S. (2009). *This Time Is Different: Eight Centuries of Financial Folly*. Princeton, NJ: Princeton University Press.

Epilogue

The response to the COVID-19 crisis

The central banks response to the COVID-19 crisis

The COVID-19 pandemic was the first test the Federal Reserve and other central banks were submitted to after the 2007/2009 crisis and the financial reforms enacted thereafter.

The business closures and travel restriction policies triggered a deep economic downturn. Amid escalating market turmoil, market participants wanted to hold cash or something that resembles cash as closely as possible.

A "flight to safety" in financial markets became an abrupt and extreme "dash for cash" in which investors sold off even safe assets such as long-term government bonds in order to obtain short-term highly liquid assets.

Even the long-viewed presumption that the market for US Treasuries is the world's deepest and most liquid financial market was seriously questioned when the investors' heavy supply overwhelmed the capacity of dealers to intermediate the market.[1]

Central banks had to take extraordinary action to stabilize markets.

The first initiative taken by the Fed was, acting as lender of last resort, to lower the rate it charges banks for loans from its discount window. However, as explained in Chapter 5, experience tells that banks are reluctant to borrow from the central bank because of the stigma associated with that borrowing. To counter this stigma eight big banks agreed to borrow from that source of funds.

The Fed lent up to $2.3 trillion to support households, employers, financial markets, and state and local governments. Besides that, it purchased massive amounts of securities including Treasury securities and mortgage-backed securities. Between mid-March and mid-June, the Fed's portfolio of securities held outright grew from $3.9 trillion to $6.1 trillion (Cheng et al., 2020).

The Fed also obtained the approval of the Treasury Secretary to invoke emergency lending authority under Section 13(3) of the Federal Reserve Act as it did during the 2007/2009 financial crisis. This allowed the Fed to revive several of the facilities implemented during the Great Recession and implement some new ones.

In the first place, it reestablished the Primary Dealer Credit Facility, under which the Fed offered low interest rate loans to primary dealers in exchange of equities and investment grade debt securities as collateral. Primary dealers are banks but also investment banks and brokers. The latter have no access to either discount window borrowing or the Term Auction Facility (TAF), which are both restricted to depository institutions.

A Commercial Paper Funding Facility was announced for the purchase of US dollar-denominated 3-month commercial paper directly from eligible issuers. It helped normalize issuance of commercial papers and injected liquidity to this market where investors were unwilling to advance funds for longer than a few days forcing businesses to issue commercial paper on a near-daily basis.

The Fed also re-launched the Money Market Mutual Fund Liquidity Facility to lend to banks against collateral (commercial paper and Treasuries) they purchase from prime money market funds (MMFs). This was necessary in order to address the MMF run triggered by the pandemic and the consequent lockdown. The scale of investor redemptions threatened to exhaust these funds' holdings of their most liquid assets.

Treasury pledged assets from the Exchange Stabilization Fund (ESF) to protect the Fed against losses in these programs.

As explained in Chapter 3, the MMF reform required prime funds to switch from a stable to a floating NAV calculation. The fact that the share price is no longer fixed implies that when many investors redeem their shares simultaneously, this can adversely affect the value of the fund shares for the remaining investors. The "first-mover advantage" creates incentives akin to depositors in bank runs: investors have an incentive to move their money out before others do.

US non-banks were especially hit when prime MMFs withdrew as marginal buyers of commercial paper after facing large outflows. MMFs are non-banks' main dollar lenders.

As market participants drew down their investments in money markets, many MMFs tried to liquidate their assets (largely commercial paper) to meet redemptions; when they found the markets effectively closed, they came very close to regulatory liquidity thresholds (10% daily and 30% weekly liquid asset requirements) which would have forced them to suspend withdrawals. This could in turn have triggered contagion to other funds and severely exacerbated the overall stress in the financial system. The Fed intervention prevented this from happening.

These events show that there is a conflict between the fact that investors seemingly conceive of MMFs as equivalent to deposit accounts and the liquidity characteristics under stress of some of the underlying assets, like bank commercial paper, on which these funds depend for liquidity (Cunliffe, 2020: 12/13).

The COVID-19 crisis showed that MMFs remain a source of systemic risk. For this reason, it is worthwhile reevaluating the money market mutual funds regulation framework.

The US central bank vastly expanded its repo operations to provide a practically unlimited amount of money to money markets. Additionally, it encouraged banks to use their capital buffers to increase lending.

The Fed also restarted the financial crisis-era TALF aimed at lending to holders of asset-backed securities.

Thus, the Fed was so applying one of the lessons left by the Great Recession crisis: the first step in fighting a crisis is to stabilize the financial system because without credit, the real economy will suffocate regardless of almost any other policy response.

In an unprecedented move, the Fed established two new facilities in order to support US major corporations as well as three programs for small- and mid-sized businesses. Not only did the Fed lent directly to corporations but it also purchased existing corporate bonds. In fact, "the Covid-19 crisis almost claimed a new and unexpected victim: the US corporate bond market" (O'Hara and Zhou, 2020: 2).

The corporate bond market was badly hit:

> over the crisis period, dealers, particularly the non-primary dealers, shifted from buying bonds to selling bonds, exacerbating market illiquidity, and resulting in a cumulative negative $8 billion inventory position for the dealer community. These negative inventory positions further drove up transaction costs, fueling the liquidity crisis.
>
> (O'Hara and Zhou, 2020: 3)

The Fed response had immediate effects: bond transaction costs dropped from their peak of over 90 bps in March right before Fed interventions to about 40 bps by the end of April (O'Hara and Zhou, 2020: 4).

The Fed acted in this case as a market maker of last resort, as Buiter and Sibert (2007) first and Mehrling (2011) later had advised.

As mentioned in Chapter 3, the changes made after the financial crisis to derivative markets implied in particular the requirement that derivatives trades be prudently collateralized against counterparty failure and – where sufficiently standardized – centrally cleared. As a result, derivatives markets went into the COVID-19 crisis with much greater underlying collateral in the system to protect against counterparty credit failure.

The increasing collateral required to protect against counterparty credit failure were met and there were scarce defaults. Although there was an initial decline in liquidity, central bank intervention was an important factor in restoring market liquidity.

While, during the 2007/2009 financial crisis, the Fed resisted backstopping municipal and state borrowing, during the pandemic crisis the Fed announced it was ready to lend directly to state and local governments.

Many of the aforementioned facilities were structured as Fed-controlled special purpose vehicles because of restrictions on the types of securities that the Fed can purchase.

As a matter of fact, the usage of most facilities was low; the US central bank announcement was enough to calm the markets as it was Mario Draghi's statement in 2012 that the ECB was "ready to do whatever it takes to preserve the Euro."

Using another tool that was important during the Great Recession, the Fed cut rates and extended the maturity of swaps to other central banks.

As we have seen, Section 13(3) of the Federal Reserve Act has remained the weapon of last resort in the US government's arsenal when responding to significant liquidity events in the financial sector. Despite the fact that many of the tools that were essential to resolve the 2007/2009 crisis have been eliminated or curtailed, Section 13(3) has stayed as the source of authority for Federal Reserve lending in critical situations not only to banks and non-bank financial institutions but also to corporations and municipal and state governments.

Section 13(3) survived myriad arguments in favor of restricting the Fed's ability to provide emergency lending which were displayed during and after the discussion of the Dodd-Frank Act. Once again pragmatic considerations prevailed over the theoretical ones concerning what open-ended emergency lending supposedly means for the taxpayer. The real-world economy is far away from theoretical fantasies aimed in many cases at pleasing vested interests.

However, an important and perhaps uncomfortable question remains: is it OK that emergency lending in the US depends on such an obscure clause as Section 13(3)?

The CARES Act

Besides the Fed's moves, there was also an initial $2 trillion fiscal response to support businesses and households.

As recently as in November 2019, Fed Chairman Jerome H. Powell had expressed his doubts on the fiscal policymakers' willingness or ability to support economic activity during a downturn because – he argued – the federal budget was on an unsustainable path, with high and rising debt (Powell, 2019).

In spite of this prevention, only four months later, in March 2020, Congress passed the Coronavirus Aid, Relief and Economic Security (CARES) Act, a $2-trillion economic stimulus bill. As it happened with the Fed, the real world also imposed its agenda in the fiscal front.

- 30% of the $2 trillion was destined to individuals who received a $1,200 direct payment for those earning up to $75,000 per year and lower sums for higher earners.
- 25% was aimed at stabilizing big businesses in hard-hit sectors, like airlines and airline contractors.
- 19% was earmarked for loans and grants to small businesses.
- State and local governments were beneficiaries of 17% of the stimulus package.

The remaining 9% was set aside for public and health service, mainly to make up the lost revenue caused by focusing on the outbreak as well as increasing the availability of ventilators and masks.

However, as public funds were compromised, a valid question is whether they could have been better used if part of them were addressed to a public works program to reactivate the depressed economy, increase aggregate demand and create jobs. It is doubtful whether markets and businesses are themselves able to create sufficient employment to make up for the losses in jobs and income caused by the pandemic.

A new wave of debt crises?

The COVID-19 pandemic has pushed debt levels to new heights. As Georgieva et al. (2020) assert, "about half of low-income countries and several emerging market economies were already in or at high risk of a debt crisis, and the further rise in debt is alarming."

Ecuador and Argentina led what may be a new wave of sovereign debt restructuring. In fact, average debt ratios are projected to rise as a result of increasing fiscal deficits triggered by COVID-19-related expenditures in a context of a global economic slowdown.

In the absence of a sovereign bankruptcy regime, the resolution of sovereign debt crises – as shown in the two aforementioned cases – is a matter of contract renegotiation between the sovereign and its creditors.

The renegotiation of Argentina's debt introduced some innovations which may favor the debtor countries' bargaining power in future debt renegotiations. One of them has been the use of "re-designation," which allows the exclusion of series of bonds from the voting pool. When Argentina's offer failed to attract the support of a supermajority of bonds across the original voting pool but nonetheless succeeded in attracting sufficient support to meet the voting thresholds from a subsection of bond series, re-designation allowed to achieve a restructuring with respect to these series only.

Another innovation has been the so-called Pac-Man strategy which allowed the Argentine government to get bondholders to deal with it one at a time.

These innovations allowed arriving at a remarkably speedy and consensual agreement neutralizing those bondholders whose unwillingness to agree to restructuring terms supported by a substantial majority of the bondholders could have imperiled the restructuring transaction.

It took less than six months for the Argentine government to successfully restructure most of its $65 billion debt with 99% per cent of its private creditors. The agreement extended maturities on the debt and lowered interest rate payments from an average of 7% to about 3%.

In April 2020, the G20 announced the Debt Service Suspension Initiative which covers 73 International Development Association (IDA) and UN Least Developed Countries that are current on their debt service to the IMF and World Bank. Under the initiative, official bilateral creditors commit to suspend debt service payments. More than 40 countries applied to participate in the initiative which, however, left out many middle-income countries badly hit by the pandemic. Although private creditors were called upon to participate on comparable terms no private creditor has shown interest in the initiative.

Conclusions

The COVID-19 pandemic triggered a "dash for cash" in financial markets. The pandemic crisis showed that even sovereign bonds can become illiquid.

Central banks had to take extraordinary action to stabilize markets.

In the US, the Fed invoked emergency lending authority to revive several of the facilities implemented during the Great Recession and implement some new ones.

In an unprecedented move, the Fed established two new facilities in order to support US major corporations as well as three programs for small- and mid-sized businesses.

Treasury pledged assets from the Exchange Stabilization Fund (ESF) to protect the Fed against losses in some of these programs.

The COVID-19 crisis showed that the secondary market for Treasuries cannot safely and efficiently handle surges in investor trading demands without the intervention of the Fed.

> Although the Fed accomplished what it needed to do, as a design principle, the lack of a robust private-market structure should not be acceptable based on the notion that the Fed can rescue the market as a last resort.
>
> (Duffie, 2020: 2)

The author concludes that "the risk of an accident in the plumbing of the Treasuries market, by which trades are cleared and settled, already suggests the need for a more robust system of central clearing" (Duffie, 2020: 4), particularly, given the historically high and growing ratio of federal debt to GDP and the ballooning stock of outstanding Treasury securities relative to the capacity of dealer balance sheets.

Besides the Fed's moves, there was also an initial $2 trillion fiscal response to support businesses and households.

At the world level, while Australia and the United States deployed the largest fiscal stimulus – more than 10% of their GDP – the size of budgetary measures has been less than 3% of GDP in Italy, France and all emerging market economies (EMEs), except South Africa (Alberola et al., 2020: 3).

However, as public funds were compromised, a valid question is whether they could have been better used if part of them were addressed to a public works program to reactivate the depressed economy, increase aggregate demand and create jobs.

The COVID-19 pandemic pushed sovereign debt levels to new heights. Ecuador and Argentina might be only the first countries in a new wave of sovereign debt restructuring.

Note

1 Growing federal deficits have caused the stock of marketable Treasuries to grow significantly. The total amount marketable Treasuries has also grown dramatically relative to the quantity of Treasury inventories for which primary dealers obtain financing (Duffie, 2020).

References

Alberola, E., Arslan, Y., Cheng, G. and Moessner, R. (2020). The Fiscal Response to the Covid-19 Crisis in Advanced and Emerging Market Economies. *BIS Bulletin* 23, June.

Buiter, W. and Sibert, A. (2007). The Central Bank as the Market Maker of Last Resort: From Lender of Last Resort to Market Maker of Last Resort. *VOXEU – CEPR*. https://voxeu.org/article/subprime-crisis-what-central-bankers-should-do-and-why.

Cheng, J., Skidmore, D. and Wessel, D. (2020). What's the Fed Doing in Response to the COVID-19 Crisis? What More Could It Do? *Brookings*, July 17. https://www.brookings.edu/research/fed-response-to-covid19/.

Cunliffe, J. (2020). *Financial System Resilience: Lessons from a Real Stress*. Speech. Investment Association Webinar, London. https://www.bis.org/review/r200610a.pdf.

Duffie, D. (2020). *Still the World's Safe Haven? Redesigning the U.S. Treasury Market After the COVID-19 Crisis*. Hutchins Center Working Paper # 62. June. https://www.brookings.edu/wp-content/uploads/2020/05/WP62_Duffie_v2.pdf.

Georgieva, K., Pazarbasioglu, C. and Weeks-Brown, R. (2020). Reform of the International Debt Architecture is Urgently Needed. *IMFBlog*. October 1. https://blogs.imf.org/2020/10/01/reform-of-the-international-debt-architecture-is-urgently-needed/.

Mehrling, P. (2011). *The New Lombard Street. How the Fed Became the Dealer of Last Resort*. Princeton, NJ: Princeton University Press.

O'Hara, M. and Zhou, X. (Alex) (2020). *Anatomy of a Liquidity Crisis: Corporate Bonds in the COVID-19 Crisis*. doi:10.2139/ssrn.3615155.

Powell, J. H. (2019). The Economic Outlook. Testimony before the Joint Economic Committee, US Congress. November 13. https://www.federalreserve.gov/newsevents/testimony/powell20191113a.htm.

Conclusions

In this volume I have analyzed the main financial reforms which took place during and after the 2007/2009 financial crisis. The conclusion is, in general, that although most of them go in the right direction, they are insufficient. In particular:

1 SIFIs are now stronger and more protected than in 2007. This means that they may be immune to relatively small shocks. It will take time for a new financial crisis to blow up.
2 Although the Fed lacks some of the weapons used in 2007/2009, section 13(3) stays as the source of authority for Federal Reserve lending in critical situations, as it was during the COVID-19 crisis. However, this raises an awkward question: is it OK that emergency lending in US depends on such an obscure section of the Federal Reserve Act?
3 What may happen if a global systemically important bank needs to be resolved is still an untested issue. Political costs could be deemed too high and some sort of bailout may be considered necessary in spite of the legal constraints.
4 The Dodd-Frank Act fails to recognize that a large part of the funding of the financial system is no longer in the form of insured deposits but rather in the form of non-deposit financial liabilities. Consequently, it fails to bring the shadow banking component of the financial system under the regulatory umbrella in a systematic way.
5 The COVID-19 crisis showed that MMFs remain a source of systemic risk. For this reason, it is worthwhile reevaluating prudential regulation of the money market funds.
6 The pandemic crisis taught that even sovereign bonds can become illiquid. In the US, the Fed had to take very aggressive actions to restore liquidity to the Treasury market.
7 Excessive risk-taking by financial institutions was a factor that significantly contributed to the incubation of the financial crisis. Legislation has not eliminated incentives to take risks that would be excessive from a social perspective.
8 In spite of their key role in the financial meltdown, credit ratings agencies emerged practically untouched after it. The essential problem is that the primary sources of revenue for their ratings continue to come in the form of fees that are paid by the security issuer. The argument in favor of the issuer-pays

model is that in the investor-pays one there may be a "free-rider" problem as non-paying investors could benefit from easy access to the rating lists. However, with today's technology, the free-rider problem should no longer be an obstacle to implement the investor-pays model.

9 Excessive concentration of loans in any one sector, region or kind of assets exposes the financial system to the risk of heavy losses which would affect it as a whole. For this reason, as part of their macro-prudential policy, central banks should establish the acceptable limits of concentration risk and the mechanisms to monitor and control that the system behaves within them.

10 It is also recommended to strictly require from any financial institution to state clearly and unequivocally whether their activities are within or outside the regulatory perimeter to make sure people know what sort of institution they are dealing with and the kind of risk they are subject to.

11 The US financial regulatory system is highly fragmented. It seems advisable to build a unified regulatory system where lines of accountability are clear and transparency is improved across all products.

12 In the present monetary regime, there is a flagrant contradiction: a purely national currency as the dollar is the global anchor currency. A new global monetary system is required to provide at least for an international lender of last resort and to remove the "exorbitant privilege" that allows the United States to run large external deficits while financing them with its own currency.

13 Economic crisis is one of the pathologies economics has yet to study better in order to provide society with an answer about its deep causes and how to prevent their occurrence.

Appendix: Financialization and the 2007/2009 crisis

According to Epstein (2001: 1), "financialization refers to the increasing importance of financial markets, financial motives, financial institutions, and financial elites in the operation of the economy and its governing institutions, both at the national and international level."

According to Lapavitsas (2011: 611):

> financialization is posited as a systemic transformation of mature capitalist economies that comprises three fundamental elements: first, large non-financial corporations have reduced their reliance on bank loans and have acquired financial capacities; second, banks have expanded their mediating activities in financial markets as well as lending to households; third, households have become increasingly involved in the realm of finance both as debtors and as asset holders. The crisis of 2007–9 is directly related to these developments.

The analysis of financialization has a remote precedent in Hilferding's (1981, [1910]) study on the role of bank capital in the economy of the early 1900s, which today might well appear prophetic.

As a result of the process which took place during the last 40 years the financial sector and financial activities play nowadays a key role in the economy as a whole. Financial firms are no longer stand-alone entities but a diverse set of interconnected components that distribute risk and are exposed to it. Bank failures may have strong negative externalities for other banks and the real economy as a whole with large economic and social costs associated with the chain reaction they may trigger.

This has led Minsky to label this new economic system as money manager capitalism in which money managers replaced corporate managers as the masters of private-sector economic activity. Perhaps it should be added that corporate managers now behave mostly as money managers, so the line between them has actually blurred. As Lapavitsas (2011: 620) remarks, large corporations have become "more independent from banks and more heavily involved in financial activities on their own account."

Money-managing institutions – such as pension and mutual funds, bank trust departments, and the annuity arms of insurance companies – rather than individual investors have become the holders of the largest share of US corporate stocks and bonds.

On the other hand,

> the growing influence of money managers forced business leaders to become increasingly focused on quarterly profits and the stock-market value of their corporations – in other words, on shareholder value. This pressure spurred many non-financial corporations to scale back costly and often aging manufacturing operations; engage in mergers and acquisitions at an unprecedented pace; and turn their attention to the sorts of borrowing, investing, and lending traditionally associated with financial firms.
>
> (Whalen, 2020: 186)

In today's economy, both corporate and money executives manage other people's huge amounts of money which they invest either in financial or in real assets. As Adam Smith put it a long time ago, referring to joint-stock companies,

> the directors of such companies, however, being the managers rather of other people's money than of their own, it cannot well be expected, that they should watch over it with the same anxious vigilance with which the partners in a private copartnery frequently watch over their own.
>
> (Smith, 1827: 311)

On one hand, in the case of non-financial corporations the production of goods has become just a by-product of their main activity focused on valorizing capital through mergers, acquisitions, takeovers and other financial instruments of the kind.

On the other hand, the manufacturing of innovative financial products is the bread and butter of the financial system. The securitization of subprime mortgages into mortgage-backed securities and collateralized debt obligations as well as the vast array of other equally highly complex, tailor-made financial instruments designed in the years previous to the 2007/2009 crisis are just examples of this innovative financial activity which culminated with the referred crisis. The shadow banking system, with its plethora of rather obscure entities resulting from regulatory arbitrage, is another one.

It has been argued that a by-product of the financialization process has been the increasing share of the rentiers in national income at the expense of wage-earners and households, who have faced stagnating real wages and increased indebtedness, respectively. For this reason, Stockhammer (2012: 40) argues that "the polarization of income distribution is a root cause of the crisis in the sense that it contributed to the imbalances that erupted in the crisis."

Mian et al. (2020) argue that the rising income inequality since 1980 in the United States has generated a large increase in saving by the top of the income distribution, which they call the saving glut of the rich and has been on the same order of magnitude as the global saving glut. The authors argue that this saving glut has been closely linked to the large accumulation of household debt of the bottom 90% of the income distribution. They conclude that "the growth in the financial sector since the 1980s appears to be driven to a large degree by the channeling of savings by some households into borrowing by other households" (Mian et al., 2020: 4).

Fifty years ago, there was only one large speculative market: the stock exchange. This has radically changed during the past half century. Deregulation and technology have made possible that almost anything can be the object of large-scale exchange, from commodities to derivatives. Intangible goods have become more and more relevant in exchange markets. The growth of trading in securities has been explosive, particularly in derivatives, so-called because they derive their value from the value of other securities. Once a derivative security is created, further layers of derivative securities can be created upon it and so on. A proliferation of new financial products was part of all this process: repos, swaps, options, collateralized debt obligations and other protagonists of the latest financial crisis. As Jesus multiplied the bread and fish, the financial system multiplied the financial instruments to bet on.

Subprime mortgages were the main protagonists of the 2007/2009 crisis. As Geanakolpos (1996) explained, a whole pyramid scheme was built upon them. Big mortgage pools were bought and split into different "tranches". These collateral mortgage obligations (CMOs) "are promises secured by pools of individual promises … There is a pyramiding of promises in which the CMO promises are backed by pools of promises, which are backed by individual promises which are backed by physical homes" (Geanakolpos, 1996: 5). The instruments being traded were hard to understand even for experts and often impossible to value.

The main ingredients for the financial crisis were already laid out. When the housing bubble exploded and mortgage defaults soared, it was discovered that many securities in which people had invested trillions of dollars were actually far riskier than people originally thought they were. The crisis blew up. The security pyramid crashed like a house of cards and billions of dollar wealth evaporated all of a sudden.

What is the bottom line of the financialization process up to now? Van der Zwan (2014: 121) argues that:

> gaining access to credit markets after years of racial and gender discrimination made finance an achievement for large segments of the population, who were previously excluded from the world of home mortgages and credit cards. Only in the most recent years have these economic and political gains been transformed into losses: of homes, of jobs and of a general sense of security. Yet while the subprime mortgage crisis has rendered visible the fictitious nature of this financial imaginary, it is hard to visualize an equally powerful alternative.

References

Epstein, G. (2001). Financialization, Rentier Interests, and Central Bank Policy. Manuscript, Department of Economics, University of Massachusetts, Amherst, MA, December.

Geanakolpos, J. (1996). *Promises, Promises.* Cowles Foundation, Yale University. https://economics.yale.edu/sites/default/files/files/Workshops-Seminars/MicroTheory/geanakolpos-080326c.pdf.

Hilferding, R. (1981 [1910]). *Finance Capital: A Study of the Latest Phase of Capitalist Development.* London: Routledge and Kegan Paul.

Lapavitsas, C. (2011). Theorizing Financialization. Work, Employment and Society. *SAGE* 25(4): 611–626. http://citeseerx.ist.psu.edu/viewdoc/download?doi=10.1.1.669.4781&rep=rep1&type=pdf.

Mian, A., Straub, L. and Sufi, A. (2020). *The Saving Glut of the Rich and the Rise in Household Debt.* National Bureau of Economic Research. NBER Working Paper Series. WP 26941.

Smith, A. (1827). *An Inquiry into the Nature and Causes of the Wealth of Nations.* Edinburgh: University Press. https://rba.gov.au/publications/workshops/research/2019/pdf/rba-workshop-2019-sufi.pdf.

Stockhammer, E. (2012). Financialization, Income Distribution and the Crisis. *Investigacion Economica* LXXI: 39–70.

Van der Zwan, N. (2014). Making Sense of Financialization. *Socio-Economic Review* 12: 99–129.

Whalen, C. J. (2020). Understanding Financialization: Standing on the Shoulders of Minsky. In V. A. Beker (ed.), *Alternative Approaches to Economic Theory.* New York: Routledge, Abingdon, pp. 185–206.

Index